ABERDEEN UNIVERSITY STUDIES SERIES
Number 157

Shetland and the Outside World
1469–1969

Shetland and the Outside World
1469–1969

EDITED BY
DONALD J. WITHRINGTON

Published for the UNIVERSITY OF ABERDEEN
by
OXFORD UNIVERSITY PRESS
1983

Oxford University Press, Walton Street, Oxford OX2 6DP
London Glasgow New York Toronto
Delhi Bombay Calcutta Madras Karachi
Kuala Lumpur Singapore Hong Kong Tokyo
Nairobi Dar es Salaam Cape Town
Melbourne Auckland
and associated companies in
Beirut Berlin Ibadan Mexico City

Oxford is a trade mark of Oxford University Press

Published in the United States by
Oxford University Press, New York

© The University of Aberdeen 1983

All rights reserved. No part of this publication may be reproduced, stored in a retrieval system, or transmitted, in any form or by any means, electronic, mechanical, photocopying, recording, or otherwise, without the prior permission of Oxford University Press

British Library Cataloguing in Publication Data
Shetland and the outside world 1469–1969
1. Shetland Islands—History
I. Withrington, Donald J.
941.1'35   DA880.S5
ISBN 0-19-714107-2

Library of Congress Cataloging in Publication Data
Main entry under title:
Shetland and the outside world, 1469–1969
(Aberdeen University studies series; no. 15)
Includes index
1. Shetland—History—Addresses, essays, lectures.
2. Shetland—Economic conditions—Addresses, essays, lectures.
I. Withrington, Donald J.   II. University of Aberdeen.   III. Series.
DA880.S5S45   941.1'35   82–2207   AACR2
ISBN 0-19-714107-2

Typeset by Phoenix Photosetting, Chatham, Kent
Printed and bound by Mackays of Chatham Ltd

Contents

	LIST OF PLATES	vi
	CONTRIBUTORS	vii
	INTRODUCTION DONALD J. WITHRINGTON	1
I.	The Scots settlement in Shetland GORDON DONALDSON	8
II.	Geographical location: environment and history ALAN SMALL	20
III.	The pledging of the islands in 1469: the historical background BARBARA E. CRAWFORD	32
IV.	Udal law KNUT ROBBERSTAD	49
V.	The post-Norse place-names of Shetland W. F. H. NICOLAISEN	69
VI.	Hanseatic merchants and their trade with Shetland KLAUS FRIEDLAND	86
VII.	The Netherland fisheries and the Shetland Islands H. A. H. BOELMANS KRANENBURG	96
VIII.	Five centuries of Shetland fisheries ALISTAIR GOODLAD	107
IX.	Shetland history in the Scottish records MARGARET D. YOUNG	119
X.	The discovery of Shetland from *The Pirate* to the Tourist Board JOHN M. SIMPSON	136
XI.	Population and depopulation WILLIAM P. L. THOMSON	150
XII.	Shetland and Norway in the Second World War MAGNE SKODVIN	181
XIII.	Economic changes since 1946 STUART B. DONALD	198
XIV.	Social changes during the quinquennium JOHN J. GRAHAM	216
	INDEX	235

List of Plates

Between pages 120 *and* 121

1. Sixerns and Hanseatic bøds at Fethaland, North Roe
2. A crofter's cottage
3. Haymaking at Bennegarth, North Roe
4. Crofting community—alive
5. Crofting community—dead (Uyea, North Roe)
6. Lerwick from the south
7. The herring boom: Lerwick fishing station
8. John Brown (?) and his team of gutters: late 19th century

Acknowledgements:
for nos. 1–5, 7, 8 The Shetland Museum, Lerwick
for no. 6 Dennis Coutts, Lerwick

Contributors

BARBARA E. CRAWFORD: M.A., Dip.Arch., Ph.D.; Lecturer in Medieval History, University of St. Andrews.

STUART B. DONALD: M.A.; formerly County Development Officer, Shetland County Council.

GORDON DONALDSON: M.A., Ph.D., D.Litt., F.B.A.; Emeritus Professor of Scottish History and Palaeography, University of Edinburgh.

KLAUS FRIEDLAND: D.Phil.; Archivist, City of Lübeck; Lecturer at the University of Kiel.

ALISTAIR GOODLAD: M.A., Ph.D.; formerly Assistant Professor, and Fellow of the Institute of Social and Economic Research, Memorial University of Newfoundland.

JOHN J. GRAHAM: O.B.E., M.A.; Headmaster, Anderson High School, Lerwick.

H. A. H. BOELMANS KRANENBURG: D.Econ.; Sea Fisheries Museum of the Netherlands at Vlaardingen.

W. F. H. NICOLAISEN: D.Phil., B.Litt.; formerly at the School of Scottish Studies, University of Edinburgh; Professor of English and Folk-Lore at New York State University, Binghamton.

KNUT ROBBERSTAD: D.Phil.; Emeritus Professor of Law and Udal Law at the University of Oslo.

JOHN M. SIMPSON: M.A.; Senior Lecturer in Scottish History, University of Edinburgh.

MAGNE SKODVIN: D.Phil.; Professor of Modern History, University of Oslo.

ALAN SMALL: M.A.; Reader in Geography, University of Dundee.

WILLIAM P. L. THOMSON: M.A.; formerly Principal Teacher of History and Geography at the Anderson High School, Lerwick; Rector of Kirkwall Grammar School.

DONALD J. WITHRINGTON: M.A., M.Ed., F.R.Hist.S.; Senior Lecturer in Scottish History, University of Aberdeen.

MARGARET D. YOUNG: M.A.; Assistant Keeper, Scottish Record Office, Edinburgh.

For
John Spence
Mortimer Manson
Tom Henderson

Introduction

THE PAPERS in this collection remain, by and large, in the form in which they were delivered in 1969 at the Shetland Historical Congress, a meeting called to commemorate—rather perhaps than to celebrate—the five hundred years' anniversary of the pledging of the islands to Scotland by Christian I of Denmark and Norway. That conference, for those who attended it, was a truly memorable occasion; and the lectures here printed had a vital part to play in a week suffused with good things. Those of us who previously had known little or nothing of the islands, 'soothmoothers' and foreigners alike, were intellectually and emotionally captured by all we saw and heard; and we all went away with a deep respect and affection for the Shetlanders.

Those last months of the 1960s, it can now be seen a decade later, were very notable indeed in Shetland life—actually deserving that too-often abused term, a watershed. Since the end of the Second World War, times in Shetland had been hard: but the energetic, diligent and increasingly perceptive Shetlanders had fought back—and did so as much, if not more, by their own efforts than by waiting passively for the British government to act. In the 1960s Shetland was attracting investment monies from Scandinavia, and local investment in new projects was rising steadily. By 1969, indeed, Shetlanders had also used such initiative in seeking out newly-available development funds from government sources that, while comprising only six per cent of the population within the Highlands and Islands Development Board area, they were laying claim to seventeen per cent of its funds. Mr Donald provides this information in his essay on the Shetland economy since 1946; Dr Goodlad notes in his paper that in 1969, too, the fishing was good—we should note the very hopeful concluding remarks in his essay, for they underline the entirely unexpected decline in fishing in the 1970s. In 1969 new manufacturing was developing fast, and a new buoyancy had appeared generally in the economic structure. In short, the future for Shetland looked bright at last, even though the struggle had been a hard one. The first discoveries and then the exploitation of North Sea oil, with so much of the activity to be based in Shetland, were still to come, hardly to be forecasted by our speakers. The hints of the new prosperity which they saw were still essentially bound in with the old ways: in fish and fishing, in wool and knitting, in pony-breeding, and in new technical developments that were still traditionally based—fish processing, machine-knitting, silverwork, stone-polishing. The Shetlanders were rightly proud of their efforts; they had pulled themselves up, very largely, by their own bootstraps and had done so within the expanding context of a still distinctively Shetland way of life.

How that was to change, how quickly the foreseeable future was to be overturned! As the members of the Congress sat contemplating their analyses of the gradual emergence of that finely-balanced community of the late 1960s, a community making the most of what seemed to so many outsiders to be remarkably meagre resources, so were being heralded such changes as had been unknown in Shetland for many centuries—perhaps since 1469 and its aftermath. While some of the predictions and some of the judgments we heard at the Congress in 1969 were soon to be overtaken by the tumultuous events of the 1970s, and despite the unfortunate delay there has been in publication, no attempt has been made to 'update' the essays which follow nor to amend the arguments and conclusions. By retaining the particular flavour of 1969 in these lectures, there has been given an added strength to the volume—for the essays now constitute, themselves, an historical record, evidence of judgments made, aspirations and exasperations felt, at that crucial moment before the oil boom of the 1970s. Here, indeed, is a late glimpse of pre-oil Shetland—of a Shetland when Sullom Voe was still an untidy and all-but-deserted monument to the wartime devastation of a peaceful corner of Northmavine, when Shetland hotels provided fine value and their usual generous hospitality for £10 a day or much less, when industrialization in the isles meant the founding of a small knitwear factory or the intermittent shock to the nose of the establishment of a fish-processing plant.

What then, as it is mirrored in these essays, did both Shetlanders and incomers see as the particularly important elements in the evolution of Shetland by the late 1960s? Firstly, there were three distinct groups of reasons for confirming that 1469 was a highly significant date. For one thing, Scottish influences markedly increased—Scots looked northwards to their new possession and Shetlanders came to look southwards rather than eastwards to

Scandinavia. By the early years of the seventeenth century, indeed, as Professor Donaldson noted, some 25–30 per cent of surnames in the islands were Scottish; while Norn was still the usual language of the islanders, they both understood and used the speech of the Scottish mainland Scots, that is, not Gaelic—in their contacts with strangers. Professor Nicolaisen pointed out that one of the most frequent place-name types in post-1469 Shetland, in a countryside that was already then well-filled with Norse names, is that of 'A of B' (as in 'Noup of Noss')—a form of place-name which, rather surprisingly, has Gaelic origins and seems to have been transferred to Shetland by immigrants and colonists from north-east Scotland. Well before the eighteenth century, it must be concluded, Scottish 'infiltration' was very considerable, and has tended to be underestimated by Shetlanders wishing to emphasize the continuing strength of Norse tradition.

In economic terms, too, 1469 proved decisive. The old, tight controls which had been imposed on markets and on trading by the Scandinavian rulers, mainly through and in favour of the staple at Bergen, were relaxed and removed. Thereafter Shetland was increasingly opened up to the 'wider world', in particular to the Hanseatic merchants and to Dutch fishermen. Dr Friedland estimates in his essay that in the sixteenth century a German merchant from one of the Hansa towns might spend as much as one-third of his seafaring life in Shetland. Dr Krannenberg and Dr Goodlad both remark on the strength of Dutch influences in Shetland in the seventeenth century, when as much as 35–40 per cent of all herring sold in Holland was probably caught off Shetland—and the Dutch presence was to be stronger still in the nineteenth century. Dr Goodlad provokingly reminds us that in the centuries which followed 1469 Shetland can be seen as occupying the centre of the European fishing world, not the fringe.

Thirdly, politically and legally 1469 was crucial too. The pledging of the islands ushered in a century of increasing activity by Scottish landed interests, a period that was then capped by a half-century of brutal dominance under the Stewart earls and the feudalisation of their territories. Meanwhile the older udal law did not disappear, a point underlined for us by both Dr Crawford and Professor Robberstadt. Just as seventy or eighty years after 1469 the Bergen staple was still trying to enforce its regulations on Shetland traders, so too as late as the early years of the seventeenth century we find Norse law still being observed—the surviving court books show. obvious connections with the lawbook of Magnus the Lawmender and no formal attempt was made to replace the existing law practice by that of mainland Scotland until 1611. As Dr Crawford and Dr Friedland both note, it seems to have been Christian I's firm intention to redeem the pledge he had made, and therefore Shetlanders sensibly retained the law of the Lawmender. But Dr Crawford and Professor Robberstadt also remark on one essential change that was made in 1469: the settlement with Scotland, while it may have left the day-to-day operation of udal law largely untouched, ceded the payment of skatt to the Scottish crown—and he who received skatt also obtained the formal allegiance of the taxpayer. How vital, then, was that change? How crucial was that transfer of allegiance to be? How important should it have been (or not) in legal judgments about such subsequent issues as the ownership of the St Ninian's Isle treasure? Professor Robberstadt's essay provides fascinating comment on such matters.

Thus the pledging of the islands to Scotland brought change, sometimes quickly, sometimes much more hesitantly. It introduced new connections, weakening some of the older Norse relationships, bringing Scots and Dutch and Germans into novel contacts which, variously and more-or-less intermittently, were to remain strong for four centuries or more. Generally these influences were those introduced by outsiders, by incomers who exercised a particular economic or social or political force on the island population. Within this grouping of outside influences, confining the native spirit and weakening native traditions, one has been most frequently remarked upon—the Scottish landlord: and it has produced what Mr Graham refers to as a long-standing Shetland blood sport, 'hunting the laird'. But Mr Thomson argues cogently that it was pressure of population on scarce resources, rather than any deliberate and debilitating landlord policy, which led directly to the notorious sub-division of crofts in the high period of fishing tenures. Mr Graham condemns those same fishing tenures, not so much because they were necessarily cruel contracts enforced by heartless landlords but because they drew the tenantry into a passive acceptance of their fate which was then supported and deepened by their religion. In an editorial in the *New Shetlander* in 1969 just before the Congress opened, Mr Graham put the same point in an especially pungent way: 'If the quincentenary is to be at all meaningful, there is one thing we should celebrate above all—the approaching end of that age-old Authoritarianism, a monstrous growth which, shielded by the walls of Landlordism,

Church, School and State, has overshadowed the lives and hopes of ordinary folk for far longer than five hundred years.' Dr Goodlad is also prepared for some reassessment of landlordism and of tenant-submissiveness: for him the worst feature of the era of haaf-fishing—and he would wish for a modification of the traditional 'heroic' interpretation of that era—was the tightness of the control imposed, on tenants and on landlords alike, by a peculiar economic and social system; the late eighteenth-century attack on the outright dominance of the merchant-landmasters by a few native and incomer merchants was welcome—it was the latter who stimulated the growth of the cod-fishing which, in Dr Goodlad's view, far surpassed the haaf; the haaf fishers were driven to their renowned gallantry at sea by the 'whims of Scottish landmasters', but when the cod fishers ranged even further offshore for their catches they did so on their own initiative, because they were 'their own masters to a significantly greater extent'. Again, Mr Thomson—analysing the fundamental causes of nineteenth-century emigration from the islands—sees one in 'a loosening of ties', in that release into a greater reality of independence and initiative which followed the move abroad. The implication of these commentaries is clear enough: even in the worst times of the past five centuries, if sometimes held in such restraint as to be all but invisible, the essential character of the Shetlander remained—there was resilience in the face of terrible adversity, there was a holding to traditional values in the face of social and cultural attack on them, there was always an insistent (if quietly observed) independence of spirit. And if earlier times had conspired to offer few opportunities for the islanders openly to demonstrate that resilience and independence of spirit, had the more recent past shown them more clearly?

Here, in concentrating on the last hundred years or so, we reach a further aspect of the 'wider world' connections of Shetland which are discussed in these essays. There was, firstly, as Mr Thomson demonstrates so well, a new readiness to emigrate, to leave the homeland and to explore the opportunities of the nearer or more distant world when comparable opportunities were not available in Shetland. In relatively prosperous times at home, for example c. 1815–c. 1830, there was little emigration: but after the harsh years of 1839–49 very large numbers left and continued to leave. Even the great herring boom in the late nineteenth century did little to slow down the movement away: Dr Goodlad reminds us that the herring fishing in its high period was largely organised by outside (Scottish and foreign) interests, not by home-based merchants and curers, and produced less and less continuing expansion for Shetland itself than has been usually presumed. After the peak census year for Shetland's population in 1861, there was a steady decline decade by decade until the 1970s. The value of the emigrant Shetlanders to the 'wider world' soon became renowned—in America, in Australia and New Zealand, in mainland Britain; their going, as Mr Thomson showed, left behind a troublesome age-structure and a still greater stimulus to emigration. Since the date of the Congress, with the expansion of oil-interests in the 1970s, some 5000 immigrants have come into the islands and there has certainly been less native emigration. What remains to be seen is whether the 1980s, with the main oil-boom past, will continue to restrain movement out of the islands.

But the 'wider world' came to Shetland for other reasons in the past century or so. Early tourism, as Mr Simpson notes, provided a romantic, even a mystical, view of the northernmost isles. The Second World War brought tens of thousands of enforced travellers into a more immediately realistic vision of Shetland life and it left many of them (including the Norwegians of whom Professor Skodvin spoke) with a new and intensely warm regard for Shetland and its people—while it gave the UK government a novel if short-lived interest in the islands. But as the strategic importance of Shetland declined after the war, so it faded from the forefront of government policy, even apparently from government awareness. A studied ignorance returned: even in 1969, as Mr Donald sadly comments, 'it seems impossible to persuade the central authorities that a community as remote from London as Prague or Genoa has its own peculiar problems or prospects'. Indeed, the later 1960s saw the publication and discussion of the Wheatley Report on local government reform: unbelievably (in the northern isles at least) it recommended that Orkney and Shetland should be submerged into a Highland Region which was to stretch from Bute to Muckle Flugga—and mainland ignorance, the cavalier ignoring of cultural distinctions and of community-orientations and even of the problems of communication which distance brings, seemed as marked as ever it had been. What was not known in 1969 was that good sense would in the end prevail, if only after much hard talking: Orkney, Shetland and the Western Isles were to be saved from the worst excesses of Wheatley. The emergence of the all-purpose Shetland Islands Council could not have been much better timed: it soon produced a welcome sharpening of powers of bargaining, on behalf of a local community it knew well, in discussions with oil companies and with successive governments at Westminster, and used them to remarkably good effect. The hopefulness of 1969 was well judged. If one thing in particular comes through from all of the papers delivered to the Congress, it is the ultimate strength of that 'sense of community and local identity' to which Mr Graham referred in the final sentence of the final lecture. It was a vital factor in the fight to gain partial independence at least, in the battle over local government reform; it can be seen in the subsequent emergence of the Shetland Movement, characteristically ready to ally its cultural and social concerns with a keen awareness of the importance of economic and political issues; it is there in the quality and variety of local publications; it is to be seen in that judicious concern for the distant or the immediate past, in the determination to seek out the realities of tradition, which produced the Historical Congress of 1969 and since then has provided for the appointment of an archivist (and very recently of an assistant to work on a predominantly oral history project)—to make available the wealth of locally-held historical records and also to stimulate the use of that cornucopia of Shetland material in the Scottish Record Office about which Miss Young spoke to the conference.

Since 1469 Shetland has experienced a succession of varying 'invasions': the oil invaders are only the latest, if among the most dramatic and powerful. Characteristically, Shetlanders have adapted where necessary to the incomers but they have also often assimilated them—processes which appear to have combined to strengthen corporate identity and the 'sense of community'. May the next five hundred years serve to enhance them still further.

DONALD J. WITHRINGTON

October 1981

CHAPTER I

The Scots Settlement in Shetland

GORDON DONALDSON

WITH THE transaction of 1469, the kingdom of Scotland reached its final frontier in the north, and the present extent of the United Kingdom of Great Britain was thereby determined; and Scottish influence has been a feature of Shetland history since 1469 in a way it had not been before. A distinction is to be drawn between the situation in Shetland and that in Orkney. Far less happened in Shetland, in the way of Scottish infiltration, before 1469, than had happened in Orkney before 1468. To that extent 1469 may be regarded as a far more significant date in the history of Shetland than 1468 is in the history of Orkney. For Shetland 1469 was very largely the beginning of a new era in its history, whereas no one would suggest that 1468 was in any sense the beginning of a new era for Orkney. In 1469 Shetland was still essentially Norse, in race, in language and in institutions, whereas in 1468 Orkney was already very largely Scotticised.

The reason for the difference was not directly geographical. It did not lie simply in the much greater proximity of Orkney to the Scottish mainland, and the somewhat greater proximity of Shetland to Norway. Nor was it substantially economic, though, in days when wealth and prosperity were measured mainly by the fertility of the soil, the economic attraction of Orkney to Scots was incomparably greater than was that of Shetland.

The main reason for the distinction between the situation in Orkney and in Shetland is to be found in the earlier political history of the two groups of islands. The earls of Orkney had been half-Scottish by race since before 1200, and almost wholly Scottish from a point not long thereafter.[1] It is true that the rule of those earls was not quite continuous, but by the fifteenth century, even when there was not a Scottish earl, the administration of Orkney was nonetheless in the hands of Scotsmen.[2] However, before Scottish influence had become very noticeable in the earldom—in 1195 to be precise—Shetland had been detached from the earldom and after that had been ruled not by Scots but by governors appointed directly from Norway. Orkney was thus ruled by earls of Scottish race and ultimately by earls or officials who were in every sense Scots, and those earls and officials were inevitably the channel whereby Scottish influence penetrated into Orkney. Shetland, on the other hand, under direct rule from Norway, was bound to be in a different position. Not only was there rule from Norway, but lands in Shetland were owned by Norwegians, and long after 1469 there were many individuals and families whose interests were so divided between Shetland and Norway that it would be hard to say whether they should be reckoned as Norwegians or as Shetlanders.[3]

The most striking illustration of the sharp contrast between Orkney and Shetland is to be found in the linguistic field. The Norse tongue was well on the way to being superseded in Orkney before 1468, whereas in Shetland it continued to be in general use for a long time after 1469. Already in the 1430s—a generation before 1469—the lawman of Orkney was using Lowland Scots.[4] In Shetland, by contrast, right on through the sixteenth century there are quite a number of documents in Norse, and the last of them belongs to so late as 1607.[5] This evidence suggests that there was a time-lag of something like a hundred and fifty years between the point at which the Scots tongue prevailed in Orkney and the point at which it prevailed in Shetland. Behind this linguistic contrast, and at least partially explaining it, there must have lain a considerable immigration of Scotsmen to Orkney before 1468. Of such immigration there is in fact ample documentary evidence.

While Orkney and Shetland were in different situations politically, there was one channel through which, already before 1469, Scots could find their way into Shetland as well as into Orkney, and that was the church, because the diocese of Orkney, unlike the earldom, always included Shetland. There were Scottish bishops in Orkney from the late fourteenth century, and Scottish bishops in Orkney were apt to mean Scottish clergy in Shetland. The archdeaconry of Shetland, like the bishopric of Orkney, was held by Scots long before 1469[6] and, again like the bishopric, was held in the fifteenth century by a succession of Tullochs—Malise, David and Thomas[7]—who were no doubt kinsmen of the Tulloch bishops. Possibly the archdeaconry might have been rather a special case, because it was, after the bishopric itself, the most valuable benefice in the whole diocese. But some of the Shetland vicarages, too, were uncommonly valuable as vicarages went, and quite likely to attract careerists.[8] The evidence for the parishes is scanty, but in Yell, for example, the name of the parish priest in 1405 was Gudbrandr Magnusson and in 1477 it was John Chalmer, an obvious Scot.[9] Some of the bearers of Scottish names who appear in Shetland in the sixteenth century may have been descendants of Scottish clerics who had come in before 1469. Certainly some of the Scottish surnames which occur in Shetland had been held by clergy in Orkney before 1469—for example Nisbet and Cant. Besides the clergy themselves there were their dependants, and the Coplands seem to have originated with a client of Bishop William Tulloch.[10]

But while Scottish churchmen were thus arriving in Shetland, there was hardly any economic or political reason for Scottish laymen to find their way to Shetland before 1469. There was indeed a certain infiltration, if only by way of Orkney and its Scottish earls. Whatever the precise political or legal position which the family of St Clair held in Shetland before 1469, that family did have a certain interest and certain properties in Shetland from 1379 onwards,[11] and it is hard to believe that all the numerous Sinclairs who appear in Shetland so soon after 1469 had arrived there after that date. Others, besides Sinclairs, who obviously reached Shetland by way of Orkney were the Frasers or Frissels, who were in Orkney as early as 1439, and appear in Shetland a century later.[12] In any event, it seems unlikely that all the Scots who appear on record in Shetland soon after 1500 were recent arrivals, or first-generation immigrants: in some cases the first bearer of a Scottish surname who happens to be recorded in Shetland was clearly not himself the first of his family to live there, for some of them have Shetland Christian names—Magnus Nisbet in Unst in 1551 and Magnus Tulloch in Northmavine in 1545[13]—from which one may perhaps deduce that they had Shetland mothers.

These, however, are mere qualifications of the general picture. While our evidence is far too scanty to admit of firm conclusions, it does suggest that, while there were Scots in Shetland in 1469, they were few and far between.

For the period after 1469, or rather after 1500, evidence becomes more plentiful. After the transfer of the islands to Scotland, as before it, the church continued to be a main instrument of Scottish immigration. Among all the Shetland clergy who are on record in the sixteenth century, only one looks as if he might possibly have been a native—Robert Malcolmson, who was vicar of Dunrossness in 1550;[14] and there was Magnus Norsk, minister of Unst from 1593 to 1632, who was presumably a Norwegian.[15] All the others were Scots, and most of them left traceable descendants in the islands—for example, Cheyne, Edmonston, Gifford, Hay, Murray, Sinclair and Wishart. Others lasted for only a generation or two in the male line—Fallowsdales, Hills and Lauders for example—but no doubt continued through females.[16] Sometimes kinsmen of the cleric, as well as the cleric himself, arrived in Shetland: the Cheynes are a conspicuous instance of this and their appearances suggest that Archdeacon Jerome Cheyne passed the word around his kinsmen that there were opportunities in Shetland.[17] Sometimes, too, it seems that two or three generations of a Scottish family might hold office in the church. For example, Henry Murray was vicar of Holm in Orkney in 1473, another Henry Murray was a priest in Kirkwall in 1547, and John Murray was curate of Bressay in 1547: Magnus Murray, who was vicar of Walls in 1562, with his Shetland Christian name and his Scottish surname, looks like the son of a Shetland mother by one of those earlier Murrays.[18]

The migration of Scottish laymen into Shetland was a complex and many-sided movement, in which three elements at least can be detected. The first was the desire for land, which in those days was the great investment and the great speculation: it is noticeable for example, how Englishmen were competing for concessions of land in Ireland before they looked for land in America; and similarly Lowland Scots sought land in the Highlands and the Islands of their own country before they in turn looked for concessions of land in Ireland or in America. The landed men are, next to the churchmen, the easiest to trace. First among them stand the Sinclairs, who were evidently in Shetland before 1469, and clearly consolidated their position thereafter. Sir David Sinclair was a leading figure in Shetland by 1485,[19] and members of this family held the office of foud, or chief magistrate, almost continuously for a century.[20] With the Stewart earls and their following, other names appear which were to be well known in Shetland, notably the Bruces, who collectively should perhaps be considered to have first place among Shetland proprietors. The first Bruce, Laurence Bruce of Cultmalindie, was a half-brother of Earl Robert, the first of the Stewart earls. To trace the ramifications of a family in the process of migration, it is not sufficient to look only for bearers of its surname. Laurence Bruce's first wife was a Kennedy, and this may explain why we find an Elspeth Kennedy and a Hucheon Kennedy among the inhabitants of Shetland at that time. Again, the first Bruce of Simbister may have been related to Cultmalindie, but he was certainly a native not of Perthshire, as Cultmalindie was, but of East Fife; his wife, however, was Marjory Stewart, a niece of Earl Robert, and this may have been the true origin of his Shetland connection.[21]

The second element was commerce, which led to the appearance in Shetland of Scottish traders. Although the main trade of Shetland was still the trade with the Hanseatic ports, there was a small but significant number of Scottish traders, operating mainly in Dunrossness and coming chiefly, it would appear, from Dundee and Kirkcaldy. In addition to traders, a certain number of fishermen came to Shetland from Orkney, Caithness and perhaps elsewhere in the south.[22]

The third element was a small infiltration of those whom we can call generally specialists—under which term are comprehended officials, with their legal and professional knowledge, and also craftsmen of various kinds. In Scalloway about 1600 there was a little group of craftsmen, all with Scottish names: George Mitchell and James Short, tailors; John Ross, mason; Alexander Gray, shoemaker; and Archibald Murray, a wright, with an apprentice called Francis Inglis.[23]

There was, indeed, a fourth way in which Scotland made an impact on Shetland in the sixteenth century. From time to time raids were made on the islands by marauders from Lewis, and the need to defend the islands against the incursions of foreigners from 'the highlands of Scotland and other barbarous parts', as it was phrased, was taken quite seriously.[24] However, these sporadic raiders are unlikely to have affected the racial composition of the inhabitants.

Behind these specific elements in the migration, there is a wider background. This Scottish settlement in Shetland at that period is to be seen within the general context of the expansion of the Scottish nation. In the whole enormous picture of Scottish emigration over the centuries one phase was the expansion of the Scots within the geographical bounds of Scotland itself. There was settlement and plantation, sometimes only attempted, sometimes successful, in parts of the western Highlands and Islands. This was essentially planned. But there was also a parallel, though more spontaneous, movement of Lowland Scots into these northern islands.[25] This was in the period before the Scots began to look seriously to lands across the oceans as targets for their emigration, outlets for their vitality and ambition. Some kind of estimate of the racial composition of the people of Shetland as it was in the early seventeenth century can be reached from an analysis of the names which appear in the Court Book for 1602–4[26] and in the Index to the Records of Testaments,[27] which cover people who died in Shetland between roughly 1600 and 1648. The figures are certainly revealing. In the Court Book, out of about 1600 names, there are 550 persons with names suggestive of Scottish descent—that is, almost exactly one-third of the total. In the Index of Testaments, out of about 1050 names, about 315 have names pointing to Scottish origin—i.e., rather less than a third. A slight difference between the proportion disclosed in the Court Book and that disclosed in the Testaments is to be expected: after all, the Court Book deals with people who lived in Shetland, the Testaments with people who died in Shetland, and a certain number of Scots came to Shetland for a time for one reason or another but returned to Scotland before they died. For this reason, the figures in the Testaments probably come a little closer to indicating the proportion of Scots who were actually settled in the islands—a figure of rather less than a third.

This general survey of Shetland as a whole can be supplemented by a more detailed examination of Yell and Fetlar.[28] In Yell, out of about 140 people mentioned in the Court Book, some thirty had names of Scottish origin, about a dozen are doubtful, leaving roughly ninety names which are clearly those of the old native population—a proportion of not very far from a quarter of Scottish origin. In Fetlar, out of some 350 inhabitants whose names are on record between about 1600 and 1650, something like eighty had names which can be pronounced with some confidence to have sprung from Scottish immigrants—again something rather under 25 per cent. One would expect the proportion of people of Scottish origin in Yell and Fetlar to be rather below the average for Shetland as a whole, because there are some indications that in other areas—notably Dunrossness—the proportion of Scottish settlers was above the average.

Certain specific Scottish names are especially prominent in this period. In the Index of Testaments, there are no fewer than 43 Sinclairs, which is a fairly high proportion of about 1000 names in all. There are 12 Tullochs, 11 Strangs, 5 Bruces, 8 Nisbets (all but one of them in Yell) and 7 Spences. In the Court Book there are 85 Sinclairs an even higher proportion than in the Testaments, 16 Bruces, 9

Strangs, 7 Nisbets and 5 Spences. Of Stewarts, there are 9 in the Court Book and only one in the Testaments, which might also suggest that on the whole they went back to Scotland to die. Dr Barclay's editions of the Court Books for Orkney and Shetland for 1612–3 and 1614–5[29] likewise show that Sinclair had a long lead as the commonest surname in the two groups of islands, with Spence as a poor second.

There is no comparable evidence for earlier times, which would make it easier to determine exactly when the flood of Scottish immigrants came. The only substantial lists of names of earlier date are the lists of the Complaints of the Commons of Shetland in 1577.[30] In these lists, the proportion of Scottish names is on the whole lower, ranging from nil in some parishes to 15 per cent in Tingwall and Nesting, 20 per cent in Yell and Unst and—not unexpectedly the highest figure—over 30 per cent in Dunrossness. However, this is not necessarily an indication that there had been a tremendous influx of Scots between 1577 and 1600, for these lists are selective in a way that the Court Book and the Testaments are not. The complaints were against the innovations made by Bruce of Cultmalindie, and it is more than likely that there was more dissatisfaction with his régime on the part of native Shetlanders than on the part of Scottish incomers.

It must be acknowledged that a pattern based on names alone is subject to certain qualifications. In the first place, the surname shows only one single line of descent, and it would therefore be conceivable that an individual with a Scots name might be 90 per cent of native blood. But then it is equally true that an individual with a native name might be 90 per cent Scots in blood, so the various possibilities probably cancel out and the names give a good enough indication of the racial composition. A more serious qualification is this. On the whole, genuine patronymic names indicate Norse descent, but this is not always true, for occasionally the children of Scots settlers conformed to native practice and adopted patronymics. Thus, in the early seventeenth century, the daughter of Thomas Gray was Annie Thomasdochter, the son of Hucheon Kennedy was Magnus Hutchison.[31] The same happened in later times. It is always said, no doubt with truth, that the Hughsons in Shetland, or some of them, are descended from a Scotsman, Hugh Noble, who arrived in Shetland about 1700. Even in the nineteenth century this kind of thing could happen. Magnus Davidson, who died in Yell in 1862 at the age of 61, was the son of David Christie.[32] As long as the patronymic system operated, the children of Scottish immigrants could adopt patronymics and thereby lose the indication of their Scottish origin. Besides, some of the Scottish settlers would themselves have surnames of patronymic type, such as Anderson or Henderson, impossible to disentangle from real patronymics unless one has the name of more than one generation. For one reason or another, therefore, there are Scots settlers, or the descendants of Scots settlers, disguised under names of patronymic form. These qualifications in respect of the evidence of patronymic names mean that an analysis based on surnames is likely on the whole to under-rate the Scottish element in Shetland.

It is hard to believe that there was much traffic in the other direction to offset this qualification. It cannot often have happened that a native Shetlander, who ought to have been known by a patronymic, would adopt a Scottish surname, though no doubt it might happen occasionally. There is also the possibility of a native name being modified to take a Scottish form. There is the conspicuous example of the transmogrification of Sigurdson or Shuardson into Stewartson and then into Stewart. Not all the Stewarts in Shetland are descended from the Stewart earls or their dependents. How true it is that not all Stewarts are sib to the king! So much, then, for the situation in the early seventeenth century, when several agencies had clearly been operating to produce a very substantial immigration from Scotland into Shetland. There has not been a period since when there has been anything comparable. For one thing, after 1600 the Scots were beginning to an even greater extent to find an outlet for their energies in settlement in the new world across the oceans; and, as emigration overseas developed, emigration to the peripheral areas of Scotland itself was likely to slacken off.

It seems likely that the outstanding importance of the sixteenth century, as the period when the Scots made most impact on Shetland, is reflected in the language. A good deal of the Lowland Scots which appears in the present-day Shetland dialect seems to be sixteenth-century Scots. It was at that time that the Scots tongue came in, and in no later period was there an immigration considerable enough to supersede the sixteenth-century idiom by the Lowland Scots of later times.

However, while there was never again a flood, or even a flow, of Scots into Shetland after the sixteenth century, the infiltration did continue, though reduced to the proportion of a trickle. It is not difficult to detect factors which have all made their small contribution from time to time and have brought a few more Scots to settle in the islands. The church continued to play its part.[33] While it is not unknown to find a native Shetlander as minister of a Shetland parish, it has on the whole been rare. And some of the Scots who came in as ministers remained—one might almost say they came to pray and remained to prey—giving us the families of Nicolson, Henry, Mitchell and Grierson (though Henry, it should be said, is also a truncated patronymic and not all the Henrys are necessarily descended from the early seventeenth-century minister of Walls). Something of the same may apply to schoolmasters, but until the history of education in Shetland is written one can hardly do more than speculate. There was, as in earlier times, the occasional merchant. From the Register of Deeds of the Stewartry, it is evident that about a score of Scottish merchants were operating in Shetland in the 1690s.[34] They belonged mainly to Dundee and the Aberdeenshire ports, and since among them there are names found in Shetland in later times—Greig, Ross and Torrie—it seems that some of them settled in the islands. And, again as in earlier times, there have been specialists of every kind—professional men like doctors and lawyers, an occasional official, as well as tradesmen and technicians.

It seems unlikely that the presence in the islands of members of the armed forces brought much admixture of southern blood to Shetland before the twentieth century, but it is not to be forgotten that Fort Charlotte was garrisoned intermittently in earlier periods. Even before Fort Charlotte was built there was for a time a garrison in Shetland, and there is the tradition that the Shetland name Doull derived from a soldier called MacDougal who was a member of the Cromwellian garrison of Scalloway Castle.[35]

But settlers of all the categories—ministers, merchants, specialists and strays—were not quite the whole story. The one single development in the last three hundred and fifty years which led to an appreciable Scottish settlement in Shetland was the herring fishing, in its great days in the late nineteenth century and the beginning of the twentieth. There was a period of half a century or so, before and after 1900, when the herring fishing reached vast proportions, bringing hundreds of boats and thousands of men to Shetland each summer. They came from many places in Scotland and from some places in England, as the advent of the steam drifter extended the range of the boats. The record year was 1905, when over 1,000,000 barrels of herring were cured in Shetland and there were, so it seems, some 1700 boats and 20,000 men engaged in the fishing. Apart from those actually on the boats, the herring industry involved a number of subsidiary or ancilliary occupations—coopers, for instance, gutters and packers, as well as the fish merchants and salesmen and the men employed on the hulks lying out in the harbour with their stores of coal. It may well be that the whole industry represented, numerically, the biggest impact the outside world has ever yet made on Shetland; if, however, that distinction really belongs to the Dutch fishery, it would still be true that this more recent phase represented the maximum Scottish impact on Shetland.

Not many of this great company settled in Shetland, or were other than seasonal visitors, but even a small proportion of such a vast total could clearly be significant. Some of them certainly did settle, and there are some Scots names in Lerwick today which originated with Scots fishermen who settled there. Nor was the movement confined to Lerwick. When the herring industry was at its height, the bulk of the curing was done elsewhere throughout the county, and in 1905 there were actually more herring stations in Baltasound than there were in Lerwick. Consequently, some Scots fishermen settled in various parts of Shetland.[36] It has to be remembered in this connection that members of fishing communities seem to find migration easy. After all, life in a fishing community is much the same in any port, whether it is in Shetland or Buchan or the Western Isles or northern Ireland or north-east England, and one can find any number of examples of people moving from one of those communities to another.

The effects of the herring fishing on the population of Shetland can to some extent be measured, for the census returns have given the place of birth of all persons and it is possible to pick out the non-natives. It is true, of course, that the census returns include others than permanent immigrants or settlers, but even so the figures are significant. In 1861—that is, before the herring fishing had reached significant proportions—the number of non-natives in Shetland was only about 600, out of a population of 31,000—a mere 2 per cent or so. In 1901 the number was over 1400, out of a population of over 26,000, a percentage of 5. In 1911 the number was nearly 2400, out of a total of over 25,000, a percentage of about 9. I have no doubt that if a census had been taken in 1905 or 1906 the percentage would have been higher still. In 1931 the total was nearly 1500 out of a total of 21,500, a percentage of 7—a slight drop, you will notice, reflecting the decline of the herring fishery. The census of 1921 is a special case. As a rule the census was taken in April, a date long before the herring fishing started, but in 1921 it was taken on 19 June, when the fishing had started, though it had not yet reached anything like its peak. In 1921 there were over 2500 non-natives in a population of under 25,000, a percentage of slightly over 10—the highest percentage ever recorded. And it is worth noting that in 1921 the census returned no fewer than 107 residents in Shetland as Gaelic speakers, which must be easily the record for the county, and reflects, of course, west Highlanders who had come in for the herring fishing. Possibly the figures for 1921 would include a certain number of holiday-makers, or tourists, but not many tourists were coming to Shetland in June in those days, and in 1921 they would certainly have been discouraged by a coal strike which had upset the steamer service.

The study of the movement of Scots into Shetland, is, like the study of any other migration, not one study but many studies—the studies of thousands of individuals. All that this paper does is offer some generalisations and give a few examples.

One theme in our minds in this Congress is the position of Shetland as the link between Norway and Scotland, indeed between many parts of the continent and Scotland, and therefore, while we are going to give a good deal of attention to the continental side, we must not lose sight of the Scottish side.

NOTES

1 The pedigrees are most clearly and simply shown in the tables in J. Storer Clouston, *History of Orkney* (Kirkwall, 1932), 382–5.
2 *Ibid.*, 229, 236–7, 240–9.
3 Gilbert Goudie, *Celtic and Scandinavian Antiquities of Shetland* (London, 1914), 89, 107–24, 129–30.
4 J. Storer Clouston (ed.), *Records of the Earldom of Orkney* (Scot. Hist. Soc., 1914), 71–2.
5 Goudie, *Antiquities*, 109–10.
6 The precise succession is difficult to determine, for there were several rival claimants, but the following names appear as those of holders or claimants between 1360 and 1425: William Jonson, who may be identical with William Wood; William of Buchan, succeeded (perhaps illegally) by Walter of Buchan; William de Lancea, chaplain of Alexander Stewart, 'the Wolf of Badenoch'; and David Craigie [*Records of the Earldom*, 15, 27; *Calendar of Papal Registers, Petitions*, i, 566; *Calendar of Papal Registers, Letters*, iv, 385; E. R. Lindsay and A. I. Cameron (eds), *Scottish Supplications to Rome, 1418–22* (Scot. Hist. Soc., 1934), 239]. It appears that in the archdeaconry, as in the bishopric, it was appointments made by the Avignon Pope which took effect during the Schism, but Adam Easton, an English cardinal, was provided by the Roman Pope and was succeeded by Angus of Kirkness (*Scottish Supplications*, 241–2).

7 *Diplomatarium Norvegicum*, xvii (1), 378, 438, 460, 509; MS Register of Supplications in Scottish Record Office, 502, 94v.
8 G. Donaldson (ed.), *Thirds of Benefices* (Scot. Hist. Soc., 1949), 1–2.
9 *Diplomatarium Norvegicum*, i, no. 606; *Cal. Papal Registers, Letters*, xiii, 569.
10 J. B. Craven, *History of the Church in Orkney to 1558* (Kirkwall, 1893), 109, 113, 115.
11 J. Anderson (ed.), *Orkneyinga Saga* (Edinburgh, 1873), pp. lxvi–lxx.
12 *Records of the Earldom*, 72; Goudie, *Antiquities*, 141.
13 Goudie, *Antiquities*, 81, 105.
14 *Registrum Magni Sigilli*, iv, 525.
15 The tale that he was a Scot who went to Norway to learn the Norwegian tongue so that he could communicate with his parishioners is inherently absurd.
16 Many of those families can be traced in Francis J. Grant, *Zetland Family Histories* (Lerwick, 1907). For Fallowsdales and Lauders, see G. Donaldson, 'The early ministers of the North Isles', in *Shetland News* (Sept. 1943).
17 G. Donaldson, 'The archdeaconry of Shetland in the sixteenth century', in *Shetland News* (1946).
18 *Records of the Earldom*, 196, 276, 339; Goudie, *Antiquities*, 51, 146; *Thirds of Benefices*, 151.
19 *Records of the Earldom*, 73, 86, 91; Goudie, *Antiquities*, 84 and n, 196.
20 Goudie, *Antiquities*, 93, 142, 144.
21 F. J. Grant, *Zetland Family Histories*, 11, 21.
22 G. Donaldson, *Shetland Life under Earl Patrick* (Edinburgh, 1958), 53, 68–70.
23 *Ibid.*, 73.
24 *Ibid.*, 77–8.

CHAPTER II

Geographical Location: Environment and History

ALAN SMALL

THE SHETLAND Islands extend for some 100 km. from north to south and Lerwick, the capital, lies at 60°46′N. 0°51′W. The landscape of Shetland, and its history, can only be fully appreciated when the implications of this position are realised. Norway lies a mere 320 km. to the east and, as man's skill in boat-building rose, contact across the North Sea was a natural consequence. Although the northern tip of the Scottish mainland is some 150 km. to the south, the Orkney Islands and Fair Isle acted as 'stepping stones' which allowed early settlers to reach Shetland more than 4,500 years ago.[1] To the north and west, however, the sequence of intervisible islands is broken, with the Faroes over 300 km. distant. Thus movement into the North Atlantic beyond Shetland did not come until early Christian times, when monks such as Dicuil founded anchorite settlements in the Faroes in the immediate pre-Viking period.

This intermediary position between Scotland and Norway can also be clearly seen in the geological features of the area, Shetland being essentially a region of old hard rocks contrasting strongly with the tertiary basalts of the Faroes. Mica schists and gneisses of Palaeozoic age, post Moine in date, form the core of the landscape, cropping out over much of the Mainland, Yell and Unst. These give an undulating landscape which rises in places to over 300m. Bands of limestone run from north to south through the outcrops of schists in the central Mainland and western Unst. These limestone bands, being less resistant to erosion, tend to form broad valleys (e.g. Weisdale) and often provide some of the largest continuous stretches of reasonably

GEOGRAPHICAL LOCATION

fertile soil in Shetland: Tingwall offers an excellent example of this. Diorites and granites have been intruded and frequently produce higher ground such as that of Ronas Hill, the highest point in Shetland, rising to just over 450m. Only the north-east area of Shetland has been intensively studied from the geological viewpoint.[2] The outcrops of serpentines, epidiorites and hornblende-schists in south-eastern Unst appear to be a continuation of the Dalradian structures in Banffshire and may also be continued in western Norway. They were subjected to orogenic movements and regional polyphased metamorphism in Caledonian times and, as Flinn has suggested,[3] some of the Shetland faults may be associated with that of the Great Glen: the general strike is from north-north-east to south-south-west, and the dip on the whole is gentle.

The Old Red Sandstone (Devonian) lies unconformably on the Dalradian structures, mainly in the west Mainland and the eastern peninsulas of the south Mainland. These sandstones are closely related to those of Caithness and Orkney, and they have provided a flatter, more gentle landscape whose soils are reasonably fertile and consequently have attracted (comparatively speaking) fairly dense settlement.

Although the main features of the Shetland landscape were established long before the ice age, glaciation is responsible for much of the detail of the topography. Some early work was done on this aspect of Shetland on a brief visit by Peach and Horne,[4] later criticised by Home.[5] More recently Charlesworth commented on the area[6] but no detailed studies were published till the 1960s when Chapelhow followed earlier authors in proving, on the basis of striations and erratics (probably from the bed of the North Sea), that Shetland was overrun by ice expanding from the Scandinavian ice-cap.[7] This conclusion can be supported by Scandinavian erratics found in other parts of Shetland, notably at Boddam in Dunrossness and North Haven in Fair Isle.[8] It would seem likely, however, that some local glaciation had occurred before this, since the height and area of Shetland would have been sufficient to allow the development of local ice-caps; but all evidence of this appears to have been removed by the Scandinavian ice. Hoppe has maintained that after the Scandinavian ice retreated, valley glaciers flowed out in all directions from the central part of the Mainland.[9] Chapelhow's discovery of a peat bed under some 5½m. of till at Fugla Ness in North Roe has proved the existence of a succeeding period when the climate must have been better than today, for pollen analysis has revealed both birch and pine in the deposit.[10] Another period of local glaciation centred on Ronas Hill then took place. As in earlier phases, there were no doubt several stages of advance and retreat of these local glaciers.

The glacial phase brought considerable modification to the Shetland landscape: it was responsible for much of the rounding of the topography, the widening and deepening of the valleys and geos, and the creation of an abundance of rock basin lakes. Morainic deposits are also numerous, with notable examples to be found near Cunningsburgh. A shallow cover of till occurs on much of the lower ground. There are no raised shorelines in Shetland because there has been a significant rise in sea-level since glacial times. At many sites peat beds dip under the sea and in 1965 peat was recorded at a depth of some 10m. off Whalsay and in Lerwick harbour.[11] Numerous archaeological sites below high water mark confirm the rise in sea-level.

After the glacial period, the islands were subjected to intense periglacial weathering and solifluction.[12] The granite outcrops were severely frost-shattered and many of the screes now covered in vegetation (common, for example, in Unst) were formed at this period. Solifluction is still effective today, particularly where vegetable cover is limited.[13] Climatic factors are responsible for a virtually continuous process of peat formation from glacial times except, possibly, during the Atlantic climatic phase when, as we have seen, birch and pine may have grown in parts of the islands. The fragments of these trees which have been preserved in peat bogs suggest, however, that they never attained any great girth. In these almost treeless islands peat has been invaluable as a source of fuel and islands such as St Ninian's Isle are said to have been depopulated as a result of the exhaustion of their fuel supplies.[14] The peat-covered hillsides sometimes tend to give a monotonous landscape.

The importance of the sea in all aspects of Shetland life cannot be overrated. Shetland is so exposed, in practically every direction, that its coasts are subjected to severe erosion. The power of the sea can be demonstrated by the many massive blocks, several tons in weight, which have been hurled on to cliff tops more than 30m. above sea level. The rising sea-level has, by exposing fresh surfaces over the centuries, accentuated the process of coastal erosion. Erosion has also caused the appearance of transient depositional features, e.g. tombolos linking inshore islands to the Mainland, of which the finest example is at St Ninian's Isle. Low sandy shorelines are uncommon in Shetland but some extensive sandy tracts occur, such as those at Sandwick in Unst, at Sands of Breckin in North Yell and at Quendale on the south Mainland. These sands blew inland, sweetened the naturally acidic soils and made them attractive to early agriculturalists: but in each of the examples just quoted the sand ultimately overran the settlements.

Normal erosional processes are still active in forming the Shetland landscape. Although the small area of the islands precludes the existence of major rivers, active gullying is common on hillsides. Indeed, Shetland is particularly susceptible to this form of erosion because the cool damp climate allows the vegetation cover to rehabilitate itself only very slowly after it has been broken.

Geographical location is the basic factor affecting the climate of Shetland. Since it lies on the 60°N. parallel, there is a negative radiation balance: and this energy deficit is redressed by the latent heat released by condensation, with considerably more precipitation than evaporation and with advection from the more southerly latitudes. The islands are dominated by the Tropical and Polar Maritime air masses and, particularly in summer, frequently lie in the frontal zone between them. In winter the Arctic Front can bring snow with north or north-easterly winds. Depressions tend to form along the Polar Front and they move eastward from the Atlantic, channelled by a jet-stream in the upper air at about 8,000m. Therefore Shetland has prevailing south-westerly winds, at ground-level and in the upper air, all the year round; and during and since the 1960s their southerly component seems to have increased. These winds bring a considerable amount of warmth in winter and create the anomaly of large positive temperatures. In summer, however, they can cause cooling by carrying in cold air from the sea. The high winter temperatures have often been attributed to the warm water brought by the North Atlantic Drift but, while this is important, there is no doubt that an atmospheric circulation influenced by the south-westerly and westerly airstreams is the dominant factor.

The statistics of the day-to-day weather of Shetland in Table 1 show that no month has a mean temperature below freezing point. Uppsala, Helsinki and Leningrad, which lie on the same latitude as Lerwick, all experience four winter months when the mean temperature is below freezing-point and this indicates clearly the positive temperature anomaly discussed above. Although snow lies in Shetland on an average of 20 days per year its insular position usually ensures that it clears very quickly. The same factor keeps low the

Table 1
CLIMATIC STATISTICS

	Temperature 1921–50 °C	Rainfall 1916–50 mm.	Number of days with rain	Sunshine (average number of hours per day)
Jan.	3.4	114	25.2	0.74
Feb.	3.3	84	22.4	1.64
Mar.	3.9	79	20.4	2.93
Apr.	5.3	69	20.8	4.40
May	7.6	56	15.5	5.20
Jun.	9.7	53	15.7	5.32
Jul.	11.9	64	17.4	4.24
Aug.	11.9	71	17.3	3.87
Sep.	10.3	94	19.5	3.50
Oct.	7.7	112	23.2	2.22
Nov.	5.6	117	24.8	1.13
Dec.	4.3	112	25.9	0.41

range of annual temperatures, with mean temperatures never rising above 12°C in July or August which are the warmest months. But it should be said that on a freak summer day the temperature has been known to rise as high as 28°C. On the whole, however, the islands are marginal in respect of crop-ripening in years with cool and wet summers and this fact explains the serious famines of 1740, 1783–84 and 1802–04 among others. A high incidence of cloud cover also keeps low the number of hours of sunshine: these average about 1,090 per annum or 24 per cent of the possible. Length of day is also significant here, the sun being above the horizon for only 5 hrs 39 mins on the shortest day. But on June 21st the sun is above the horizon for as long as 18 hrs 48 mins and this 'simmer dim' can help to alleviate some of the crofters' problems. On the other hand, fogs are common in summer and relative humidity is consistently high, the average monthly figure being between 85 and 89 per cent—due in part to the many lakes and the close interlocking of land and sea, with no point in Shetland being more than 4½ km. from salt water.

The archipelago has a reputation for raininess but this owes more to the spread of precipitation throughout the year than to its quantity. Precipitation occurs on average 248 days per year but totals only 1025 mm., considerably less than other areas similarly exposed to Atlantic influences (e.g. Bergen with 2210 mm.). This low rainfall can be attributed to the low relief of the islands. The wettest months are generally those from October to January while May and June are the driest.

Gales occur on 56–57 days per year and the wind blows at gale force for 2.5 per cent of the time.[15] This may not seem particularly high but the average wind speed throughout the year is 27 km. per hour and thus wind is obviously a significant factor in Shetland life. On 27 January 1961 gusts of 264 km. were recorded on the exposed cliff-top site at R.A.F. Saxa Vord. At Lerwick Observatory the maximum recorded speeds have been a gust of 170 km. on 27 January 1961 and an hourly mean of 118 km. on the same date and on 31 January 1953.[16] The gales come mainly in the winter months but high winds in late summer and autumn sometimes have a devastating effect on crops. Wind is the main element inhibiting tree growth, and the salt spray which it carries is particularly damaging to many plants.

Thus, although the south-westerly influences maintain a climate in Shetland which is fairly equable for its latitude, it combines with an impoverished physical environment to place very definite limitations on agricultural and industrial endeavours.

The geographical location of Shetland has been equally significant in prehistoric and historical colonisation. In pre-historic times the British islands must have seemed to project like a triangular peninsula from Europe, with Shetland at its apex; and it is important to note that it was possible to travel to Unst, the most northerly of the habitable islands, without ever being out of sight of land. Thus right up until c.800 A.D. Shetland was the *Ultima Thule* of early settlers. Those reaching these northern isles had already passed through Britain, and Shetland acted as a zone of cultural fusion where prehistory was marked by a continuation of old ways long after they had been replaced further south.

Mesolithic settlers may have reached the islands but, as they would almost certainly have occupied low and sandy coastlands, any trace which they may have left must now be under water, due to the rising sea-level. The first positive evidence of settlement is in Neolithic times, sometime after 2,900 B.C.[17] Calder has shown that the graves and houses of these Stone Age people are widely distributed throughout Shetland.[18] The primary settlement appears to have been related to the Megalithic movement along the western sea-board of Scotland. Some of the Neolithic cairns are of styles peculiar to Shetland and emphasize the isolation of the islands. The beet-shaped cairn, for a long time thought to be a local Shetland type, has now been shown to exist on the Scottish mainland but covered there by a long cairn or barrow.

Even at this period one can discern the influence of environmental controls which have played so great a part in human activity in later times. The distribution of oval houses is coastal and they are frequently surrounded by one or more small fields up to 18m. × 80m. in size. A large quantity of grain was discovered at Ness of Gruting, which confirms the existence of an agricultural economy, and several sites have produced the bones of oxen, sheep and ponies, suggesting a crofting-type economy.[19] While there is only limited evidence for hunting and fishing in this period, both seem likely. In Shetland the remains of houses show them tending to cluster together in groups, in direct contrast to the apparently dispersed settlement pattern in Orkney where a much more pastoral economy was being pursued. The distinctiveness of the two archipelagoes here reflects the major physical differences between them. Orkney has a much flatter landscape and richer soils which have developed from till originating in the Old Red Sandstone. These soils will have yielded a richer pasture than those in Shetland, will have covered a much greater percentage of the area of the islands and thus obviated the need for so much cultivation and for the concentration of settlement in limited areas. It seems that driftwood, probably of North American origin and transported by the North Atlantic Drift, was used in Shetland to roof the dry-stone houses of the inhabitants, confirming that there was no local growth of timber of constructional quality at this period.

The Stone Age in Shetland seems to have continued into the early centuries B.C., because relics of Bronze Age type which are common in Scotland are notably absent in the islands. A bronze smith had certainly reached Jarlshof in the late seventh or sixth century B.C.,[20] while the site at Clickhimin has produced a Late Bronze Age farmstead similar to that of Jarlshof:[21] recent work by Goodlad has also revealed a Middle Bronze Age domestic site on the Island of Trondra off Scalloway.[22] But the cubicled houses and the material culture of the Late Bronze Age farmers appear to be derived from Neolithic antecedents and the present writer is not satisfied that it is possible to distinguish clearly between Neolithic and Bronze pottery in some Shetland contexts.

The arrival of new settlers from the south in the sixth and fifth centuries B.C. heralded a much higher density of population than Shetland had previously experienced. It is thought that deteriorating climatic conditions, associated with the Sub-Atlantic climatic phase, caused shortages in the supply of food in Europe and led to migration on a large scale. Several waves of new peoples moved into southern Britain and the reverberations of the consequent political and social disturbances resulted in movement into the northern isles. The first groups, identified by pottery of Late Hallstaff/Iron Age A tradition, made a peaceful colonisation of the islands; but later, well-organised bands of Celtic settlers arrived in Shetland and brought with them concepts of building on promontories and of erecting ring forts which were akin to those of the western seaboard of Britain. Hamilton points out that this specialisation accompanied a political development which saw Shetland become part of a maritime confederacy based on the Orkney Islands.[23] By the turn of the millenium the building of brochs had been perfected. Shetland has nearly a hundred broch sites, including at Mousa the best preserved example which exists.[24] These centuries of fort- and broch-building indicate the disturbed political conditions among the Scottish tribes of the Early Iron Age. As the Roman advances of the first century A.D. engaged the military strength of the peoples of central and western Scotland, the northern isles returned to the peaceful existence of a remote political backwater. Thirteen Roman coins have been found in Shetland but they must all have reached the islands in later times, while the fragments of Roman glass and other objects which have been recorded represent imports through trade or piracy rather than Roman settlement or even Roman visitation.

Although these changes brought new constructional concepts, new iron-working techniques and an increased population to Shetland, they did little to alter the basic way of life of the people. The sea and the limited resources of the land continued to provide a subsistence economy and the environment dictated settlement patterns which followed a distribution similar to that established 2,000 years before. Brochs probably went out of use by the end of the first century A.D. when they no longer had strategic value, and they were replaced by wheelhouses and by open settlements. During this period there can be no doubt that Shetland became part of Pictland. A stone (now lost) of the early Class 1 type was found in 1879 at Sandness[25] and fine examples of Early Christian stones were later recovered from Papil[26] and Bressay.[27] Other fragments relating to the same period have been recorded as coming from Uyea and Lerwick.[28] Professor David Wilson has drawn attention to the Pictish character of the St Ninian's Isle treasure and ogham stones have been discovered at St Ninian's Isle, Cunningsburgh and Lunnasting. These finds all point to the existence of at least some level of population in the islands when the Vikings arrived about 800 A.D., although the archaeological record suggests that by then the inhabitants had suffered a severe economic decline, perhaps caused by a combination of the factors we have seen already—Shetland lay at the apex of the continental angle of Europe, it was an archipelago approachable only over difficult seas and it offered only a limited cultural environment.

With the coming of the Vikings within the years 790–810 A.D. the relative position of Shetland dramatically altered. No longer was it at the end of the known world; instead, suddenly, it lay at the closest point to the source of the newcomers. That complex of economic, social, technical, political and psychological factors which stimulated and maintained the flow of colonists need not be examined here,[29] but it should be remembered that by the end of the ninth century the population of Shetland had risen to over 20,000; that is, the same as it was to be in the nineteenth century.[30] This suggests that a declining Pictish society was submerged by the new arrivals and that Shetland became a zone of cultural replacement rather than the area of fusion and absorption which it had been in the preceding millenia. The focal position of the environmentally richer Orkney Islands, in relation to the Norse colonies established in Caithness and the Hebrides, ensured that they became the political centre for the invaders' activities. Much more is therefore known in detail of Viking times there. Shetland has no equivalent of the *Orkneyinga Saga* and only two Viking sites have been excavated—at Jarlshof[31] and Underhoull.[32] Enough is known, however, to show that the ninth century established that pattern of life which was to exist right up to modern times in Shetland.

Viking settlements probably occupied every bay head where there was land suitable for cultivation and grazing, where there was adequate water supply and where conditions were suitable for pulling up boats.[33] The limited arable but extensive grazing available in some areas led to the grouping of farmsteads in either tightly knit or scattered townships, just as they are today. Economic life also followed a similar pattern, with little growing of grain but with a heavy dependence on animals. Fishing and home industries were also important, so that one can see in the Viking settlements the origins of the traditional Shetland way of life.

Shetland remained part of the earldom of Orkney until 1195 when it came directly under the control of King Sverre of Norway for tax and tribute. The direct ties of Shetland with Norway were effectively continued for longer than they were in Orkney where, from 1231 through the Anguses and then after 1321 through the Strathearns, government was by Scottish earls: in Orkney, as Professor Donaldson has made plain, the process of 'Scotticisation' went ahead much more quickly and was well advanced long before the impignoration of the late fifteenth century. This again brings home the problem of distance as a geographical factor; for Shetland, lying far from the political centre of both Norway and Scotland, gradually sank back to its pre-Viking position of isolation and was slower to adopt change.

Even before the late twelfth century, migration to the northern isles on a large scale had ceased, and the inhabitants probably regarded themselves as Shetlanders rather than as Norwegians. Norway weakened politically and Shetland, while still remaining Norwegian, again became part of the earldom of Orkney in 1379 under the first of the St Clair earls. Then, in 1397, the Union of Kalmar brought Denmark, Sweden and Norway under a single king, so that it was Christian I of Denmark and not a Norwegian ruler who pledged Shetland to Scotland five hundred years ago.

The complex of events which led up to the pledging of the islands is a matter for the political historian and need not concern the historical geographer. Two points, however, must be borne in mind: firstly, the geographical orientation of Shetland was beginning to change even before the impignoration and, though the islands retained their Scandinavian language and culture, the concept of a Viking-dominated Norwegian Sea had by then vanished; secondly, Scotland tended to regard the islands as lying off the Scottish coast and, since they lay much closer to Scotland than to Denmark, it was desirable that they should be Scottish territory. The whole concept of the location of Shetland changed radically and although Denmark made repeated efforts to redeem the pledge (in 1549, 1550, 1558, 1560, 1585, 1589, 1640 and 1660 among others) Scotland studiously avoided these claims, continuing to regard Shetland as an integral and natural geographical part of Scotland.

NOTES

1 Where dates are given in the prehistoric section of this paper they are based on the 5730 ½-life of C^{14}. Recent work on tree ring chronologies has shown that at 5000 B.P. these dates may be older by as much as 1000 years. For comment on this and curves which may be applied to the usual dates, see E. K. Ralph and H. N. Michael 'Problems of the Radio-Carbon Calendar' in *Archaeometry, 10* (1967), 3–11, and Sir Mortimer Wheeler *et al.*, 'A symposium on the impact of the natural

sciences on archaeology' in *Philosophical Transactions of the Royal Society of London*, Ser. A, *269* (1970), 1–185.
2   'On the deformation of the Funzie conglomorate' in *Journal of Geology*, *64* (1956), 480–505; 'On the nappe structure of North-East Shetland' in *Q[uarterly] J[ournal of the] G[eological] S[ociety of] London*, *114* (1958), 107–36; 'Continuation of the Great Glen Fault beyond the Moray Firth' in *Nature*, no. 4788 (1961), 589. D. Flinn *et al.*, 'On the age of the sediments and contemporaneous volcanic rocks of western Shetland' in *Scottish Journal of Geology*, *4* (1968), 10–19. L. J. D. Fernando, 'Petrology of certain felspathised rocks from Herma Ness, Unst, Shetland Islands' in *Proceedings of the Geological Association of London*, *52* (1941), 110–30. M. S. Amin, 'Matamorphic differentiation of talc-magnesite-chlorite rocks in Shetland' in *Geol[ogical] Mag[azine]*, *89* (1952), 97–105; 'Notes on the ultrabasic body of Unst, Shetland Islands' in *ibid.*, *91* (1954), 399–406. F. C. Phillips, 'The serpentines and associated rocks and minerals of the Shetland Islands' in *QJGS London*, *83* (1927), 622–52; 'Petrographic notes on three rock types from the Shetland Islands' in *Geol. Mag.* 65 (1928), 500–07. H. H. Read, 'On the quartz-kyanite rocks in Unst, Shetland Islands, and their bearing on metamorphic differentiation' in *Mineral[ogical] Mag[azine]*, *23* (1933), 317–28; 'On the segregation of quartz-chlorite-pyrite masses in Shetland igneous rocks during dislocation metamorphism with a note on an occurrence of boudinage-structure', in *Proceedings of the Liverpool Geological Society*, *16* (1934), 128–38; 'The metamorphic geology of Unst in the Shetland Islands' in *QJGS London*, *90* (1934), 637–88; 'On zoned associations of antigorite, talc, actinolite, chlorite and biotite in Unst, Shetland Islands' in *Mineral. Mag.* *23* (1934), 519–40; 'Metamorphic correlation in the polymetamorphic rocks of the Valla Field Stack, Unst, Shetland Islands' in *T[ransactions of the] R[oyal] S[ociety of] Edinburgh*, *59* (1937), 195–221.
3   *Nature*, no. 4788 (1961), 589.
4   B. N. Peach and J. Horne, 'The glaciation of the Shetland Isles' in *QJGS London*, *35* (1879), 778–811, and *Geol. Mag.*, *2* (1881), 65.
5   D. M. Home, 'Valedictory address' in *Transactions of the Edinburgh Geological Society*, *3* (1880), 357–64.
6   J. K. Charlesworth, 'The late-glacial history of the Highlands and Islands of Scotland' in *TRS Edinburgh*, *62* (1959), 887–9.
7   R. Chapelhow, 'On glaciation in North Roe, Shetland' in *Geographic Journal*, *131* (1965), 60–70.
8   T. M. Finlay, 'The Old Red Sandstone of Shetland' in *TRS Edinburgh*, *56* (1930), 671–94.
9   G. Hoppe *et al.*, 'Fran falt och forskning naturgeografi vid Stockholm's Universitet' in *Ymer* (1965), 109–25.
10 Chapelhow, 'On glaciation'.
11 G. Hoppe, 'Submarine peat in the Shetland Isles' in *Geografiska Annaler*, Ser. A, *47* (1965), 4.
12 Solifluction is the gradual down-slope movement of most soil under the influence of gravity. It is very pronounced under periglacial conditions when there is a rapid oscillation between freezing and thawing.
13 D. H. N. Spence, 'Studies in the vegetation of Shetland Islands. The serpentine debris vegetation of Unst' in *Journal of Ecology*, *45* (1957), 917–45.
14 G. Goudie, *The Celtic and Scandinavian Antiquities of Shetland* (Edinburgh, 1904).
15 S. G. Irvine, 'Hurricanes in Shetland' in *Weather*, *17* (1962), 34.
16 S. G. Irvine, 'An outline of the climate of Shetland' in *ibid.*, *23* (1968), 392–443.
17 See footnote 1.

18 C. S. T. Calder, 'Excavations in Whalsay, Shetland 1954–5' in P[roceedings of the] S[ociety of] A[ntiquaries of] S[cotland], 94 (1963), 28–45; and 'Cairns, neolithic houses and burnt mounds in Shetland' in ibid., 96 (1965), 37–86.
19 C. S. T. Calder, 'Stone-Age house-sites in Shetland' in ibid., 89 (1957), 340–97.
20 See J. R. C. Hamilton, *Excavations at Jarlshof, Shetland* (Edinburgh, 1956), 4, 23.
21 J. R. C. Hamilton, *Excavations at Clikhimin, Shetland* (Edinburgh, 1968), 25–33.
22 C. A. Goodlad, 'Shetland: Trondra' in *Discovery and Exploration* (1966).
23 J. R. C. Hamilton, *Clikhimin*.
24 J. W. Paterson, 'The Broch of Mousa' in *PSAS, 41* (1922), 172–83.
25 See G. Low, *A Tour through the Islands of Orkney and Shetland* (Kirkwall, 1879).
26 G. Goudie, 'Notice of a sculptured slab from the Island of Burra, Shetland' in *PSAS, 15* (1881), 199–209. See also A. Small *et al.*, *St Ninian's Isle and its Treasure* (Aberdeen, 1972).
27 J. R. Allen, *The Early Christian Monuments of Scotland* (London, 1903), ii, 1–15.
28 *Ibid.*, 16–18.
29 These are discussed by the present writer in 'The historical geography of the Norse Viking colonization of the Scottish highlands' in *Norsk Geografisk Tidsskrift, 22* (1968), 1–16.
30 A. Brøgger, *Ancient Emigrants* (Oxford, 1929).
31 J. R. C. Hamilton, *Jarlshof*.
32 A. Small, 'Excavations of Underhoull, Unst, Shetland' in *PSAS, 98* (1967), 225–48.
33 See the maps in A. Small, 'The distribution of settlement in Shetland and Faroe in Viking times' in *Saga-Book, 17* (1969), 145–55.
34 G. Donaldson, *Shetland Life under Earl Patrick* (Edinburgh, 1958).

CHAPTER III

The Pledging of the Islands in 1469: the Historical Background

BARBARA E. CRAWFORD

IN DEALING with the centuries between the sagas and 1468 we are looking at a period in the history of the north which has been neglected by historians. These centuries are dealt with in three chapters of Storer Clouston's *History of Orkney*[1] (where he entitles them the 'Dark Period'), whereas the earlier period of the sagas merits eighteen chapters. This is, of course, for the very good reason that the historical material from these centuries is very thin compared with the unsurpassed source of information about the eleventh and twelfth centuries which we have in the sagas and, particularly, in Orkney's own saga, the *Jarlsaga*. But the documentary information from the thirteenth and fourteenth centuries is more clearly historical material whereas the sagas were intentionally literary and were written for dramatic effect. A period of three centuries is a long time, moreover, and many developments must have taken place during them which altered the situation in the islands; the picture we get in the sagas of life under Earl Thorfinn tells us very little of the situation in the mid-fifteenth century under that equally great earl, William Sinclair. From the point of view of our understanding of the events of 1468–9, one scrap of documentary material from the intervening centuries is worth a whole stanza of the sagas. And in any case Shetland itself figures very little in the *Jarlsaga*.

A starting point for a study of this dimly-observed period is the year 1195, which marks a great break between the old order of the sagas and the new. Its events are among the last to be mentioned in the *Jarlsaga*. Before 1195 Shetland, along with Caithness, was part of the domain of the great Norse earls of Orkney. We know this from the sagas and also from one charter in which Earl Harold Maddadson is called 'earl of Orkney, Shetland and Caithness'.[2] But after 1195 Shetland was taken away from the earls and thereafter bound much more firmly to the Norwegian crown. The reason for this is well known: Earl Harold, if not directly involved, had given tacit support to an attempt to remove King Sverre from the throne of Norway. The band of 'island beardies', as they were called, had started out from the Orkneys, led by a son-in-law of the earl, in support of a pretender who had sheltered there and been well-received by the earl. It is no surprise that King Sverre laid great feud at Earl Harold's door 'and said it was his doing that the band of men had been got together',[3] and at the resulting judgment conditions were imposed on the earl which meant the end of the situation in the northern isles which was mirrored in the sagas. Firstly, King Sverre took Shetland from the earl with all taxes and dues and, says the saga, 'the Orkney Earls have not held it since'.[4] Secondly, the freedom of the earls was severely curtailed: Harold is said to have been reappointed earl of Orkney on certain conditions, undoubtedly the most irksome of which was the appointment of royal officials alongside him (if the various murders of officials by earls and earls by officials in the next few decades is anything to go by).

From this year for the next two centuries Shetland and Orkney developed along completely separate paths, with very little evidence of contact between them in the secular sphere. Ecclesiastically there must have been some contact as the two groups of islands were in the same bishopric, but, because Shetland was separated in secular affairs from the earldom, this made for a great degree of individual development even in ecclesiastical matters. Before looking at the history of Shetland during these two centuries, however, let us first look more closely at the earldom of Orkney.

Harold's submission to Sverre is only the first of several occasions in the thirteenth century when conditions are known to have been laid on earls of Orkney by kings of Norway. This century saw the culmination of royal authority in all three Scandinavian kingdoms. Norway emerged unified for the first time with one king as effective head of the legislative and judicial systems. Along with this internal consolidation went the expansion of royal power over Greenland and Iceland, and from the evidence of 1195 and other events during the century it is clear that royal authority was being extended over the

Orkney earldom too. Exactly the same development can be seen in Scotland. The Scottish kings were determined to control their Norse vassals and William the Lion and Alexander II both marched against the earl of Caithness and Orkney or sent armies against him in an effort to subdue him and enforce his allegiance to them. Confiscation of land and enforcement of fines were the punishments, as they were in Orkney, and Harold Maddadson was again the earl who bore most of the brunt of this process. Throughout Europe the thirteenth century saw the consolidation of royal authority; national boundaries were being defined and in such an atmosphere there was to be little room for a powerful international earldom such as that of Orkney and Caithness. The days when northern Europe had been the Vikings' oyster were over, and the Orkney earls were caught in the mesh of growing administrative efficiency and royal control. If they didn't play their hand carefully they would be crushed out of all recognition between the opposing pressures of Scottish and Norwegian royalist ambitions: indeed, in the process of consolidating their kingdoms the two kings clashed over the islands lying around the Scottish littoral. In the year 1263 Magnus, earl of Orkney and Caithness, saw both his feudal sovereigns at war with each other. He is usually thought to have come down on the side of his Scottish sovereign, but the saga tells us that he sailed from Bergen with the Norse fleet and was given a good long-ship by King Håkon, which was a mark of favour.[5] After the fleet had sailed on from Orkney however, the earl fades out of the story. Far from discovering that he was active on the Scottish side, all we hear about in the Scottish records is a crushing series of fines being imposed on the earl, and find too that many hostages were being taken from the northern earldoms by King Alexander.[6] It seems rather as if Magnus was cowed into an enforced neutrality and that, after the treaty of Perth had been drawn up between the two countries, he was reconciled to his Norwegian sovereign at Bergen in 1267: for it was said then that fresh conditions were imposed on him.[7] He certainly managed to emerge out of the dilemma in which he found himself in 1263 but did so with some further loss to the earldom of land or power or income. It is not until the next century that we can see exactly how reduced the earl's authority was over his earldom and how his independence had been curtailed.

This series of events relating to Orkney had little effect, however, on Shetland. After 1195 when the earldom was deprived of its northern half, Shetland was brought directly under royal control; that is, it was governed by royal officials who sent all skatts and dues into the royal treasury at Bergen. Evidence from taxation accounts shows close connections between Shetland and the Norwegian royal house continuing right up to the middle of the fourteenth century. Thus, as part of the 'skattlands', Shetland appears to have been granted out to members of the royal house from time to time. The skattlands were the overseas dominions of the Norwegian crown that paid their tax or skatt to the royal treasury: these were Orkney, Shetland and the Faroes, with Iceland taking the place of the Western Isles after 1266. In 1217 the great Earl Skule was granted one-third of the skattlands. As well as skatt from all the odallers' estates in Shetland, the crown received income from its own estates there, most probably composed of the land that had belonged to the earldom before 1195 as well as of the lands which had been forfeited to the crown by those odallers who had fallen in the battle of Florevaag and which had not been redeemed by their descendants. They must have been valuable to the crown, for Duke Håkon after he had acceded to the Norwegian throne in 1299 directed in his will that the rents from his estates in Shetland and Faroe should go towards the building of the Apostles' Church in Bergen, specifically stating that once the building had been completed the rents were to return to the crown.[8] And in 1350 when King Magnus Eriksson handed certain lands and powers over to his sons, he reserved for his own use and revenue the skattlands, i.e. Iceland, Faroe and Shetland.[9]

From these pieces of information we can guess that the administration of Shetland was well-organised and fully in royal control. Indeed, the very earliest documents known to have been written in Orkney *or* Shetland are records of a judgment at the lawthing of Shetland in which Thorvald Thoreson, an official of Duke Håkon, was involved.[10] These date from 1299 and 1307, and their survival is no doubt due to their relevance to the royal income. It is possible that Shetland and Faroe were linked together in their administration by the crown. Certainly, when they formed part of the ducal appanage, a decree of Håkon's mentions that Sigurd, lawman in Shetland, travelled with the bishop of Faroe to the Faroes with a new lawbook for the islands.[11] The connection between the two groups of islands is to be seen, too, in the many records of Shetlanders marrying Faroese during these centuries, and also in the fact that men owned land in both groups of islands.[12] There is evidence from this period that a number of important Norwegian families owned land in Shetland, but whether they had received these estates in grants from the crown, or by marriage with Shetland heiresses, is not known.[13] What is significant is that during this period all of Shetland's links were northwards, and not at all southwards towards the earldom from which it had been taken away.

With the fourteenth century we enter on a new era, for Norway's once strong, outward-looking monarchy was declining. This was partly due to the growth of a feudal nobility in Scandinavia which was struggling to take political control into its own hands, leaving the Norwegian kings less time or authority to attend to the affairs of their overseas dominions. It was also due to a major economic factor in the growth of the Hanseatic League of North German cities and ports which was obtaining a financial strangle-hold on the Scandinavian monarchies. The growing practice of making feudal grants of royal land and income tended in the long run to reduce royal control: the evidence suggests that the earls of Orkney benefited from this and were themselves given a feudal grant of the royal land and rights in Orkney along with their earldom. There are indications too that there was great turbulence in the islands, with different factions fighting for control. The effects of the Black Death may well have contributed towards this disruption; these were disastrous in Scandinavia, and we cannot imagine that Orkney or Shetland escaped unscathed. Economic values most probably depreciated, and this meant above all a loss of income for the great landowners. In this power struggle between nobles and monarchy, Orkney and Shetland were drawn together as they became a theatre of action for the first time since 1195. Finally, as Scots became involved in the fight for land and power and as Norwegian influence weakened, Scottish influence becomes evident—in Orkney at any rate.

Trouble appears to have started soon after the turn of the century, for we know from an agreement between King Håkon V of Norway and Robert I of Scotland in the year 1312 that Scots had been invading Orkney and Shetland, seizing the rents of the king of Norway and imprisoning his steward.[14] There is particular evidence of much turbulence after the death of Malise, earl of Strathearn, Caithness and Orkney, who had inherited the earldom from the Angus line. He died about the middle of the century and left no fewer than five heiresses. For twenty-six years, from 1353 to 1379, their husbands and sons fought over the titles to the earldoms of Caithness and Orkney. Two of them were Scots, and the clash of different inheritance- and legal-systems undoubtedly made the contest all the more complicated and bitter. From this period probably dates the first settlement of Scots on land granted to them by whoever had power in Orkney at the time. In 1379 we discover Henry Sinclair promising not to alienate (or to sell) any lands or islands of the earldom away from the king and also issuing a charter in Scotland which announced his inability to do so—an indication that something of the sort must have been going on beforehand. In 1369 an agreement between the bishop of Orkney and Håkon Jonson, a Norwegian nobleman who may have had some commission from the king of Norway, tells of the seizure of royal rents and the arrest of men and confiscation of their property in both Orkney and Shetland.[15] Nor did this state of lawlessness cease, for in 1375 when the eldest heir of Earl Malise was granted authority in the islands his contest with the bishop of Orkney was mentioned, as was the possibility that foreigners or natives would attempt to force him or his officers from what was his and the king's by right.[16]

These were turbulent times, and the last act of the drama between the heirs of Earl Malise was to be played out in Shetland. Exactly what did Earl Henry Sinclair, first of the Sinclair earls and grandson of Earl Malise, receive when in 1379 he was appointed 'to rule over [the] lands and islands of Orkney, and raised . . . to the state of earl over the foresaid lands'?[17] It is usually said that this grant included Shetland which was at long last restored to the earldom of Orkney, and that it remained part of the earldom until 1468.[18] The installation document of the new earl—a full and most interesting charter—is however of the 'lands and islands of Orkney'; Shetland is never mentioned as being included in the grant, and therefore one must doubt if it was included. Here, as elsewhere, it has been assumed that Shetland was included when Orkney alone was named, but the history of the area since 1196 emphasizes the separate existence of the two groups of islands and shows them to be quite distinct administrative entities. Shetland *is* mentioned once in the installation document, when the new earl promised to defend his new possessions if anyone should invade the lands of Orkney 'or also the land of Shetland', but that is no indication that Shetland had therefore been rejoined to the earldom in the grant. What does confuse the problem is that several times in his document there is mention of the 'earldom and lordship'. Shetland was, indeed, known as the 'lordship of Shetland' after the islands had been handed to Scotland, but never before 1469 (or, rather, 1472). Evidence from the years after 1379, although meagre, indicates that Shetland was still a separate entity then. In 1418 John Sinclair, brother of Earl Henry II, received a grant of all Shetland with all royal rights.[19] But there is no evidence that Shetland was ever accounted part of the earldom before 1469, or indeed afterwards. The fact that the Scots then referred to Shetland as a 'lordship' shows that they certainly regarded Shetland as quite separate from the earldom.

But, despite the fact that Shetland appears to have remained separate from the earldom throughout the period before 1469, there is no doubt that the Sinclair earls acquired land in Shetland, and we will now return to the struggle which Earl Henry had with the last remaining claimant of the Strathearn line, his cousin Malise Sperra.

Malise Sperra is one of those enigmatic historical figures about whom we know sufficient to arouse interest but not enough to satisfy our curiosity. He was named Malise after his grandfather, the earl of Strathearn, Caithness and Orkney. His mother had been married to Guttorm Sperra, who appears to have been a Swedish nobleman, with Shetland connections—an Ivar Sperra had been important in Shetland earlier in the century. Malise evidently had close Shetland connections, which most probably resulted from estates inherited from his father. The remarkable thing about Malise Sperra is that he is remembered in public records long after his death. There is an entry in the exchequer rolls for Scotland from the year 1438 about lands belonging to the 'former lord Malise Speir', nearly fifty years after his death.[20] And in the Orkney rentals, which date from about the year 1500, there are several references to land which had been 'Sir Malise Spar's';[21] these rentals do not refer to many people by name and the earls themselves are rarely mentioned, but here a lesser member of the earldom family is perpetuated about 120 years after his death. When he died, probably in the year 1391, the event was worthy of being recorded in the *Icelandic Annals*. What then is known about the life of this man?

Most of our evidence concerns his struggle for power in the north with Henry Sinclair. In 1379 he, and his cousins Alexander of Ard and Henry Sinclair, formally laid claim to the earldom before King Håkon Magnusson. Malise was the loser, and in his installation document the new earl, Henry Sinclair, had to promise that his cousin would drop his claim to the earldom so that the king would be caused no more trouble by him or his heirs. Malise in fact remained behind in Norway for a year, as hostage for the performance of certain assurances by his cousin, the new earl. He was allowed to return to Scotland in June 1380, and in the following years appears to have made persistent attempts to win land and power for himself in the north. In October 1386 a judgment of the king's council in Bergen declared that the lands of Herdis Thorvaldsdatter (who had been an important landowner in Shetland) belonged to John and Sigurd Hafthorsson and not to Malise Sperra who had occupied them.[22] In November 1387 a document in the form of an amnesty or submission was drawn up by Malise in which he condoned any injuries done by the earl of Orkney to his men or goods and promised payment for any injury committed by his men to the earl.[23] Malise seems to have been losing out all round, but then comes one piece of evidence that he gained a position of importance in the Norwegian kingdom. This is the accession document of Erik of Pomerania[24] which in 1389 was signed and sealed by the earl of Orkney who was second in the list of witnesses, and also by Sir Malise Sperra, one of eleven other secular and ecclesiastical councillors of the kingdom of Norway. His signature indicates that Malise was then both royal councillor and a man of importance in the Norwegian kingdom. Perhaps, indeed, he had been given an official grant of Shetland to compensate for the judgment against him in the case of the lands of Herdis Thorvaldsdatter. What we do know is that, for some reason, the antagonism between the earl and Malise flared up again, and soon after this the two came to blows in Shetland. 'Malise Sperra slain in Shetland with seven others by the earl of Orkney', says the *Icelandic Annals*: and the standing stone can still be seen on the road between Scalloway and Tingwall where he is supposed to have been killed.

The first question raised by this incident is, what was Henry Sinclair doing in Shetland? This is the first evidence for centuries that any earl had set foot in Shetland. The earls had not, as far as we know, owned any land there from the time that Shetland was taken away from them in 1195. It looks very much as if Earl Henry—who certainly appears to have been a remarkable man—was determined to incorporate Shetland within his earldom, in fact if not in law. He was thus, of course, going directly against his oath of fealty to his Norwegian overlord. Some corroboration for the guess that he did clash with the king of Norway in Shetland is given in a contemporary account, the much disputed *Voyages of Nicolo and Antonio Zeno*.[25] This is a garbled and enigmatic version of two letters written by two Venetian travellers who stayed for several years with the lord of a group of islands in the North Sea. He was called by them 'Zincmi'—which can only be understood as a corruption of Sinclair

—and the account tells that about the year 1390 this Sinclair won a victory over the king of Norway, and that there was a great struggle between them in the islands of Shetland, which lay in the lordship of the king of Norway. If this tallies with the fight with Malise Sperra then it looks as if Malise did lose his life while fighting on behalf of the king of Norway and that he had received from the king some authority which gave him the standing of a member of the Norwegian Council. Thus equipped, Malise was a rival to the earl's own power and influence in the north, and, since he had a claim to the earldom, he was a particularly dangerous rival. More than that, it appears that Henry Sinclair was also the ultimate heir to his cousin's possessions. Malise was childless and, in the event of his death, all his lands would revert to his only surviving aunt, Isabella of Strathearn, who was the mother of Henry Sinclair. That this is what did happen is clearly stated in the *Genealogy of the Earls of Orkney*.[26] Malise Sperra was thus, on two counts at least, certainly more advantageous to Earl Henry dead than alive. After his death the Sinclair influence in the north was assured and the kings of Norway had lost their last champion, never really managing to counter Sinclair power again. Particularly as regards Shetland, the Sinclairs now appear to have at least some influence; and the evidence we have of Shetland affairs in the next few decades mostly relates to Sinclair connections. If Malise had had Shetland lands through his father's family, these would now have reverted to the Sinclairs, and they probably comprised the first Shetland estates of the earls since 1196. It is significant that in 1391, the same year as Malise's death, a charter was drawn up in Kirkwall in which David Sinclair resigned to his brother, the earl, all claim and right which he had from his mother Isabella to any lands in Orkney *or* Shetland.[27] This charter is witnessed by three Shetland notables, and it is the first documentary evidence since 1195 of any connection between the earls of Orkney and Shetland, or of the possession by the earls of any Shetland estates.

Among the witnesses to this charter was an Alexander of Clapham, probably of the Fife Clephane family and thus a hanger-on of the earls from the south. He evidently managed to win favour with the king of Norway, for in 1412 an 'Alexander von Klapham' received a grant of all royal possessions (including all royal rights in Northmavine).[28] And then in 1418 John Sinclair, brother of the second Sinclair earl, received a grant of all Shetland with all royal rights.[29] Malise Sperra's death, therefore, had important repercussions for Shetland: it opened the way to the Sinclair family and all the Scottish influences which they brought with them, influences from which Shetland had hitherto been kept absolutely free. Nevertheless, it is important to recognise that the Sinclair holdings in Shetland were purely odal possessions and were not part of the earldom estates. Shetland was still a separate entity from the Orkney earldom, as we can see from the grant to John Sinclair. The family nature of the Sinclair lands in Shetland is seen in a charter dating from 1498, after the islands had become part of Scotland, in which thirteen sons and daughters of Earl William Sinclair, the last earl, handed over their odal portions of Shetland estates, and in particular Sumburgh which they had inherited from their father, to their brother, the famous Sir David Sinclair.[30] These lands which had been held by the last earl had, therefore, *not* gone to the crown in 1469: they were private odal possessions and not part of the official earldom holding. How does that reconstruction of the relationship of Shetland with the earldom of Orkney affect our interpretation of the transactions of the years 1468 and 1469?

The story is well-known of how the islands of Orkney and Shetland were pledged to Scotland by Christian I of Denmark and Norway for the marriage dowry of his daughter. Relations between Denmark and Scotland had been bad for several years before 1468, and there was no better way of healing this breach and of having a treaty of friendship than by arranging a contract of marriage between the ruling houses of Oldenburg and Stewart.

The cause of the bad relations was basically the annual payment of one hundred marks which Scotland was supposed to make in perpetuity to Norway, and later to Denmark, for the cession of the Hebrides and the Isle of Man in 1266. By the end of the thirteenth century non-payment of this due had already been causing trouble, but there were spasmodic attempts to continue payments during the fourteenth century. In the fifteenth century persistent defaulting on payments led Christian I finally to request the French king (Charles VII) to intervene on his behalf in the deadlock. In the end the two countries met for negotiations, under the chairmanship of Charles, at Bourges in 1460. The Scottish attitude was unequivocal. They had made no effort to meet the Danish king's demands for payment. But the suggestion of a marriage to heal the breach found the Scots fully prepared with their demands: they insisted that both Orkney and Shetland should be handed over to Scotland as part of the Princess Margaret's dowry, as well as 100,000 crowns for her adornment. James II had his plans carefully laid, although they were not realised on that occasion because of James' sudden death. Eight years later, when the matter of James III's marriage had become an immediate problem, negotiations were again opened—but this time on a Scottish initiative, it appears.

Christian's attitude to the whole question of his island colonies of Orkney and Shetland is difficult to define. It is easy to propose him as the villain of the piece, bartering away portions of his Norwegian dominions with no intention of ever redeeming them, pandering to the susceptibilities of his Norwegian subjects by pledging the islands and hoping to save face thereby. But Christian had mortgaged so much of his kingdom at one time or another that the question of saving face in front of his subjects cannot have been very important to him, especially when they were from the northern and poorer half of his kingdom. Besides this, no king has ever willingly parted with any of his territory which was capable of bringing him in a tidy income. And there seems little doubt about the significant value of Orkney and Shetland to the Norwegian and Danish kings. The last earl had certainly been difficult about forwarding royal skatts to the treasury at Bergen, and Christian made several vain attempts to summon him to Copenhagen: in fact Christian had turned to the lawman and bishop of Orkney to help him against the earl and so get in his dues from the islands. The elaborate administrative arrangements which the Danish and Norwegian kings had made in the attempt to ensure themselves of their skatts and rents from the earldom and from Shetland certainly point to the importance they gave to the income from the islands.

Christian's attitude in 1468 was, however, dictated by his financial circumstances; and his penury was legendary. In 1468 itself he was heavily involved in costly wars in Sweden: and these are particularly referred to in the document pledging Shetland to Scotland, where this stated that the hindrance caused by the insults of Christian's enemies and rebels were to blame for his inability to provide a cash dowry for his daughter.[31] The Scots, having made their demands in 1460, undoubtedly repeated them in 1468: that is, the handing over of both Orkney and Shetland or no marriage treaty. Christian was clearly incapable of offering any satisfactory cash equivalent to the Scottish demands and did not even have sufficient financial resources to give himself a bargaining position of any strength. In the circumstances he can be said to have done his best. He agreed to pledge—but not give outright—Orkney alone, instead of 50,000 of the 60,000 florins of the Rhine named as the dowry money.[32]

Shetland was neither handed over nor pledged. The fact that it was Orkney alone which was pledged at first seems to indicate Christian's resistance to Scottish demands rather than his acquiescence in them. True, he had to hand over Shetland in the next year too; but not before he had made some effort towards collecting the 10,000 florins which he had agreed to pay in cash before then. The evidence for this has recently come to the fore: it is on record that on 19 April 1469—seven months after Orkney had been pledged in the marriage contract, and five weeks before Shetland was pledged—the chamberlain of Denmark was granted by Christian the right to keep the money which was being raised from the tenants of his estates in the form of a tax 'levied', it was said, 'to pay our daughter's dowry for Scotland'.[33] Small wonder that the 10,000 florins were never raised if Christian was busily granting away the money being collected for it! By 19 April, however, Christian may have realised the impossibility of his ever raising the sum in time before the Scottish legates had to return home; and perhaps he had already decided that he would have to pledge Shetland instead, as the Scots had demanded. Nonetheless, the document does prove that Christian made at least some effort to raise the money by levying a tax, in order to avoid his having to cede Shetland as well as Orkney.

Shetland was pledged to Scotland on 28 May 1469, for 8,000 florins only, as is clearly stated in the document drawn up on that date.[34] There is no mention anywhere of the 2,000 florins which would have made this sum up to 10,000, the sum stated in the previous year. Whether it *was* paid, or whether Scotland remitted a certain amount as a friendly gesture to her new ally, is not certain. As the latter seems unlikely, it may be that the 2,000 florins *were* paid.

Let us now consider more closely what was in fact transacted by the documents which pledged Orkney and Shetland. The language of the Shetland document is almost word for word the same as the Orkney one. This can mean one of two things: either the circumstances in the two groups of islands were exactly the same and there was no need for the Shetland document to differ in any way; or they were different but the distinctions were not understood by the Scots—who, after all, only wanted a blanket-cover to assure themselves of any rights to which they would be due as wadsetters. This was not an age remarkable for its tolerance of other people's traditions, and it is probable that the significance of odal possession, of the legal position of the Orkney earldom as opposed to the Shetland 'foudrie' and of administrative grants as opposed to feudal ones, were lost on the

Scots. This seems to be certainly the case if their attitude towards the institutions of the northern isles in later centuries is anything to go by. The marriage contract states that Christian resigned 'all and sundry our lands of the islands of Orkney', and in the Shetland document 'all and sundry our lands of the islands of Shetland, with all sundry rights and their rightful pertinents whatsoever', and this seems to reflect the Scots' feudal assumptions, their seeing the situation through eyes accustomed to a feudalised society and expressing it in the feudal terms which they always used. They were merely assuring themselves of everything that they could legally get their hands on, whether these were actually the same in Orkney and Shetland or whether they differed. It is possible that both documents were in effect drawn up by the Scottish legates at Copenhagen: they are dated, for instance, by the day of the month as in other Scottish documents of the period, and not by the particular feast day of the Church which was the customary way of dating documents in Denmark. If the documents indicate how the Scots saw the rights to which they were due in both groups of islands, then they do not necessarily provide an exact reflection of the situation. The lack of any distinction in the phraseology of the Orkney and Shetland documents need not mean that there was no distinction between the two groups of islands, especially when—as has been seen—their historical development had not been at all the same.

There were royal estates in both Orkney and Shetland which had probably been first acquired by King Sverre after his victory over the Orkney and Shetland men at the battle of Florevaag. In Orkney they had at first been administered for the crown by bailiffs or 'sysselmen' but, not surprisingly, the earl had managed to get a grant of these royal estates in Orkney. A claimant to the earldom, Alexander of Ard, was put in charge of all royal income from Orkney in 1375, and by 1425 it was sufficiently established that the earl usually held the royal estates, for the people of Orkney to write to the queen of Norway saying that the earl, William Sinclair, was the most acceptable debtor for all those things which were known to pertain to the king in Orkney.[35] Christian therefore transferred the superiority of these royal estates, as well as the superiority over the earldom which he had it in his power to grant to the claimant with the best right.

In Shetland, however, the earls had no official rights; the king's lands were held in grant by an official, the 'foud', just as they were in Orkney by the earl. In practice the situation appeared very much the same in the two groups of islands, despite the historical differences, and so the same phrases sufficed in both the Orkney and Shetland documents. The first occurrence of the peculiarly Shetland title of 'foud' is in Alexander von Klapham's grant of the royal lands in Northmavine in 1412. This title was apparently reserved for those who were given a grant of royal authority over the islands. For example, John Sinclair in 1418 was given a grant of Shetland with all royal rights 'in feodalem concessionem'; how long he held the office is not known, and the only other record of such a grant before 1469 is to a member of the Henderson family who is said to have received a commission from King Christian in 1450.[36] But it is most probable that Shetland would, at the time of the pledging of the islands in 1469, have been granted out to some official and granted out in the same feudal concession as it had been to John Sinclair in 1418. When he pledged Shetland, therefore, King Christian was pledging his feudal superiority of the royal estates there, just as he had pledged his superiority of both the royal estates and the earldom in Orkney the year before.

In the transfer of the islands, the 'rights pertaining to the King of Norway by royal right' were really more important than the actual landed possessions of the kings. In both Orkney and Shetland these rights were financial and judicial, with an income being provided also from the profits of justice. This income was, indeed, far more important to the king than the rents from his royal estates. Among the many payments owed to him was skatt, the annual monetary tax from the odallers. The Dano-Norwegian kings had no control over the odallers' possessions and were not, in feudal terms, the superiors of the odallers. But despite their non-feudal freedom of possession, the odallers still all had to pay skatt to the king (and in Orkney also to the earl). The Latin word for skatt is 'tributum' and, as in all payments of tribute, there went also an acknowledgement of authority. On the same day that Shetland was pledged by Christian he wrote to the inhabitants of Orkney and Shetland telling them to be dutiful and obedient as well as to pay their skatt yearly to the kings of Scotland until the islands had been redeemed by Christian or his successors.[37] So by rendering their skatt, the islanders were also to render allegiance to their new king, and this was really the most important aspect of the pledging.

Many problems and uncertainties must therefore have been aroused by the pledging of Orkney and Shetland to the Scottish crown in 1468 and 1469. The transfer of these islands, where a distinctive form of society existed, to a country accustomed to a different form of land-holding was not a straight-forward transaction. This was particularly the case with the earldom of Orkney which was a completely distinctive dignity, quite different from anything else in the Scandinavian north, and not at all the same as a Scottish dignity of the same name. But it was a powerful earldom in that it was capable of giving the earl much wealth; and the Scottish crown, in order to secure the earldom in its own hands for the future, engineered another transaction a year later on 17 September 1470, when William Sinclair resigned to the crown 'all right of his earldom of Orkney' in exchange for the castle of Ravenscraig in Fife and other privileges.[38] This transaction may have been the means by which the Scottish crown got possession of Earl William's inherited lands in Orkney—although not apparently of his acquired lands—although the only piece of property mentioned in the document was the castle of Kirkwall. The most important factor however, was the earl's resignation of his right. This right, which any member of the earldom family had claim to under odal law, appears to have remained very much alive right up to the fifteenth century. The struggle between the grandsons of Earl Malise to get a grant of the earldom in the 1370s has already been mentioned. In the 1379 charter of the new earl, Henry, a clause was devoted to Malise Sperra that he should 'cease from his claim and altogether demit his *right* . . . to the said lands and islands'. Another clause talks of the possibility of forfeiture 'so that we and our heirs hereafter shall have no *right* of claiming the foresaid earldom', and the earl mentions also 'our *right* which we have now obtained in the said earldom'.[39] It is this right which in 1470 the earl was renouncing for himself and his heirs; just as in 1391 his great-uncle David had resigned to his brother, the earl, any right and claim that he had 'in the parts of Orkney or Shetland' which came to him through his mother, in return for a compensatory piece of land elsewhere.

In the 1470 'excambion' it is very clearly said to be his right of the earldom of Orkney which Earl William Sinclair resigned. There is no mention of Shetland, and if Shetland was not part of the earldom then Shetland cannot have been included in this resignation. The northern group of islands was a quite separate entity and it so remained until 1469 for, as has been mentioned, it was not joined again to the earldom in 1379. Nor is there any evidence that the last earl, William Sinclair, was given a grant of Shetland. So when the charter of 1470 mentions only the earl's right of his earldom it can be concluded that this did not include any right to Shetland. Two years later, in 1472, the Scottish parliament formally annexed the earldom of Orkney and lordship of Shetland to the crown, to be granted in future only to legitimate sons of the king.[40] For the first time there occurs the phrase 'lordship of Shetland', and it is significant that this is when Shetland is first mentioned in the Scottish records after the pledging. 'Lordship' seems, therefore, to be a purely Scottish title, no doubt a translation of the Norse 'foudrie'. It certainly indicates that the Scots regarded Shetland as entirely distinct from Orkney. But after 1472 grants made by the kings of Scotland to tacksmen are of the 'lands and lordships of Orkney and Shetland'. Thus, from the beginning of Scottish rule, the two groups of islands were formally joined together and administered together, the first time since 1195 that this had been done.

The purpose of the 1472 annexation was to proclaim publicly that the dignities attaching to the earldom and lordship, which in the past had pertained to others than the royal family, were from henceforth to be granted only to legitimate members of the Scottish royal family. It signifies, of course, the importance attached to these northern possessions. It also signifies that the crown considered that their acquisition was permanent, for it would surely never have countenanced that a prince of Scotland might be an earl of the kingdom of Denmark, which would have been the case had the islands been redeemed. In fact the Scots ignored all attempts to offer redemption money for the islands during the forthcoming century, and the Stewarts were to act directly against the high-sounding terms of the annexation when they gave the dignities of Orkney and Shetland to their base-born sons.

NOTES

1   J. S. Clouston, *History of Orkney* (Kirkwall, 1932).
2   *Diplomatarium Norvegicum*, ii, no. 2.
3   *The Orkneyinga Saga*, trans. A. B. Taylor (Edinburgh, 1938), 358.
4   *Ibid.*
5   *The Saga of Hakon* (Rolls Ser.), chap. 318.
6   *Exchequer Rolls*, i, 13, 19.
7   *Norges Gamle Love*, 1st ser., iii, 403.
8   *Diplomatarium Norvegicum*, iv, no. 128.
9   P. A. Munch, *Det Norske Folks Historie* (Christiana, 1859), v, pt. i, 515.
10 J. S. Clouston (ed.), *Records of the Earldom of Orkney* (Scot. Hist. Soc., 1914), nos. xxviii, xxix.
11 *Norges Gamle Love*, 1st ser., iii, 33–9.

12 *Records of the Earldom*, 28–31.
13 The heiress Herdis Thorvaldsdatter, who married the Norwegian treasurer, is a notable example. Her father 'Torvald de Shetland' was lord of Papey (*Diplomatarium Norvegicum*, vii, no. 134), which belonged to Duke Hákon Magnusson at the end of the thirteenth century (*Records of the Earldom*, 67).
14 *Ibid.*, no. i.
15 *Ibid.*, no. viii.
16 *Ibid.*, no. x.
17 *Ibid.*, no. xi.
18 J. Mooney, *The Cathedral and Royal Burgh of Kirkwall* (Kirkwall, 1943), 175; A. W. Brøgger, *Ancient Emigrants* (Oxford, 1929), 192.
19 *Diplomatarium Norvegicum*, ii, no. 647.
20 *Exchequer Rolls*, v, 54.
21 A. Peterkin, *Rentals of the Ancient Earldom and Bishoprick of Orkney* (Edinburgh, 1820), 59, 76.
22 *Diplomatarium Norvegicum*, i, no. 501.
23 R. A. Hay, *Genealogie of the Sainteclaires of Rosslyn* (Edinburgh, 1835), 57.
24 *Diplomatarium Norvegicum*, xviii, no. 34.
25 'The Voyages of Nicolo and Antonio Zeno', ed. R. H. Major, *Hakluyt Society*, 1st ser., i (1874).
26 *Bannatyne Miscellany*, iii, 81–2.
27 *Diplomatarium Norvegicum*, ii, no. 525.
28 *Ibid.*, no. 623.
29 *Ibid.*, no. 647.
30 A. W. and A. Johnston (eds.), *Orkney and Shetland Records* (London, 1907–13), vii, 97.
31 B. E. Crawford, 'The earldom of Orkney and the lordship of Shetland' etc., *Saga Book of the Viking Society*, xvii, 175.
32 J. Mooney (ed.), *Charters . . . of the City . . . of Kirkwall* (Third Spalding Club, 1952), 96–102.
33 W. Christenson (ed.), *Reportorium Diplomaticum Regni Danici*, ii (Copenhagen, 1929), no. 2580.
34 B. E. Crawford, 'The earldom of Orkney', *Saga Book*, xvii, App.; 'The pawning of Orkney and Shetland', *Scottish Historical Review*, xlviii (1969), App.
35 *Diplomatarium Norvegicum*, vi, no. 423.
36 From an account in the Edmonston family papers, of which Col. Edmonston of Buness, Unst, kindly gave me details.
37 A. Huitfeldt, *Historiske Bescriffuelse om huis sig haffuer tildraget under . . . Her Christiern den Første* (Copenhagen, 1599), 190.
38 *Registrum Magni Sigilli Regum Scottorum*, ii, nos. 997–1002.
39 *Records of the Earldom*, no. xl.
40 *Acts of the Parliaments of Scotland*, ii, 102.

CHAPTER IV
Udal Law

KNUT ROBBERSTAD

UDAL LAW is an old system of ownership of land, older than the feudal system. It has, of course, been modified with the passing of time but it still forms the foundation of the law on land ownership in Norway; and the Norwegian odal system has the same origin as the udal law of Shetland and Orkney. The word udal or odal may be found in several old languages: Swedish, Danish, Gothic, German, Frisian and Anglo-Saxon. The meaning of the word was particularly related to ownership of land which had been inherited from an ancestor. In Anglo-Saxon, and perhaps also in the old Norse language, it was also the name of a character of the older runic alphabet (ᛟ), meaning o. With the Norse settlement in Shetland there came the introduction of Norse names of farms and of institutions (such as, for instance, lawman, lawthing) and we must conclude that the Norsemen also introduced, and enforced, their own views on both ownership and the law of ownership.

In the *Orkneyinga Saga*, written about 1200 A.D., we may read about odal law in Orkney in the time of King Harald Fairhair (Hårfagre, king of Norway from 872) and the Earl Torv-Einar, the Earl Sigurd the Stout (d. 1014) and of the Earl Ragvald (d. 1158).

There is reason to believe also that in Shetland the land law was a Norse odal law, even in this first period (i.e. down to the year 1274 A.D.).

What is left of the texts of Norwegian law at this time has been excellently translated into English by Laurence M. Larson in *The Earliest Norwegian Laws, being the Gulathing Law and the Frostathing Law*.[1] These were laws written down in the 11th century and partly in the 12th century; while Gulathing law was in force in western Norway, Frostathing law applied to the northern parts of the country.

These law-books show that odal law then implied complete ownership of land, combined with certain odal rights for the odal family: that is, a right of pre-emption for the kinsmen of the owner in case he wanted to sell the land; a right of redemption by kinsmen if the ownership was transferred in some way or other to another person; and a right for kinsmen to lease land from the owner if he wanted to let it. At first the land must have become odal land as soon as ownership went from an owner to his son, or even before that occurred. In both Gulathing law and Frostathing law it is important to note that odal men appear as a distinct social class. The fine [wergild] which had to be paid when an odal man was killed was, according to Gulathing law, twice as much as it was for any other freeman and half the amount paid for the killing of a baron. The odaller was thus half way to being a nobleman.

As early as during the reign of King Harald Fairhair it was customary for the royal family—and even other families—to register the burial mounds of their ancestors, which were named odal mounds.[2] After the coming of Christianity we find that witnesses, giving evidence in odal cases, usually enumerate the ancestors of disputants 'til haugs og til heiðni', which means 'until the time of the man in the heathen burial mound'.[3]

In the age of Christianity the rights of kinsmen were so reduced as to apply only when the land had been the property of the family for six generations (Gulathing law) or four generations (Frostathing law). This was obviously of advantage to the king who as a rule could not confiscate odal land for crimes, and of advantage too to the church which wanted to come into possession of land either by gift or by sale.

Since this period when older odal rights were being transformed, the Norwegian legal system has contained provisions both for full ownership with odal rights for the kinsmen and for full ownership without any odal rights for the kinsmen. When Norwegians nowadays speak of odal right, they think mainly of the rights of the kinsmen. In Shetland and the Orkneys udal right chiefly refers to full ownership, thus pointing out the difference from the feudal system.

King Magnus Håkonsson, called 'Lagabøte' (i.e. the Lawmender), revised the laws of his kingdom. His *General Lawbook* actually contained one and the same code for each of the four law districts of Norway: Gulathing, Frostathing and the two law districts in the eastern part of Norway. This code was independently accepted by the four lawthings, each lawthing acting as a separate legislative body. It was considered then as a revised edition of the laws of St Olav, the patron of the kingdom, and was often called St Olav's law. The new code was first accepted by the Gulathing in 1274 and is sometimes referred to as the earlier Gulathing law.

The General Law was also introduced in Jemtland, a law district belonging to Norway until 1648.[4]

King Magnus set up a new legal code for Iceland in 1280 in the *Jonsbok*. The national law of Iceland (Grågås, dating back to 930 A.D., revised and written down in 1113) contained no odal rights for the kinsmen; that is, no odal rights of pre-emption or of redemption. The Icelandic owners had full ownership of their land. We may assume that the pioneers who settled in Iceland were powerful masters who did not want to share their power, even with their own children or kinsmen. It is known, indeed, that early settlers were forced to sell land to new immigrants in order to obtain a reasonable population in their districts. After 1262 Icelanders were subjects of the Norwegian king, and the code which King Magnus sent in 1280 was, for the major part, identical with his General Law. But the althing of Iceland did not approve of the precepts of odal rights for the kinsmen and these rights did not, therefore, become part of the *Jonsbok*.

King Magnus also set up a law for the towns of his kingdom. More than seventy per cent of its provisions are taken from the General Law, but none relate to odal rights for kinsmen. Instead of this it was determined that the *king* should have a right of pre-emption when the owner of ground in a town wanted to sell it. The reason for this must be connected with the fact that the old Norwegian cities were mostly founded on royal estates.[5]

The General Law of the Lawmender was also introduced in the Faroe Islands, whose population were also subjects of the kings of Norway. Until then the Faroe Islands had had an althing, but when the *Lawbook* came into force the althing was transformed into a lawthing—and this exists even today, at least in principle. It was in fact the Gulathing version of the *Lawbook* that was adopted for the Faroe Islands. (The odal law book of the Faroese lawmen from the 14th to the 16th century was called the *King's Book*. It was probably a gift from the king, and it is still extant in the Royal Library of Stockholm in Sweden.) It was the Gulathing version of the *Lawbook* which also came to be introduced in Shetland and Orkney.

Before the introduction of Magnus' new code, Shetland had had its own lawman and its own central thing or assembly. Most probably the assembly was, from the beginning, an althing or assembly of all men; as in Faroe it was transformed into a lawthing in virtue of the new *General Lawbook*, when this code was introduced.

That Shetland had its thingwall can be seen in the name of Tingwall church and in the tingholm or ness where the lagretta had its place when considering cases. According to Norse custom the Shetlanders must also have had a Lagberg or thingbrekka, where the lawman publicly recited the law to the people. This thingbrekka customarily sloped towards the east and it is plain to see that the slope to the east of Tingwall church must have been excellently suited as a Lagberg for Shetland, corresponding to the one known in Iceland and, to some extent, to the one in the Isle of Man.

In 1194, after the famous battle of Florevaag near Bergen, the king placed Shetland directly under Norwegian administration, as he did the Faroe Islands in 1195. This change may have resulted in less marked influence from Orkney and a stronger influence from Norway in Shetland affairs.

An early example of judicial process in Shetland, respecting udal law according to the *General Lawbook* of King Magnus, may usefully be given here. In a judgment in Tingwall on 19 May 1307 the lawman Ivar, with the advice and consent of the king's men and the lawrightmen, declared that certain merks of land in Kollavåg in Yell were forfeit on account of a mortgage for a fine due to the king. But the court made the reservation that the land might be redeemed by the odal men if they made valid payment for the land. The tribunal in this case was a law court in accordance with the *General Lawbook*, and the right of redemption reserved in the sentence corresponds with prescripts in the same law book concerning land given as payment of fine to the king for manslaughter (L IV, 2 and X 1, 5).[6]

When the *General Lawbook* had been introduced in the Faroe Islands, the Faroese demanded supplementary laws on certain local affairs and especially on sheep farming. One such amending addition was provided in 1298 by Magnus Lagabøte's son, the Duke Håkon Magnusson (from 1299 to 1319 king of Norway as Håkon V). The wishes of the people in this matter were presented by Bishop Erland (1269–1308) of the Faroe Islands and by the lawman Sigurd of Shetland who was sent there by King Håkon V.

The contents of the *King's Book* of the Faroe Lawman may be regarded as typical of such a book. The Faroese book comprises: the

General Law of King Magnus; some amendments (rettarböter) prescribed by later kings; local provisions given by the Lawthing itself concerning local affairs (such bylaws were not to replace any provision of the General Law); and notes on important judgments which were passed by the Lawthing.

In 1469 Christian I, king of Denmark and Norway, had to mortgage his lands in Shetland and his royal rights there, for the sum of 8,000 Rhenish florins, the money to be paid by himself or a future king of Norway in the St Magnus Cathedral in Orkney.

The Rhenish florin was a coinage issued by four German electoral princes, and consisted of 2.7 grammes of pure gold. Thus the sum of 8,000 florins was the equivalent of 21.6 kilograms of pure gold (or something like £8,000 or 160,000 Norwegian kroner, in 1969 money). No interest was stipulated perhaps because both kings were Catholics, and interest on credited money was forbidden in the law of the Church. Instead of interest, the mortgagee was to have the revenue of the mortgage. This is the story of the dowry, which may have its origin in an ambitious wish of Christian I, the son of a German count, to have a royal son-in-law. The fact that the sum was 8,000 florins out of 10,000, implies a sincere wish to have Shetland redeemed.

It was no unusual thing for this particular king to pawn the revenues of districts or of towns to a vassal, who then governed the district until it was redeemed. Christian I pawned the towns of Kiel and Flensburg in 1469 and several districts of Holstein and even the duchy of Slesvig. He pawned many fiefs in Denmark and Sweden and even the royal revenues of the towns of Skien in Norway. His queen, Dorotea of Hohenzollern, paid some of the debts and took over the right of the pawnee.[7]

Shetland had its lawbook on the basis of which its law was settled during the years of Norwegian rule. It is vital to remember that the mortgaging of Shetland did not abolish the existing law of the land. The lawman of Shetland continued to exist into the 16th century and the lawbook of Shetland was clearly still in use in 1602.[8] Thus on 27 July 1532 Nils Tomasson of Aith in Bressay, also called Nicol Reid, was elected lawman of Shetland.[9] He passed a sentence on 1 July 1538 in Gardie in Reafirth parish in Yell in accordance with the Gulathing law, and this decision was confirmed by the Norwegian king's court in Bergen on the 6 July 1538.[10] Again, in 1538, the king of Denmark and Norway made Gerwald Willemsson lawman of Shetland.[11] As late as 1576, indeed, the king of Norway appears to have sent a certain Lawrence Carnes to be lawman according to an agreement with Robert Stewart. In the same year 1576 the old lawrightmen of the whole of Shetland gave evidence that all men ought to come to the lawthing, those who had 'land or heritage or grit takkis (great tacks) of the King'. This duty corresponds with a paragraph of the *General Lawbook* (I.2).[12] It seems certain that judgments from the Shetland lawthing could be brought before the king's court in Bergen for confirmation—there is one reference in 1538 in the sources just mentioned—and there clearly existed a connection between the lawman of Shetland and the lawman of Bergen and Gulathing.

Why were the people of Shetland ready to maintain this legal connection with Norway? The likely answer is that they had to ask themselves what would be the situation if the mortgage was redeemed, which from their point of view might happen any time. And to the people of those days it seemed, in any case, quite natural that a decision given according to the Gulathing law might have its authority increased by a confirmation by the highest court in Bergen, including the lawman of Gulathing. There was, after all, no other superior law-court with knowledge of the Gulathing law. The connection between the lawman of Shetland and the lawman of Bergen and Gulathing would easily furnish the Shetlanders with knowledge of new decisions in Gulathing law and of new statute laws. We may have here, indeed, a reason for the abolition of the institution of lawman in Shetland.

In 1507 Prince Christian (later Christian II), acting as viceroy for his father King John, decreed that all amendments to the General Law made by Håkon V were to be in force throughout the whole kingdom of Norway, even in Iceland, the Faroe Islands and Shetland. The motive for this action is to be found in the amendment passed on 2 May 1313 (*Norges Gamle Love*, iii, 99 §1) where Håkon decreed on the right of kinsmen to inherit or redeem land: When a child has inherited land from its mother and then the father inherits the land from the child (the child having left no legitimate offspring), then the father is to inherit only the chattels permanently, and also the father is to possess the land for his own lifetime, and thereafter the land is to pass to the nearest kin in the maternal line from which it has come. (Land which a mother inherited from her child who had received it from his father was to revert to the paternal line in the same way when the mother died.) Important lawsuits had arisen in Iceland concerning rights of succession in two large estates, Grund and Mödruvellir, and the lands belonging to each of them.[13] As we noted earlier, *Jonsbok* had made no provision of special rights for kinsmen in respect of odal land and the decision in 1507 depended on whether the law of 1313 was valid or not in Iceland.[14] This legal question had necessarily to be brought before the king's court in Norway. There the question was solved in the Grund lawsuit by a sentence passed in Oslo by the viceroy and the Norwegian Council on 22 November 1507.[15] There King Håkon's law was found to be valid, as it had been confirmed by all later kings of Norway and also by the viceroy as being in force in the kingdom of Norway and even in Iceland, the Faroe Islands and Shetland.

Two days later the viceroy (Christian II) published his confirmation of all the laws of King Håkon V, and decreed that they were to be observed 'in the whole kingdom of Norway and lands under the crown of Norway, even Iceland, Shetland and Faroe as in other places here in Norway'. The viceroy warned his officials in Iceland that, if they prevented any subject from making use of Håkon's law, they would be made to feel his princely anger and revenge.[16]

There is no indication in the sources as to why Christian made his decree of 1507 include the Faroe Islands and Shetland.[17] Yet he may have had more than one of the following reasons for doing so:

(a) Whereas Denmark was an electoral kingdom, Norway was legally a hereditary monarchy. Christian used the title 'lawful heir to Norway', and had an interest in maintaining the whole territory of Norway. Orkney may have been omitted from the decree in order to avoid a dispute with the king of Scotland.

(b) King Håkon's amendment was obviously valid in the Faroe Islands from the beginning, as appears from a judgment given in Torshavn, Faroe in 1403.[18] There is reason to believe that it was valid in Shetland and Orkney as well.

(c) Important Norwegian families owned lands in both Shetland and Faroe, and they would not want the introduction of any new rules concerning succession to land, nor any obscurity about the validity of Håkon's law. The most important of these families was descended from a daughter of King Håkon V himself and her husband Havtor Jonsson. To this family belonged Håkon Jonsson, who on 25 May 1369 in Kirkwall made an agreement with bishop William, regarding the lands which Håkon owned in Orkney and Shetland.[19] The family had inherited land in Shetland from Herdis, the daughter of Torvaldus de Shetland.[20] One member of this family was in 1507 a member of the Council of Norway and another was a courtier of Christian. The Norwegian knight Knut Knuttson [Båt], who was murdered in 1519, owned lands in Shetland which produced an annual rent of one barrel of butter and four packages of wadmal. These lands was probably pawned to Archbishop Gaute (1475–1510), and it is worth noting that both Knut Knutsson and the archbishop were members of the Norwegian Council in 1507. In Faroe a considerable estate belonged to Otte Rosenkrantz, lands which remained in his family's possession for more than 150 years. And the Norwegian nobleman Trond Tordsson Benkestokk, who was a member of the Norwegian Council about 1500, also owned land in Faroe.[21] With regard to Orkney it seems that there was no real property belonging to Norwegian noblemen there in 1592.[22]

(d) The relations around 1507 between Norway, Iceland, Faroe and Shetland can be exemplified by the case of Gudtorm Nilsson, a Norwegian nobleman. He had close connections with Iceland as brother to the bishop of Holar there and as son-in-law of the Icelandic lawman Finnbogi Jonsson; he lived with his wife on the estate of Grund from about 1496 until she died in 1499, and perhaps remained for some years after. Sometime between 1505 and 1509 Gudtorm was made lawman of Bergen and Gulathing and held that office until about 1539. He died in 1540. In 1509 we find him in Shetland attending a local thing at Melby in Sandness in Vågar [Walls], a farm belonging to the king from 1505 to 1515, while in 1512 he appears to have bought one half of Sandfridarøy (now Samphrey) in Shetland.[23] The Faroe connection is less clear, but it is supposed that Gudtorm was the father of Andreas Guttormson, lawman of Faroe from 1531 to 1544.

What implications, then, did the events of 1469 have for the standing of udal law in Shetland? The pawning of Shetland comprised the royal sovereign rights, the royal revenue and crown land. According to the *Lawbook* of Magnus the Lawmender, the king shared the sovereignty with the people, who were represented by the things, especially the lawthings. Thus the *Lawbook* itself could not be abolished without the consent of both lawthing and king. But the king could, on his own, make amendments which were to be the benefit of his subjects.[24] The king could not, however, impose new taxes in districts where 'leidang' was provided in the form of military service or skatt. Meanwhile, the lawthing could enact bylaws: but these were valid only within the district concerned and could not alter nor abolish provisions of the *Lawbook*. And the lawthing could authorize new taxes proposed by the king.

With regard to the pawnee, his obligation to return the pawn in undamaged condition would effect his part of the legislative power. Christian II's part of Norwegian legislation in Shetland in 1507 shows that he pretended to have the right to legislate in such matters even in Shetland. The decree of 1507 was accepted by the althing of Iceland in 1508 and, named *rettarspiller* (spoiler of rights) by some Icelanders, remained in force until 1711. Its fate in Shetland is not known to me. Formally it was only the confirmation of an old law. Christian II must have thought that a new king of Norway should have the power of confirming these old laws even in respect of the mortgaged land, an idea that was by no means revolutionary.

In 1936, in an essay on udal law published in *The Sources and Literature of Scots Law*, W. J. Dobie wrote 'That the law of the islands was in fact based on the law of the parent country of Norway is proved by available records' and 'Without the lawbook it is impossible to reconstruct with any confidence the law of the islands, to say how far it conformed in detail to the parent law of Norway, or if it followed the progress of legislation there'.[25] But in 1954, when Professor Gordon Donaldson published an edition of the *Court Book of Shetland 1602–4*, it became possible to be more precise than this.[26] It is possible now to compare the Shetland Court Book with the *Lawbook* of Magnus the Lawmender.

The Court Book is written in Scots, interspersed with many Norse words, especially the words which had been used by the Lawmender for legal technicalities. It is one of the two oldest court books we have based on districts using Norwegian law, the oldest being the court book of the lawthing of Oslo for 1572–80. The two books have several features in common. The Shetland lawthing was presided over by Earl Patrick Stewart or his deputy and the book is written in Scots; the Oslo lawthing was presided over by a Dane, Nils Stub, who at the time was lawman of Oslo, and his court book was written down in Danish with many Norwegian terms.

The Shetland Court Book is a real treasure of information: about the lawthing itself, lawsuits and possession of land (skattald); about agriculture, udal law and royal prerogatives or regalia; about division of an inheritance by sjond and erve (schound and airff), i.e. a legal process which in earlier times was connected with the funeral feast. Most of the Court Book is taken up with details of crimes and fines. The fines are regularly imposed in marks or merks, and it is notable that the amounts are the same as stated in the *Lawbook* of Magnus the Lawmender. The Court Book for 1602–4, indeed, shows that the lawthing used the *Lawbook* of King Magnus. In some respects

Shetland was applying Norwegian laws and Norwegian legal customs much later than the year 1469. The lawman of Shetland must have been in closer communication with the lawman of Bergen and Gulathing than we know in detail. The latter was the nearest competent adviser in such matters, and the journey from Shetland to Bergen took two days with a fair wind.

In some fields, however, Shetland had its own customs. A number of regulations were specific to Shetland, as they were to Faroe. Thus their lawthings were not held on 16 June each year as prescribed by the *Lawbook,* but later in the summer and after a minor thing had been held in every parish; the stembod or 'budstikke' (a small stick which the messenger carried when summoning people to a thing) was shaped as a cross, a shape unknown in Norway where secular matters are concerned; the under-foud in Shetland must have been an official with the same status and responsibilities as the 'syslemann' in the Faroe Islands. Shetland's own lawthing also made acts and ordinances which applied only to Shetland, and these are conspicuous in the Court Book because the fines here are quoted in shillings, a few even in pounds, but never in merks.

In the *Court Book* (p. 43) there is a sentence concerning accessory to murder which was passed to 'be the inspectioun of the cheptures of the law and parteikis of the contrie in sic caises'. Those sitting in judgment evidently had (a) to look up the law to find out whether it was a case of murder or of manslaughter only, and (b) to find out what was the correct punishment according to precedents. The punishment of an accomplice had to be decided in each separate case according to the circumstances. The fact that the courts of Shetland in 1602–4 based their decisions on the *Lawbook* of King Magnus appears from the terminology, the legal conceptions applied, the rules enforced and the way of thinking—and from the fines.

This was still the situation when, in 1604, King Christian IV put into force a new edition of the Lawmender's *Lawbook,* 'revised, corrected and improved' and printed in Danish. In Shetland at that time the common man no doubt understood the Norse language of the Lawmender, even if Scottish influences must have caused some difficulties in the use of the old *Lawbook* in the courts. To use a lawbook written in Danish would only raise new and more difficulties, and further, from a Scottish point of view, the introduction of the new book must have been undesirable as it would tend to admit the fact that Shetland belonged to the kingdom of Norway. Consequently, in 1611 the Scottish privy council prescribed that the foreign laws of Orkney and Shetland should be abolished and replaced by the laws of Scotland at a moment when Shetland had no earl who could protest, for Earl Patrick Stewart was in prison and Christian IV was himself occupied with a war against Sweden (1611–13).

The act of 1611 would have proved a disaster to all owners of udal land in Shetland if they had been deprived of their land, and their estates had become feudal possessions of which the king was the owner. The king then would have been able to give away the land by feudal tenure to whom he liked. Earl Patrick Stewart seems to have made a futile effort, in 1592 or earlier, 'upon some sinister information' and 'upon some other unlawful grounds', to have the udal land feudalized.[27]

However, the act of 1611 was not given retroactive effect in this way. Udal law continued in Shetland as well as in Orkney, retaining concepts of ownership in accordance with the law of Magnus the Lawmender, 'the form of land-holding introduced by the Norsemen'.[28] How did this continuing udal system compare with the law of Norway?

Udal holding is of an allodial nature. The udaller has no feudal lord and consequently has no feudal obligations or services to perform. In the udal system there exists no presumption or fictio juris saying that the king or the crown has been the owner of the entire territory. In the *Lawbook* it is expressly stated that land presented to a man by the king, is the odal of the man, provided the gift is not offered on other conditions (L VI, 3).

In Shetland the udaller paid his customary skatt, a tax which had been introduced before the days of the Lawmender. And the weights and measures on which that tax was based could not be altered. In Norway we find in some districts that the taxes were raised by altering the weights and measures, and new taxes appeared in the 16th century and afterwards—the old tax system was not abolished until 1939. Nonetheless, two hundred years ago it was thought by some theorists that odal right entailed that no new tax could be imposed on an odaller without his consent. This is the reason why in 1814 the lower house of the Norwegian Storthing was given the name Odelsting.

Differences between udal and feudal law are to be seen in the practice of land transfers, for no written deed was or is required for the transfer of udal land. Magnus the Lawmender advised his subjects that it would be wise for them to make transfers and pledges in written form, an idea he had got from Roman law: but this warning was not to be regarded as an order, and no feudal dues were to be exacted. In later periods the transfer of land is usually based on written documents, however, and since 1623 Norway has registered all deeds—a practice called 'tinglysing', i.e. publication at the thing. While this registration is very useful it is not necessary for the acquisition of ownership of land.

When odal land was to be transferred to a new owner, the kinsmen of the owner had certain odal rights if the ownership had rested with the family for 60 years and the owner had a duty to notify his kinsmen of the intended transfer. (In Norway now the stipulation is 20 years.) The rights of kinsmen were carefully guarded. An owner could not evade his obligations towards kinsmen by the practice of upgestry or making legitimate donations to the church or others. According to the *Lawbook* an owner might make such a gift without the consent of his heirs, but he could not give away more than one-fourth of his earnings and one-tenth of his inheritance—the provision of 'tend penny and the ferd'. The original purpose of this rule had been to enable the owner to make gifts to pious institutions for the benefit of his soul. But, according to the *Lawbook*,[29] the owner could make his gift to whomsoever he liked, his son or others. The gift might consist of odal land but in such cases kinsmen had the right to redeem the land with payment, and there could be no prescription to prevent the redemption.[30]

Transactions similar to that of upgestry were practised in Norse law, but they could not remove the right of kinsmen to redeem udal land. The kinsmen usually consented to the transaction (e.g. because they did not want to maintain the old owner).[31]

The seller frequently referred to his need for money and to urgent necessity, a custom found even in Sweden: but this phrase was only an excuse to placate the kinsmen and had no significance for their right to redeem the land by paying its value. It is well to note that in Norway the right of the kinsmen is still valid, and is often practised, as in cases where the owner has gone bankrupt or has sold to a stranger.

The Court Book of Shetland in 1604 mentions that some confusion prevailed then about the sale of lands. Evidently some people, who did not know about or did not like this aspect of udal law, wanted to buy land. It was prescribed that nobody should buy or sell any kind of land without first having offered the land to the nearest of the seller's kin, according to the custom of the country. If the next of kin refused to buy, the land was to be offered to the earl (*Court Book*, p. 150):

the seller was regularly a man in financial straits, and his next of kin was usually either a son or a daughter who were just as poor as he was. It can be seen, therefore, that the earl's new right of pre-emption was a great privilege, and one derived from the kinsman.

When an owner died, his property went to his heirs: a daughter only got half as much as a son—a sister's part as against a brother's part; the inheritance was of one farm only, it became a condominium. An 'inheritance feast' was usually held on the seventh day after the death of the owner, when the division among the heirs took place. This was called the sjaund (i.e. the seventh day) or shynd.

According to a statute passed in Bergen in 1539, however, the eldest son was to take possession of the whole farm, and had to pay rent to his brothers and sisters for the use of their parts. If there were sufficient farms to be inherited, then every brother and sister was to have one each. It seems that simple primogeniture had been introduced in Orkney in 1535—and maybe the Bergen legislators were copying an attractive example formulated in Orkney or Shetland.

According to the *Lawbook* of King Magnus, the odaller had a high ranking. This appears from the fines applied for trespassing. If the land belonged to an odaller the fine for trespass was stipulated at 6 uris (oras); if the owner was a common man or a foreign immigrant the fine was 4 uris only; and if he chanced to be a baron the fine was to be 9 uris.[32] The provision was included in Christian IV's edition of the *Lawbook* in 1602, and remained in force in Norway until 1687.

'Full ownership' in odal law implied, and in principle still implies, complete right of disposal of the land in all legal ways. The owner himself chose the manner in which he wanted to use and cultivate his land. The systems of skattald, runrig and so on, which have existed in Shetland and Orkney for hundreds of years, are very similar to those used in the Gulathing district of Norway until a hundred years ago, and similar in some respects to those mentioned but not imposed in the *Lawbook* of King Magnus. In the full ownership obtained under the odal law the owners themselves decided how to use their property and, where the property was a condominium, the owners had to proceed according to laws and customs concerning joint property.

In the oldest forms of odal law full ownership included, and still includes, ownership of the foreshore. To a property belonged, and belongs, not only the shore to the lowest point of the ebb but also the ground a bit further out, to what is called the 'marebakke' (Norse: *mar-reins-bakki*, where *marr* means the sea, *rein* means borderline or border strip, and *bakki* means slope). That is, ownership extends to the line where the foreshore becomes steep, at a depth (according to the steepness of the bottom) of from 2 to 5–8 metres at the ebb tide. The same legal provision prevails in Iceland, Sweden and Finland, but in these countries the rights of the landowners extend still further into the sea. In many old Norwegian deeds the extension of the land is described by the clause 'fra fjell til fjaere' (i.e. from the mountain to the shore). The Norwegian landowner had, and has, the right to take sand and stones from his foreshore, a right to the seaweed there, to the shell-fish, and even a right to build a quay from his shore out into navigable waters. Indeed, full ownership also includes the right of hunting.

In Norway, similarly, lakes and streams belong to the land. In the 20th century there has been made one exception; the central parts of the biggest lakes are not, on the whole, to be under ownership. According to the *Lawbook* all fishing in lakes and rivers belonged to the owner, and this is still the principal rule. From mediaeval times onwards, in lawsuits concerning fishing rights, the courts have consistently decided that these rights belong either to the owner of the land or to anybody who has derived the right from him. So far as sea-fishing is concerned, it is now quite clear that the owner alone has the right to put out fishing gear which is fastened permanently, or for the duration of the fishing season, to some point on shore or near to the shore (e.g. above the foreshore border).[33] In 1468 we know that the crown of Norway had no right *inter regalia* to the fishing of salmon or any other kind of fish in the sea, in the rivers or in the fiords; and the crown still has no such rights. In Norway it is not disputed that full ownership also embraces the right to make use of property in different and new ways, or to find other ways of making profits from it. Consequently, it was, and is, the owner of the land who, for instance, could utilize waterfalls by constructing electric power plants.

In Shetland the right of a udaller to make use of the shore down to the lowest of the ebb is now well established in law,[34] and his fishing rights have been likewise established.[35] It would seem natural, indeed, that the udaller should still have the rights of full ownership and the disposition of it where this has not been disputed. And that has implications for the legal position of treasure trove, such as the St Ninian's Isle treasure. Here, again, let us look first at Norwegian practice.

Treasures wich have been found in Norway have got into the

ground in various ways. Before the introduction of Christianity, for instance, objects were buried with their owners at death. After Norway was converted to Christianity, in the reign of King Olav Trygvason (995–1000), the dead were interred in churchyards and gifts were given to the church. But the gravemounds from heathen times, situated on the estates, were not destroyed and were treated with respect. Even as late as about 1900 some odallers of Norwegian estates knew themselves to be descendants of the man who they said was 'living' in the gravemound and who had been the first to clear the land and make it into an estate, one thousand years or even more before. The breaking-up of gravemounds was chiefly carried out when 'the man in the mound' was believed to have become wicked and dangerous. Such gravemounds produced weapons and tools, but very seldom gold or silver.[36]

Again, treasures could be deposited in the earth or in rock-falls by people who believed that this was a way to ensure that they would have the use of the treasures after their death. The Icelandic saga-writer, Snorre Sturlason (1179–1241), notes that Odin made a law to the effect that every man should enjoy what he himself had dug into the earth.[37] The great treasures, however, and by far the largest number, were buried in the earth and in rock-falls in times of war and peril, a custom which has lasted right on to our own times. The gold and silver which was buried was then sometimes lost or forgotten about.

The position of treasure in Norwegian law before 1030 must have been that it belonged to the owner of the land where it was found. That was also the rule of the oldest law of Iceland.[38] When the Norwegian king, Olav Haraldsson (later St Olav), died in 1030, King Cnut of England and Denmark installed his young son Svein Cnutsson on the throne of Norway (1030–35). The head of the government was the boy's mother Alfiva (Ælfgifu), the daughter of an Anglo-Saxon ealdorman. During this reign the government of Norway had to be maintained by a foreign army, and had to introduce laws to increase the revenue of the king. One of these laws determined that treasure found in the earth belonged to the king. But these new Alfiva laws were gradually abolished. In 1040 or 1041 a provision was inserted into the older Gulathing law stating that the owner of the land was the owner of goods found on his land even though the goods might have been unearthed by another man. But in the old Frostathing law a provision was inserted at some time between 1103 and 1116 which declared that goods that had been hidden in the ground were to be the property of the finder. Therefore, King Magnus had to compromise when he made his *Lawbook*,[39]

According to that *Lawbook* treasure should be divided: one-third going to the owner of the land, one-third to the finder, and one-third to the thing. If a man could establish his odal line back to the man who was buried in the gravemound, then he was to have the owner's part. The right of the landowner to his third was part of his 'full ownership'. The law presumed, however, that the treasure had been hidden by someone in the oldest odal line, and regarded the odal heir as the owner of the land where treasure was concerned. The provision makes the three part-owners also joint-owners of the treasure. In the 1604 edition of the *Lawbook* the part-owners of treasure are stated to be the king, the odaller and the finder (with one-third to each). This same provision was adopted in Christian V's Norwegian lawbook (1687) and remained in force until 1905, when a stature of 13 July decreed that the state was the owner of all treasure trove which was of mediaeval or earlier date, with the proviso that the state paid the whole metal value to the finder and the landowner, if they were not allowed to keep the objects which have been found. A new law of 29 June 1951 amended this slightly: the state has to pay ten per cent more than the current metal value of gold and silver.

The St Ninian's Isle treasure was found in Shetland in 1958 and it was a matter of importance to decide who was the owner of the treasure. Since udal ownership in Shetland had not been abolished in 1611, I came to the conclusion that the matter ought to be solved according to udal law as laid down in the *Lawbook* of King Magnus: that is, one-third was due to the finder (the University of Aberdeen), one-third to the udal owner of the land and one-third to the crown. But the Court of Session in Edinburgh, on 2 August 1963, declared the crown to be the sole owner of the treasure in a lawsuit brought against the University of Aberdeen. At the quincentenary conference held in Orkney in 1968, it was clear that opinions differed among competent jurists in Scotland: I stick to my former opinion, and will now explain why.

The basis of the Court of Session decision is the maxim that the crown shall have what belongs to nobody else, i.e. *bona vacantia*. It is a maxim which was and is not valid in Norse law and it has never been part of the Norwegian legal system. Moreover, the right of the udaller to one-third of buried treasure is a privilege which is intrinsic in his ownership of the udal land, a right which—as we have seen—was to some extent founded on the general assumption that the treasure had been hidden by the forefathers of the udaller. It is my contention that the definition in law of 'full ownership' of an udaller must be judged on the basis of the concept of full ownership which existed from before 1611. Furthermore, there is no doubt that sovereignty over a country can exist without the sovereign having the right of *bona vacantia*: for that was, and is, the case in Norway. King Christian I could not mortage or give away a more extensive sovereignty than he himself had.

As to the foreshore I should like to add some words on the problem of defining it. I have already mentioned that the udaller's right in Shetland extended as far as the lowest point of the ebbtide, and that according to Norse law (which is still Norwegian law) the landowner's estate goes farther out, to the marebakke. Once again, here, there is a difference of concept between Norse law and Scots law, because according to Scots law the crown is the owner of the shore. It seems probable that the older Norse ruling in this matter was modified in Orkney and Shetland and that the clause 'to the lowest of the ebb' is an expression of the modified rule. This modification could not be of any advantage to the landowner: the use of the word 'ebb', which is not a Norse but an English word, indicates a mediating expedient and one of a type to be expected from a lawyer. When was the limit of the 'ebb' introduced and what legal status should it have?

The first document containing the clause was written in Kirkwall on 31 January 1480.[40] It is a deed of conveyance from James Cragy, youngest son of the deceased lawman John Cragy, who sold all heritable lands in his part of the inheritance within Orkney and Shetland 'fra the heast stane of the hil to the lawast in the eb' to his brother William Cragy, then lawman of Orkney. The next instance is a judgment, passed on 27 April 1509 by the lawman John Cragy and concerned with the boundary between Saba and Toop in Orkney, from the boundary stone 'to the lawest of the se and sand'.[41] So far as Shetland is concerned, the first mention of such a limit comes in Unst in 1528 when a deed specifies the extent of property as 'fra the hyest of the hill to the lawest of the eb'.[42] Another deed, dated 16 July 1538, from Peter Magnusson to Gilbert Cant, concerns four merks of land 'fra the heast in the hyll to the lawest in the eb'.[43]

Thus it is probable that the clause was first used in Orkney, with the 1480 document as one of the earliest instances of its use. It may be important to note that the 1480 transaction was one carried out within a family which held the position of lawman for some decades. John Cragy, father of the parties mentioned in 1480, had been lawman, the eldest son William was the actual lawman at the time, and the youngest son, John Cragy, was to become lawman (and acted from at least 1496 to 1509).

These Cragy lawmen were descended—through a sister of Earl Henry II—from the earls of Orkney,[44] and we should expect here a deep and sensitive knowledge of Orkney and its people.

If the invention of the ebb limit came from Orkney, it is worth noting that the difference between high tide and low tide is much greater there than in most parts of Norway. Most Orcadian beaches are broader and less steep than they are in Norway; and a very large proportion of the shores of Orkney go directly into the open sea or into broad fiords.

What then can the concept of the 'ebb limit' tell us about the way of thinking of the man who invented this modification of the Norse law? Whoever he was, he cannot be said to have acted as a Scots patriot, maintaining that the shore ought to belong to the crown; nor did he act as a Norwegian patriot, maintaining the marbakke border as in Norse law; but he did act as an Orcadian (or Shetland) patriot, for he invented a new concept of the limit in the light of what he saw as the rule which would be in harmony with the nature of the islands—a rule which would bring least disadvantage to the islanders, and a rule which has been ignored in the Scottish courts.

NOTES

1 Published in New York in 1935. Larson was born in Norway in 1868, became a university professor in Illinois, USA, and wrote on English medieval history.
2 *Ynglingatal; Kvalsund: de Borgund og Giske I* (Bergen, 1957), pp. 193 et seq.
3 This is expressly noted in a statute of 1316.
4 *Tidskriff, utgiven av Juridiska Foereningen i Finland*, (1961), 183 et seq.
5 The oldest of the Norwegian cities, Nidaros (now called Trondheim), was founded about 997 and was planned after the model of Dublin.
6 The document is published in *Diplomatatium Norvegicum* (vol. I, 109) and has been translated into English in the *Records of the Earldom of Orkney*), 69.
7 *Norges Gamle Love* (Christiania, 1885) iv, pp. 665 et seq. *Jon Helgason in Utiseti*, vi (Copenhagen 1951), 101 et seq. and J. Agerholt in *Arkiv for nordisk filologi*, vol. 74. Also Erik Arup, *Danmarks Historie*, ii (Copenhagen, 1932), 229, 233–7, 249–53: cf. P. J. Jørgensen, *Dansk Retshistorie*. 332. 353–7, 368–9, 436.
8 Gordon Donaldson, *The Court Book of Shetland, 1602–4*, 31.
9 Gilbert Goudie, *Antiquities of Shetland*, 93.

10 *Diplomatarium Norvegicum*, ii, 1126, *Diplomatarium Orcadense et Hialtlandense*, 41, translated in *Records of the Earldom of Orkney*, 96.
11 *Norske Rigsregistranter*, i, 57; cf. *Diplomatarium Nörvegicum*, ii, 1126.
12 David Balfour, *Oppressions of the Sixteenth Century*,(Edinburgh, 1869), 3–4 and 58.
13 The Icelandic jurist, Finar Arnórsson, has written at some length on thse lawsuits in 'Gottskalk Biskup Nikulásson og Jón Lögmaður Sigmundsson' in *Safn til Sögu Islands*, 2, flokkur (1953–4), pp. 50–69.
14 Þorvaður Erlendsson, lawman of the southern and eastern half of Iceland from 1499 to 1512, claimed that King Håkon's law was valid, and that the estate of Mööruvellir should therefore pass to himself and his family. But Finnbogi Jónsson, lawman of the western and northern half of Iceland from 1484 to 1508, took the opposite view and this, if upheld, would bring the estate of Grund to himself.
15 *Norges Gamle Love*, 2, iii, 301.
16 *Norges Gamle Love*, 2, iii, 303.
17 Christian II did not forget Orkney. On 31 July 1514 he was to write to the people there: 'Dear friends, You know that you rightly belong under the crown of Norway, even though you are pawned to the king of Scotland. But we intend to redeem your land very soon for the crown of Norway, to remain under us and the king of Norway as it ought to be by right'. *Diplomatarium Norvegicum*, i, 1042.
18 *Diplomatarium Norvegicum*, i, nos. 589–92, 611; *Diplomatarium Faeroense*, ii, 3, 11.
19 *Diplomatarium Norvegicum*, i, 404; *Records of the Earldom of Orkney*, 14.
20 *Records of the Earldom of Orkney*, 67 et seq.
21 *Diplomatarium Norvegicum*, vi, 805.
22 Balfour, *Oppressions*, 102, 'Supplication to the Scotch Parliament 1592 from the noblemen of Orkney and Shetland'.
23 *Diplomatarium Norvegicum*, vi, 651; viii, 426; iii, 1055 and 1056.
24 *Lawbook*, x, 3.
25 Stair Society publications, vol. i, 445–60 and especially 450–1.
26 It is a great help when using the Court Book to refer to another of Dr Donaldson's books: *Shetland Life under Earl Patrick* (Edinburgh, 1958), a most vivid description.
27 See the 'Supplication to the Scottish Parliament, 1592' by Lawrence Bruce of Cultmalindy and others, which is printed in Balfour *Oppressions of the Sixteenth Century*, 101 et seq.
28 Dobie in *The Sources and Literature of Scots Law*, 450.
29 *Lawbook*, v, 21.
30 *Ibid.*, vi, 7. Neither Dobie, *Sources*, 453 nor J. Storer Clouston in *Records of the Earldom of Orkney*, 77n., mentions this provision.
31 cf. Dobie, 452.
32 L VII, 20, *Norwegian Historisk Tidsskrift*, vol. 42, 339.
33 See *Lawbook*, vii, 48, which gives owners' rights of fishing 'in front of his land' just as in inland waters.
34 *Smith* v. *Lerwick Harbour Trustees*, 1903.
35 *Lord Advocate* v. *Balfour*, 1907.
36 Johs. Skar, *Gamalt or Saetesdal*, (Christiana, 1903–07) vol. i, 3, 39, 53 and vol. iv, 96.
37 *Heimskringla*, Ynglinga saga, ch. 8.
38 Grågås i and ii, *Landnamabok*, (1900 edition), 170–1.
39 Gulathing Law ch. 148, Frostathing Law part XVI, ch. 1. Part vi of the *Lawbook* on odal law has a chapter (16) which refers to goods hidden in the ground.
40 *Diplomatarium Orcadense* no. 32, printed also in *Records of the Earldom of Orkney*, 192.

41 *Records of the Earldom of Orkney*, 82.
42 G. Goudie, *Antiquities of Orkney and Shetland*, 116.
43 *Ibid.*, 142.
44 J. Storer Clouston, *History of Orkney*, (Kirkwall, 1932), 384–5.

CHAPTER V

The Post-Norse Place-Names of Shetland

W. F. H. NICOLAISEN

IN MY view, it can be demonstrated quite clearly that when the Norsemen arrived in Shetland almost 1200 years ago they not only carried with them in the vocabulary of their language a large number of words suitable for the naming of geographical features of all kinds, whether natural or man-made, but also a stock of actual names which could be drawn upon whenever applicable. The giving of Norse names to places in Shetland—and this statement has, of course, more general implications and could be said to be true of all areas into which speakers of a new language move in large numbers—was therefore not entirely a process of creating appropriate distinguishing labels from suitable lexical items. Although this spontaneous creation did take place naturally, there must have been also many occasions when a ready-made name from the homeland was pulled out of the onomastic bag, simply because such and such a feature always had such and such a name at home. In some cases, there may have been an element of nostalgia involved as well but, on the whole, I feel that the use of this kind of commemorative naming is usually overstressed, perhaps because of the important part it has played in the naming of settlements in the New World across the Atlantic in more recent times. Naturally, it is not always easy to decide which aspect is involved in the act of naming, but I suspect that in cases like Lerwick, Dale, Tingwall, Linga, Breiwick, Twatt, Voe, Melby, Houlland, which all have not only close but identical parallels in Norway and sometimes several of these, we may with some confidence consider the possibility of onomastic rather than linguistic naming: by which I mean that a ready-made name was re-applied rather than freshly created.

This is the subject I first thought of exploring in this lecture, but it is more appropriate that I should turn rather to a discussion of the place-names of Shetland after 1469 rather than before that date. I do so with some hesitation, even trepidation.

First of all, there is the regrettable fact that this is my first visit to Shetland, which makes clear my presumption in attempting an account of Shetland place-names under Scottish and British rule. Secondly, Shetland has been extremely fortunate in having experienced—mainly in the last decade of the nineteenth century but also in the ten or fifteen years which followed—the stimulating influence of that great scholar, Jakob Jakobsen, still fondly remembered by so many.[1] The existence of his book on the place-names of Shetland, now unfortunately only obtainable at a premium, has so far persuaded us in the Scottish Place-Name Survey not to conduct any systematic collecting and recording of place-names in these islands, since the more urgent task seemed to be the carrying out of field-work in areas in which Scottish Gaelic is disappearing fast. I do not know whether the expression 'carrying coals to Newcastle' is still apposite in our day and age, but if it is, then 'talking about place-names in Lerwick' carries just about the same indication of superfluity. Thirdly, and this point is linked with the last, I am only too well aware that I am addressing an audience in which at least every Shetlander present is an expert in, or at least has some knowledge of, local place-names, and among whom one in particular—a Whalsay man, a schoolmaster in Aberdeen[2]—knows a great deal more about the place-names of this group of islands and has done more research into them than I could ever know or do. Lastly, the post-Norse place-names of Shetland do not have anything like the glamour of their Norse predecessors.

Yet there are good grounds for addressing ourselves to this topic. Firstly, the place-names of the post-Norse area in Shetland have never been looked at systematically but have only had a few pages or paragraphs in even the best accounts of Shetland names published so far; their detailed investigation is more than overdue. And, secondly, it appears reasonable that an elucidation of problems and questions rather than solutions and answers may be useful to any future scholar or scholars who may want to devote time and energy to a more comprehensive study of the subject under discussion. I have therefore come from Edinburgh to bemoan the fact so little has been done in this field, to suggest what might be done and to put in a plea for work to be carried out locally, not only with regard to the

THE POST-NORSE PLACE-NAMES OF SHETLAND 71

place-names of Shetland coined or adapted after 1469 but also for those of earlier periods. There is, after all, no reasonably complete and systematic published account of the place-names of these islands. Not being a Shetlander nor a Scot, I can perhaps walk where angels would fear to tread and state categorically at the outset that the question of whether Scottish and English or Scotticised and Anglicised place-names in Shetland are desirable or not is not going to enter into or colour my arguments. I am neither celebrating their existence nor holding a wake for them: but I shall be looking at them in the way in which I would look at the place-nomenclature of any region in which one language has been superseded by another. I shall look for survivals, for adaptations, for new coinings, and for all the other phenomena associated with the place-names of what must have been for centuries a bilingual community. It is perhaps also well worth remembering in this respect that almost as much time has passed since 1469 as elapsed during the period between the arrival of the Norsemen about 800 A.D. and the year of the fateful pledging. Indeed, if we take into account a certain amount of Scottish infiltration into Shetland before that date, the Norse and the post-Norse periods are practically of equal length.

It does not need a place-name expert to tell you that the earlier of these two periods has had a much profounder influence on Shetland place-names than the second, certainly with regard to individual names. The evidence is all around us and exemplified by the many names, mainly of human settlements but also of natural features, which Shetlanders without any special instruction no longer easily understand—neither through their own dialect of Scottish nor via Standard English—but which, I believe, still give Norwegian and other Scandinavian visitors the feeling that they are not far from home. This is no idle statement, for comprehensibility plays an important part in peoples' attitudes to names. As soon as a name is no longer understood it is removed even further from the realm of ordinary words than a name of which the meaning is still clear. Then only its onomastic qualities survive since it is no longer of any practical use as a lexical item. Such a shift, from the immediately or relatively meaningful to the partly or totally meaningless, takes on immense proportions when we go beyond the obsolescence of individual name-elements within the medium of the same language[3] to the replacement of one whole language by another. Depending on the kind of replacement and its speed, we have a gradual or sudden drifting into meaninglessness of hundreds or even thousands of names. This is the sort of process which must have taken place in Shetland some time between the middle of the fifteenth and the middle of the eighteenth century, and it is not surprising therefore that linguistic and local historical scholarship has since then, but mainly during the last hundred years or so, been concerned with the retrieval of these lost meanings. The driving force behind this has been largely the community's interest in its linguistic past or its roots in general. There has also, however, one suspects, been the age-long curiosity and imagination which imbues the meaningless shape with romantic ideas and notions, identifies the lost meanings of names with the loss of an age in which everything was good and lovely, and so there seems to be some hope that the recovery of the meaning of names may also bring back (or strengthen the demand for the return of) at least some aspects of that golden time. Would the same amount of scholarship, energy and interest have been spent on such a quest if Lerwick had been known as Mud-Bay, Linga as Heather-Island, and Houlland as High-Land? I personally doubt this very much, for I never receive requests for help with the investigation of names like Bankhead, Middleton and Stonehouse although such names are by no means as clear as they look. It is a fallacy anyhow to suppose that we can handle place-names better if we know what they mean.

This is not as much of a digression as it may seem, for it explains why the Norse ingredient in Shetland place-nomenclature has had so much attention whereas the English and Scottish names have not. Our starting-point nevertheless must be this Norse nomenclature which, in the context of this paper, is simply regarded as existing at the time when the islands were pledged to the Scottish crown. That these names must have been dense and numerous on the ground there is no doubt. If it is correct that the population figure soared to the region of 20,000 at one stage of the Scandinavian period, many individual dwellings and clusters of dwellings must have been needed, and each required a name; and even if, as I suspect, the population figure was a little lower, a large number of settlement-names was still needed and doubtlessly existed. Obviously these names were not all created at the same time nor even within a few years of each other. As settlement became denser, as families grew, as new settlers arrived, the need for new names increased and must have been met. It is therefore possible to detect strata within the Scandinavian stratum, and I have recently published an attempt to disentangle these layers and to establish a sequence of names or at least of name-elements, not only for Shetland but for the whole sphere of Norse influence in the Northern and Western Isles and on the adjacent Scottish mainland.[4] This sequence does not concern us here, for all that matters to us is the fact that in 1469 there was a dense network of Norse settlement names in Shetland so that the Scottish incomers came across the *staðrs*, and the *bólstaðrs*, and the *boers*, and *kvís*, and *setrs*, and names compounded with similar elements referring to man-made settlements.[5] In addition, there were almost uncountable numbers of Norse names of natural features and of settlements which had derived their names from natural features: *víks* and *vagrs* and *ás* and *nes's* and *fjalls* and *vatns*, and dozens more. Personally, I would not entirely support the claim that every feature had a name in 1469, and certainly not that every feature had a Norse name. Quite clearly, some pre-Norse names have survived even if we can't yet ascribe all of them to any particular language.

What, then, happened to these Scandinavian names? As far as I can see, there are three main possibilities in this kind of bilingual situation when one language is increasingly ousting another.[6] Names are adapted in some way, they are replaced, or they drop out altogether.[7] And this process goes on while new names are being coined in the new language for new settlements which may spring up or for natural features which apparently had no name in the earlier language. Let us look at these various possibilities in turn.

First of all, there are the adaptations, using that word in its widest sense. Here we have a number of possibilities. Names may be fully translated, a process which requires practically full bilingualism and would therefore not be associated either with the earliest phases of Scottish influx nor with the later stages when Scots had become so dominant that there was very little left of Shetland Norn. One might be inclined to think of the sixteenth and seventeenth centuries as suitable periods when conditions were right. Or again, only one part of the name may be translated whereas the other part is left intact. This usually happens to generic elements but sometimes also affects the explanatory part of a word. Theoretically it could probably take place at any stage during a bilingual period. A third form of adaptation takes place when words of the new language are added tautologically—that is, they mean the same thing and describe the same feature as the whole name (if it is an uncompounded name) or as one element of it (if it is a compound one). This is not the same as translation because tautologies normally arise when the meaning of the original name or name-part is no longer known. They are therefore mainly late phenomena. Fourthly, there is the possibility of extensions or incorporations. What I mean by this is that a word or words belonging to the new language are added to an existing name to describe a feature nearby, i.e. the old name is incorporated in the new one. Occasionally this also happens in the case of the same name but the extension is then not tautological. Lastly, the name may be phonologically adapted; that is, it is left untranslated but its sound-shape is changed according to the sounds available in the new language. Sometimes this produces the possibility of a folk-etymology on the basis of the receiving language. Phonological adaptation may, and usually does of course, also happen as an integral part of part-translations, tautologies and extensions, and we can say straightaway that it is always the most common treatment given to existing names by the incoming speakers of a new language.

So far as Shetland is concerned all these five varieties of adaptation of older names did happen in the Norse›Scottish change-over. The first of these, full translation, is the most difficult to prove and indeed frequently unprovable unless there is conclusive documentary evidence. Jakobsen[8] cites at least two instances. These are Black Loch (in Unst) and Black Water (Nesting) which, in his terminology, 'correspond' to a name such as *Swartasjøn* from the Old Norse *svarta tjǫrn (black tarn): according to him we have a plural in West Sandwick in Yell, but on the Ordnance Survey one-inch map this is spelled in the singular form *Swarta Shun*. Jakobsen may be right or he may be wrong; the documentary evidence being what it is, we have no means of proving the case either way. I do not know of a single instance in which the written record demonstrates or suggests full translation of an existing Norse name by the incoming Scots. We are nevertheless entitled, I think, to assume that this variety of adaptation did take place to a limited extent although it is not one of the most common phenomena in other bilingual regions, even in the Gaelic-speaking parts of Scotland where we can check the various processes in present-day conditions because they are happening under our very noses.

We are in a much stronger position with regard to part-translations, of which there are several good examples in Shetland.[9] Woodwick in Unst, for instance, probably goes back to an Old Norse *við-vík, in the same way as Woodwick (Orkney) which has an earlier spelling Weidwick. Dyke-end may be a rendering of an earlier Old Norse *garðs-endi, with the same meaning.[10] In fact, this may almost be called a full translation since *-end* may well be the Lowland Scots cognate of Old Norse *endi*. Transition from Norse to Scots was often facilitated by such cognate words, and one suspects that loch-names ending in -water, like Fugla Water (Yell), Papil Water (Fetlar), Gorda Water (Papa Stour) and Gossa Water (Sandsting), originally ended in Old Norse *vatn*. Similarly in Cat Firth, Lay Firth, Colla Firth, Whale Firth and the like, firth is surely the replacement of Old Norse *fjǫrðs* by its Scots cognate. The element *land*, too, was easily 'translated', as very little sound substitution was necessary; and the same is true of *dalr* and dale, *bakki* and bank, *borg* and brough, *holmr* and holm, *hus* and house, *gata* and gate, *hǫfði* and head, *sund* and sound, and many others. (I am quoting the Old Norse forms although the Shetland Norn versions are sometimes even closer to Scots). In the case of non-generic first elements, certain adjectives lend themselves to the kind of treatment just described, particularly Old Norse *djupi which easily becomes 'deep' as in Deepdale (Sandwick and Sandness); *hvíta* which is without difficulty turned into 'white' as in Whiteness (Tingwall); *groen* for 'green', which must have been substituted at an early date in such names as Greenmow (Dunrossness) and Greena (Tingwall). Adjectives of position like *øfri* and *neðri* must also have invited quick replacement by 'over' and 'nether', and a similar correspondence existed between terms for the directions of the compass. In some instances, both the first *and* the second element have found easy substitution in this way. We have already mentioned Deepdale, in which both elements are cognates of the kind just described; Greenland in Walls would also belong here, and all these examples (but the last two in particular) are reminders that the Shetland variety of Norse and the Scots variety of English were closely related languages when the linguistic confrontation took place: they did not, therefore, create the same problems which exist, for example, in an English-Gaelic or English-Welsh bilingual community. People must have understood each other fairly quickly and easily, especially since Scots in general was very strongly influenced by Norse. The modern Shetland dialect seems to demonstrate very clearly this kind of easy amalgamation.

This brings us to the so-called tautologies, which can be quite misleading in so far as they appear to contain an element of translation and are therefore often regarded as such. In my own view this element, although natural in one way, is purely accidental in another. And it is certainly unpredictable which word in the new language is going to be used when it is applicable. In their very nature, these names presuppose that the earlier of the two (or sometimes three) tautological elements had become meaningless; consequently, they must be reckoned mostly to have arisen at the tail-end of a bilingual situation. This type of name is practically unknown in Shetland, for one suspects that, in Yell coastal names like Bay of Whinnifirt and Point of Ness, Whinnifirt and Ness are not really regarded as names of the same feature, and Head of Hevdagarth, in the same island, with its doubling of *hevda* (Old Norse *hofði*) by 'head' would also not be an instance of straightforward tautology. The almost total absence of this kind of adaptation of earlier names can only be explained by the assumption that most generic elements referring to geographical features never really lost their meaning; but were retained in the emerging Shetland variety of Scots so that there was no need for re-describing the voes, wicks, geos, and nesses by words of English origin. Indeed, most of these are still alive in Shetland today and have been used in the formation of new English names, as we shall see.

Whereas tautologies were uncalled for, the extension or incorporation of earlier Norse names in their Scotticised forms is a normal feature of post-Norse naming in Shetland. In a number of cases this extension may have taken place in Norse times and was obscured later by a kind of part-translation, but such instances are difficult to establish. That that extension is also a pre-1469 phenomenon is, I think, shown by such names as Lunda Wick (Unst) incorporating the early name Lund, Laxabigging (Melby) and the many sound-names like Uyea Sound, Hascosay Sound, Yell Sound, Bressay Sound which contain the names of adjacent islands and undoubtedly go back to names originally ending in Old Norse *sund*. Post-Norse examples would be Sumburgh Head, New Grunasound (East Burra), Wormadale Hill (Tingwall), Lerwick Harbour, and Pettadale Water (North Roe); but probably also Kirkabister Ness (Bressay) and Papa Skerry in spite of the Norse origin of *nes* and *skerry*. In these names and some others they were probably used as Norse loan-words in a Scots dialect rather than as genuine Scandinavian elements in Norse times. Such a statement as this is not easily proved, and only clearly-dated documentary evidence will help in time to solve this problem.

The most common type of post-Norse Shetland name which incorporates an earlier Norse one relating to a neighbouring geographical feature is that exemplified by the construction, 'A of B': Hill of Dale, let us say, or Noup of Noss. These names occur in abundance on the Shetland map, and have such an interesting history that we should look at them in a little more detail.[11] It must be stated at the outset that I feel that, in the interpretation of this name-type, Jakobsen was incorrect in assuming a Norse origin for this construction.[12] I have very carefully examined the various Scandinavian place-name archives and have also consulted colleagues in Norway, Denmark and Sweden; and there appears to be no trace of any similar name-type in those countries. We must therefore look elsewhere for its origins, and it is significant here that Shetland and Orkney are by no means the only regions of present-day Scotland in which this type of name is to be found. If we look, for instance, at a map showing the distribution of 'Burn of—' names (95 out of a total of 135 stream-names in Shetland marked on the one-inch Ordnance Survey maps bear such a name), we discover that the Scottish north-east also shows a remarkable density of these names. Such Shetland names as Burn of Russdale, Burn of Geosetter, Burn of Aith, Burn of Hamnavoe, are paralleled in the north-east by Burn of Birse (Aberdeenshire), Burn of Longshank (Angus), Burn of Boyne (Banffshire), Burn of Melmannoch (Kincardine), Burn of Clashgour (Moray) and many others. In my opinion, it is here that we can expect to find the roots of our Shetland name-type, for it is remarkable how often the element B in this 'A of B' construction is a name of Gaelic origin. In our selection we have Birse, Boyne, Melmannoch, and Clashgour. It is therefore tempting to derive the 'A of B' pattern from a Gaelic source and, without wanting to make this too much of a mystery, I suggest that the stages in which this development took place may have been as follows:[13]

1st stage: Gaelic *Allt an t-Sluic Leith*, i.e. burn of the grey hollow;

2nd stage: most commonly (a) Burn of Sloch Lee, with 'Burn of' translating the Gaelic *Allt (an)*, anglicisation of the Gaelic element 'B' as in Sloch Lee, and with substitution of the nominative for the genitive: or sometimes (b) where the whole name is translated; thus the Angus names Burn of Blackpots and Burn of Oldtown are strongly suggestive of being full translations of Gaelic **Allt na(n) Linneacha(n) Dubh(a)* and **Allt an t-Sean(a)-bhaile* respectively;

3rd stage: 'Burn of', followed by any (usually anglicised) Gaelic element, whether or not it has been part of an original stream-name in *allt*, e.g. Burn of Knock (Kincardine),

Burn of Corrhatrich (Moray), Burn of Badenhilt (Aberdeenshire);

4th stage: 'Burn of', followed by any defining element regardless of its linguistic origin, cf. Burn of Berryhill (Angus), Burn of Cauldcots (Kincardine), Burn of Davidston (Aberdeenshire). (The two names mentioned in the 2nd stage (b), Burn of Blackpots and Burn of Oldtown, may also belong here.)

The third and fourth stages of this development bring the complete emancipation of this new name pattern and its independence from the original stimulus. Nevertheless it must have come about in a Gaelic-Lowland Scots bilingual situation particular to the Scottish north-east, and could not and cannot emerge in the south-east where there was no Gaelic stimulus or in the present-day Highlands and Islands where Gaelic is being replaced by a variety of Standard English, and not Scots, under completely different economic and educational circumstances.

That the distribution of the 'Burn of -' type is no matter of mere chance is shown by the geographical scatter of such name patterns as 'Water of -', 'Mains of -', 'Mill of -', 'Hill of -' and others. In this respect, it is interesting to note that Shetland does not share the types 'Water of -', 'Mains of -' and 'Mill of -' with the north-east. 'Water of -' could not be used here for the naming of water-courses because its Norse cognate *vatn* had already been assigned to denote 'loch'. 'Mains of -' and 'Mill of -' were probably unsuitable because of the differences in agricultural organisation between the north-east and Shetland. 'Hill of -', on the other hand, is represented by at least 109 names on the one-inch Ordnance Survey maps, such as Hill of Dale, Hill of Canisdale, Hill of Berry, Hill of Gunnista and so on. There are even more 'Loch of -' names, in fact a total of 137, on these maps: for instance, Loch of Spiggie, Loch of Grunnavoe, Loch of Lunnister, Loch of Kettlester, etc. Not infrequently, both 'hill' and 'loch' are combined with the same name in this way, such as Hill and Loch of Basta, and of Brindister, Burwick, Colvister, Garth, Girlsta, Grista, Houlland, Huxter, Kirkabister, etc. The types Point of Coppister, Head of Mula, Saddle of Swarister, Bight of Haggrister, Bay of Quendale, Isle of Noss and Mires of Linksetter reinforce the impression of basically Scots or English usage, and at the same time make it very likely that the 'A of B' pattern came to Shetland (and Orkney) as a ready-made name-type from Scotland with Scots-speaking incomers from the north-east mainland.

By the time this pattern reached Shetland there was no trace left of its Gaelic origins. It had become well established within the variety of Lowland Scots spoken by these incomers, and its usage seems to have become very popular in the developing Shetland dialect of Scots: so much so, that almost every Scandinavian geographical term which had been borrowed into that dialect could also appear as element A in the imported construction. There are countless examples of this, of which I can only mention a few: Wick of Collaster (O.N. *vík*), Ness of Wadbister (O.N. *nes*), Taing of Noustigarth (O.N. *tangi*), Geo of Henken (O.N. *gjo*), Ward of Clugan (O.N. *varða*), Keen of Hamar (O.N. *kinn*), Holm of Skaw (O.N. *holmr*), Lee of Saxavord (O.N. *lið*), Breck of Newgarth (O.N. *brekka*), Noup of Noss (O.N. *gnupr*), Hamars of Houlland (O.N. *hamarr*), Cro of Ham (O.N. **kro*, a variety of *kra*), Stacks of Valsland [or Vataland?] (O.N. *stakkr*), and many others. The map of Shetland today tends to give the impression that this is perhaps the most common name-type at present, certainly with regard to the names of natural features. In colloquial usage the definite article is usually prefixed, and the 'f' of 'of' is elided (both under Scottish influence), so that we have de Bard o'Bressay (instead of Bard of Bressay), de Hevdin o'Waddersta (rather than Hevden of Wethersta), de Klepps o'Kollaster, de Kūl o'Fladabister, de Rogg o'Kirkabister, and so on.[14] Whether this pattern is still creative today is difficult to say, but its close proximity to ordinary appellative usage may still be keeping it alive, just as its popularity and impact are probably also due to its holding a position half-way between a proper name and a more syntactic unit used as a descriptive label. However that may be, it is undoubtedly the major contribution of Lowland Scots to the naming of Shetlanders, and to the map of Shetland, after 1469.

Nevertheless, it is not the most common type of adaptation of Norse names by incoming speakers of Scots and English, for out of the five different varieties mentioned, the fifth and last is also the most frequently employed, i.e. the phonological adaptation largely through the means of sound-substitution. The fact that Old Norse **leir-vík* has become Lerwick (and ['lɛrɪk] in Lerwick itself) and not remained *Leir-vík* as in Norway, that **þing-vǫllr* is Tingwall and not Norwegian *Tingvoll*, that **lyng-øy* is Linga today and not still *lyng-øy*, and that **hóland* has developed into Houlland and not into *Høy-land* are due to this adaptation. I am not saying that Shetland Norn would not have developed its own distinct forms anyhow—after all, Icelandic names sound quite different from their

Norwegian counterparts today. But it is more than likely that these are not the forms which have been brought about, in spelling and in pronunciation, by five hundred years of Lowland Scots and English linguistic influence. It is improbable that there would have been any 'w' in the present-day Shetland pronunciation of names like Lerwick and Tingwall without such southern influence. The introduction of metathesis into such names as Brough (several instances), Gossabrough (Yell), and Snabrough (Fetlar), all containing the Old Norse *borg*, can also be ascribed to Scots influence (cf. the word *broch* itself), although spellings like Scousburgh, Sumburgh, and Cullinsburgh sometimes obscure this fact. The visitor by air now lands at Sumburgh and not at *Sumbrough. There is no genre of names in Shetland which has not been affected by this phonological process although it is perhaps more noticeable in the major names of the islands: settlement names, names of districts, the names of the islands themselves, and the names of all the major elevations, bays, headlands and so on. On the whole, this phonological adaptation has had the effect of making many of these names totally or partly meaningless for the present-day Shetlander who has no special training in the Scandinavian languages or in linguistics.

In general, this adaptation was easy because of close relation which the two relevant languages then had, including their similar soundsystem. There is a good research topic for a linguist in contrasting the stock of sounds which Shetland Norn is likely to have had in the fifteenth century with the phonological structure of Lowland Scots of the same period and during the two or three centuries which followed: for on that basis it might be possible to predict the kind of substitution to be expected. Our linguist could also offer a quantitative analysis of the influence which Lowland Scots (and latterly Scottish-English) have had on the Shetland Norn sound-system, and that with regard to more than place-names.

So much for adaptations which do not, after all, add anything substantially new to any nomenclature:[15] but are there any independently-created new names to be ascribed to the post-1469 period? We cannot distinguish any new Norse or Shetland Norn names from those coined before 1469 unless additional extra-linguistic information is available. In the case of Lowland Scots or English names, could we rule out the possibility of full translation from Norse or of an easy adaptation to a cognate phonological and lexical system? Jakobsen,[16] for instance, derives from Norse such names as Midhouse (Delting), Northus (Unst); Westhus (Dunrossness), Easter-,

Mid- and Wester-tun (Unst), Langtun (Mainland) and Korstun (Dunrossness); but some at least of these may be of later origin since names ending in -hus and -tun are very common in Lowland Scots areas.

Sometimes it is possible to ferret out a replacement of an earlier name, such as Newhoos for an older *Skēva in Delting or West Yell for the earlier village called Strand;[17] but, on the whole, such replacements are just as difficult to determine as full translations. And even when we do know that a certain name mentioned in the sagas or in early documentary evidence has been lost,[18] we cannot know very easily whether it has been replaced by another name. This does not mean that there are no readily recognisable post-Norse names on the Shetland map today. Scots names like The Faulds in Yell and Aithsting, or The Links (in Unst and Dunrossness) belong to this category, as do modern English names like Belmont (Unst), Greenmeadow (Aithsting), Hillside (Delting), Roadside (Sandsting), Seafield (Mid Yell).[19] Fort Charlotte might be added here and Jarlshof too, as well as the street-names in Lerwick and Scalloway. Names of individual town-houses like Leagarth, Clairmont House, Rocklea, Gordon Cottage, Hillbank, and Helenlea, which one notices in the capital of Shetland, would also have their place here; but although there are plenty of these, the additional place-name material which has come into the rural areas of Shetland appears to be rather small and limited when compared with the number of Scottish personal names which have been introduced into Shetland in the last five hundred years.

Of the 500 names included on the Ordnance Survey one-inch map for the parish of Dunrossness only a maximum of 40 (or 8 per cent) can be regarded as having independent post-Norse origins, and even this figure may hide a few full translations from Norse. The names in question apply almost without exception to such less important geographical features as stones or holes or small streams or to a few late settlements. And out of the 139 inhabited settlements in Shetland listed in the 1961 Census report, *Place Names and Population: Scotland*,[20] only 9 look as though they have post-Norse names, viz. Bridgend, Freefield, Longfield, Lower Sound, Moors, Mossbank, Netherston, Northhouse and Whitefield; but, apart from Bridgend and perhaps Mossbank, the others could be adaptations. There are also five names of the 'A of B' type. It is by adaptation of existing names that Lowland Scots has made its impact since 1469.

Is there any possibility of dating this impact and of linking it to particular events? Only a diligent search of the existing documents could help us here and no one has yet made a comprehensive survey of the available sources relating to Shetland. But I have noted a number of points in my search for some kind of a chronology of naming. Perhaps it is not necessary to stress that there are very few names which can be dated as precisely as Fort Charlotte, named after the wife of George III in connection with the re-establishment of a garrison at Lerwick in 1782; or as Jarlshof, which makes its first appearance in Scott's *The Pirate* in 1821. But street-names should be readily datable from successions of street-plans and council minutes, while houses must also, in many cases, have datable names if it will not always be possible to discover why they were given the particular names they have—apart from reasons of euphony (the Victorian variety) and nostalgia. For the bulk of Shetland names, however, we must despair of absolute dating and can only hope to establish a relative chronology, for we must remember that the first reference to a place is normally not contemporary with the creation of the name by which it is called.

The first mention of something approaching a Scots place-name in Shetland seems to be a reference to the *Corss Kyrk* in Dunrossness in 1506.[21] *Newhous* and *Stansland* are mentioned in the Court Book of 1615[22] but we do not know, of course, whether these are Scottish or adapted Norse names. The pattern 'A of B' certainly existed at the beginning of the seventeenth century for the Court Book of 1615 has 'the mylne of Urafirthe', 'the . . . hill of Urafirth', 'the hous of Wasland' (or 'Vasland'), 'the hill of Quarfe', 'the ile of Moussay', 'the ile of Rue', and 'the hill of [Conn]sburch'; whereas one year earlier we find 'the loch of Coginsburch' and 'the ile of Wais', always with the definite article and still hovering on the brink between appellative and onomastic usage.[23] In the field of phonology we may note that, whereas in 1467 Tingwall is still spelt with a 'y' (Tyngvell),[24] in 1602 the Scots 'w' seems to have come to be there to stay (Tingwall).[25] The Scots metathesis of 'borg' to 'brough' is also in evidence at that time: not only for Brough in Gulberwick (which is spelt 'Bruche' and 'Burghe' in 1602) and for Sumburgh ('Soundbrughe'), but also for Hamburg as is shown by the mention of 'ane half Hambruch barrell of beiff' in 1615. The intrusive double 'l' in the spelling of Walls was still absent in 1510 ('Waas') and in 1614 ('Wais') and both spellings are very close to modern Shetland pronunciation of that place-name.

One difficulty in the dating of such linguistic changes lies in the fact that most of the relevant documents like the Court Books are in Scots, and they tend therefore to obscure rather than bring out the local pronunciation of the time. The records of Hanseatic towns are, therefore, a welcome non-Scots source for many of our names and may well be closer in many respects to local usage than are the contemporary official Scottish documents. An example of the value of non-British sources is to be found in the *Records of the Earldom of Orkney*[26] where there is a certification by the law-courts of Bergen of an agreement affecting lands in Shetland. Written in 1485, this document is in Norwegian and we get some lovely spellings—'Liwngöy' for Linga, 'Hwalsöysund' for Whalsay Sound, 'Vlstadh' for Ulsta in Yell, and some others. That Norse place-nomenclature remained stable and unchanged even after the appearance of numerous Scottish surnames and their bearers in Shetland is clearly shown in such examples as this from the Court Book: at an assize on 21 August 1612, arranged for a 'dittay contra the egiptians for schlauchter', while the names of the persons involved are Schlaitter, Magnussone, Olasone, Kaid, Mowat, Coghill, another Mowat, Foster, Nicolsone, Olasone, another Magnussone, Bult, Smith and Wischart, all the place-names are Norse.[27] It is a situation which has, to all intents and purposes, continued until the present day when the discrepancy between surnames and place-names is still very notable.

In tackling such a seemingly unrewarding subject as the post-Norse place-names of Shetland, therefore, we meet a host of questions rather than answers: but we can come to certain general conclusions in spite of the comparative dearth of material and the little work which has been done so far. When Shetland was pledged to the Scottish crown in 1469 it contained such a wealth of named settlements and of named natural features that the necessity for fresh naming was not very great. The percentage of really new Scottish names given without reference to the existing Norse nomenclature was therefore very small, and it has been infinitesimal with regard to settlement names. The only major contribution made by the Scots incomers was the introduction of the pattern 'A of B' which became dominant in the secondary naming of natural features and thus quite typical of the Shetland onomastic dialect.[28] Otherwise, phonological adaptation as part of the general linguistic take-over has been the main process of change observed. This has meant that the place-nomenclature of Shetland today has remained close to the Shetland dialect in its ingredients but has retained a large Norse element because that meaningfulness which is essential to the retention of ordinary lexical items is not required in the retention of names. Perhaps one can say that the dialect is largely but not exclusively Scots in its phonology, morphology, and syntax but that it has a strong Norse admixture in its vocabulary, whereas the place-nomenclature is basically Norse with the addition of certain Scottish material.[29]

What *is* now necessary is the systematic collection, from oral tradition and from historical documents, of the place-names of Shetland; and I would therefore support Mr John Stewart's appeal for such a collection, made in the *New Shetlander* in 1951.[30] This collection should be made regardless of the linguistic origin of the names and should, if at all possible, consist not only of lists but also of map references and tape-recorded interviews with suitable informants. I am quite sure that the Scottish Place-Name Survey, with the Shetland Folk Society, could devise and implement such a scheme, calling if necessary on help from the schools. The immediate aim would be the preservation of material for future generations but it would not exclude analysis and interpretation. A Gaelic map of Scotland is being prepared for Gaelic speakers for use in school classrooms. A similar kind of map or series of maps which would show the place-names of Shetland in the Shetland dialect would be an interesting and very desirable parallel to the Ordnance Survey sheets produced by English-speaking publishers and intended for English-speaking users. What I envisage is not an etymological map or an antiquarian map going back to pre-1469 times but one which would reflect Shetland usage today. It would provide an immediate local stimulus for the collection of names and would thus repay the labours of those who were involved in its preparation.

NOTES

1   See T. M. Y. Manson, 'The personal impact of Jakobsen in Shetland and Orkney' in *Froðskaparrit*, xiii (1964), 9–13.
2   The late John Stewart.
3   For instance, the name Hawick in Southern Scotland is now meaningless although it is a Scottish-English name.
4   W. F. H. Nicolaisen, 'Norse settlement in the Northern and Western Isles: some place-name evidence' in *The Scottish Historical Review*, xlviii (Apr. 1969), 6–17.
5   There is an excellent analysis of these by John Stewart in Alan Small (ed.), *The Fourth Viking Congress* (Edinburgh, 1965), 247–266. The same author has a

shorter account in A. T. Cluness (ed.), *The Shetland Book* (Lerwick, 167), 136–140.
6   For some general comments see W. F. H. Nicolaisen, 'The interpretation of name-changes' in *Scottish Studies*, v (1961), 85–96.
7   Like *Flókavágr* of the sagas and a number of others listed by A. B. Taylor in 'Shetland place-names in the sagas', in W. Douglas Simpson (ed.), *The Viking Congress, Lerwick: July 1950* (Edinburgh, 1954), 112–129. Losses are of no interest to us in the context of the present paper.
8   Jakob Jakobsen, *The Place-Names of Shetland* (London, 1936), 5.
9   *Ibid.*
10 'Dyke-end' may be much more recent than the phase of part-translation: many 'dyke-ends' seem to be nineteenth century in origin.
11 This type of name has been dealt with in a number of articles by the present writer in the series 'Notes on Scottish Place-Names' in *Scottish Studies*. 'See 'The Type "Burn of -" in Scottish Hydronymy', iii (1959), 92–102; 'Names containing the preposition "of"', iv (1960), 194–205; '"Hill of -" and "Loch of -"', ix (1965), 175–182.
12 Jakobsen, *Place-Names*, 6, where he suggests that de Hill o' de Waters (Yell) represents an older *Vatnahul* or *Vatnabrekk*, and Hill o' Dale an older *Dalsfell*.
13 See *Scottish Studies*, iii (1959), 97–8.
14 Jakobsen, *Place-Names*, 9–10.
15 The type 'A of B', however, might well be regarded not only as an incorporating adaptation but as a kind of new formation which has added to the existing stock of name patterns and has in this way enriched the range of Shetland place-names, especially secondary and subsidiary names.
16 *Place-Names*, 129–130. (The names are here quoted in the forms given by Jakobsen).
17 *Ibid.*, 133.
18 See note 5 above.
19 Jakobsen, *Place-Names*, 7.
20 *Place Names and Population, Scotland: an alphabetical list of populated places derived from the Census of Scotland* (London, 1967).
21 Alfred W. and Amy Johnston (eds.), *Orkney and Shetland Records*, i: Old-Lore Series, vii (London, 1907–13), 249.
22 Robert S. Barclay (ed.), *The Court Books of Orkney and Shetland 1614–1615* (Scot. Hist. Soc., 1967).
23 *Ibid.*, 107–108. One of the finest references to this type of name is in a court case in connection with 'the thifteous steilling of twa sheip out of the nes of Kebusta, and ane uther of nes of Gr[im]bista in Juni last on ane Sonday in the morneing, quhilk they pat in a boit and sauld to the Hollenderis at Brassay'.
24 Johnston, *Orkney and Shetland Records*, 51.
25 Gordon Donaldson (ed.), *The Court Book of Shetland 1602–1604* (Scot. Record Soc., 1954).
26 J. Storer Clouston (ed.), *Records of the Earldom of Orkney, 1299–1614* (Scot. Hist. Soc., 1914), 72–73.
27 Robert S. Barclay (ed.), *The Court Book of Orkney and Shetland, 1612–1613* (Kirkwall, 1962), 25–26.
28 The map-forms do not, of course, always represent local usage faithfully. As we have seen (see p. 79 above), the preposition 'of' is given locally rather as 'o'[ə] . The type as such, however, exists in oral tradition but is sometimes paralleled by the 'B–A' rather than 'A of B' construction.
29 See David Murison, 'Scots Speech in Shetland' in Simpson, *The Viking Congress, Lerwick: July 1950*, 255–260, and esp. 257.
30 John Stewart, 'The Shetland place-name collection' in *The New Shetlander*, no. 28 (May–June 1951), 7–8.

CHAPTER VI

Hanseatic Merchants and their Trade with Shetland

KLAUS FRIEDLAND

SHETLAND, AS seen in Hanseatic sources, was a very well-known foreign market of the late Middle Ages. This is obvious as late as 1700; Dutch maps about that year show Shetland with Orkney and the Faroes outlined between the Scottish and Norwegian coasts. A hundred years later the islands were no longer seen from the point of view of sea-trading merchants, and knowledge on the continent about the north began to deteriorate. Maps of those later years connect Shetland and Orkney rather with the British Isles, while the Faroes and Iceland were combined with Denmark and with the southern parts of the other two Scandinavian countries. A new edition of the same atlas in 1837 stressed still more territorial and dynastic divisions, printing only a small inset of Iceland and Faroe on the Denmark map: Shetland meanwhile was to be found only in the historical map. Even that historical reference was no longer included in 1886 in the well-known school atlas by Droysen, when Shetland was reduced to pin-point size on a map entitled 'Colonies and Communication', with the added (and incorrect) comment—'British 1468'. It was about that time that a historian of the Hansa, Professor Baasch of Hamburg, first noticed that the Hansa (or at least Hamburg) developed 'a quite lively trade with Shetland and Faroe, far more extensive than their current unimportance would suggest'.

The date 1469 is significant for the relations between the Hansa merchants and Shetland. When the Danish-Norwegian kings gave up Orkney and Shetland, they relinquished also economic and political power over northern trade. The marriage treaty with the Scottish king was intended to improve Denmark's relations with France, Scotland's ally; and the Hansa at the same time also decided to side with France. The consequent decrease of Scandinavian power encouraged the merchants to follow their trade more freely and openly. The records of the Hanseatic towns in the 1480s clearly show this development but the origins of Hanseatic trade with Shetland are of earlier date, going back as far as the beginning of the fifteenth century and—though documentary evidence is rather scanty— probably earlier. In the first half of the fifteenth century, Shetland was included as a matter of course in the Hanseatic-Danish system of staples based on Bergen in Norway. This was so because the Shetland Isles offered the nearest landmark and shelter for those who sailed from Bergen on the Norwegian coast for the Danish crown-lands of Faroe and Iceland: until 1469 they were themselves crown land. Not that the voyage across the open sea from Norway to Shetland, even in the late Middle Ages, was particularly adventurous: contemporary sources mention a time of just twenty-four hours to sail from Norway to Scotland and the present-day crossing over the same distance lasts longer. Goods from Shetland could be legally traded via Bergen as could the products of all other crown lands.

The Shetland Islands were first mentioned in their commercial connection with Norway in 1276 in the *Lawbook* of Magnus Lagaböter (i.e. the Lawmender). Roughly twenty years later the Norwegians opened up Bergen trade to the Hanseatic merchants but prohibited voyages beyond Bergen: the effect of this was to connect trade from the crown lands *to* Bergen and Hanseatic trade *from* Bergen in a single economic system. Few agreements were to function without a hitch over such a long period as this one negotiated between the Scandinavian crown and the cities on the Baltic. The system at first sight seems likely to draw trade away from Shetland, Orkney, Iceland and Faroe into the staple of Bergen and also to prevent merchants from other Norwegian towns from taking part in this trade. More careful investigation shows quite clearly that there was no hard and fast division. By the thirteenth century the individual, itinerant merchant-salesman had been replaced by larger commercial enterprises with commissioners and trading partners. As a result it is difficult to find out very easily which goods belonged to whom at any particular time. We know that goods on the way from Shetland to Bergen formerly belonged to and had been traded by Scandinavian merchants and that they were in fact bought by order of

Hansa merchants: that is to say, Hansa-Shetland trade connections were effectively in operation even before the first Hansa merchants had visited Shetland.

The earliest evidence we have of such Hansa visits to Shetland dates from about 1415. By that time the prohibition of direct trading within Norwegian crown lands was openly flouted, first by the English who sailed to Iceland about 1412 and then by Hansa merchants sailing to Orkney, Shetland and to Faroe who met up with the English in Iceland not later than 1423. The first Hansa merchants trading to Iceland came from Hamburg and Danzig, and we know that the first merchant to visit Orkney was from Lübeck. We even know that this Lübeck man was called Hinrich Sparke. We don't know who first came to Shetland and Faroe but apparently the Faroe merchants were Hamburg people and the Shetland visitors from Lübeck. The Hansa merchants, including those from Hamburg, made their way to the northern islands via Bergen, the regular fish staple of the north, but their trade did not fit into the joint Norwegian-Hansa staple scheme. Attempts to carry on direct trade met with prohibitions, the first from the 1416 congress of Hansa city deputies in Lübeck where it was decided not to allow trade to 'Orkenen, Hydlande unde to Ver', i.e. to Orkney, Shetland and Faroe. A second restriction was placed on them in 1425 by King Erik of Denmark, pronouncing against direct Iceland trade. But the Hansa administrators, far away on the continent, did not know very much of the semi-illegitimate trade in the north: when, in 1434, a clerk of Brugge copied the statute of 1416, he did not know what 'Hydland' meant and read it wrongly as 'Vinland'. (Hanse councillors at Lübeck then thought 'Vinland' was Iceland.) Here we have the first occasion when Hansa politicians tried to stop the Iceland trade, and they did so out of error: it is also the first time that Hanseatic-Shetland trade was tolerated, and this because of the same error, for in the wrongly copied document they didn't find anything against trade-communication with these islands. The size of this latter trade is difficult to judge: we learn very little, unfortunately, from the sources of the fifteenth century, probably because of the semi-illegal character of the commerce.

In fact Shetland trade did not fit into that scheme of strictly regimented trading desired by the Hansa administrators in the first half of the fifteenth century and established in 1447 by the so-called 'staple system'. It was determined that certain goods were to be carried on specified routes only, and were also to be sold only in specified markets. Shetland goods, for instance, whether traded by Norwegian or local merchants, were to be directed through the fish staple of Bergen. By this system Hansa merchants could have no part in trade with Shetland, but in fact they made contacts secretly with Shetlanders in and through Bergen. Whether the people from Shetland or the Faroes or Iceland sold goods only within the terms of the regulations of the staple in Bergen, or whether they took them there having sold them already to Hansa merchants, whether Hansa merchants sailing to Shetland initiated business there and then completed it in Bergen or whether they made specific trading agreements, such things are not easily proved or disproved.

The later statutes and decisions of the Hansa and of the Danish crown, however, mirror a fair part of the practice. In 1468 King Christian I, according to the report of a Bergen chronicler, allowed German merchants to voyage to Iceland and thus effectively disrupted the older staple system. In 1482 after Christian's death, the Norwegian Council of the Realm renewed the prohibition. King Johann supported the Council by a statute of 1483 but, surprisingly, in 1490 gave the Dutch the privilege of visiting the Shetland Islands and Iceland in the same way as 'other Hanseatic merchants are privileged to do': yet the Amsterdam merchants who were given this privilege were not members of the Hansa nor had the Hansa merchants at that time been granted any permission to visit Shetland or Iceland. In 1487 and 1489 the council of the Hansa, the Hansetag, itself placed some restriction on voyages to Iceland—the first and only definite prohibition of Iceland trade made by the Hansa. In 1494 and 1498 this Iceland prohibition was lifted but direct trade with Orkney, Shetland and Faroe was again forbidden. And this situation lasted well into the sixteenth century.

The authorities in Bergen again and again complained to the Hansetag, up to 1535, about illegal trade with these islands and this alone indicates how ineffective their objections were. Indeed, a Danish proposal in 1549, demanding that Icelanders, Faroese and Shetlanders should offer their products only on the Bergen market must have seemed very naive: it was nothing less than an attempt to turn back the wheel of history by at least a century and a half, and it had no effect at all. It is difficult to judge why the Hansa retained its statutory restrictions on trips to Shetland, Orkney and Faroe. It is a decision which seems even more curious when one considers that the voyage to the Shetland Islands and to Faroe would have been along the same sea route as that taken in the direct trade with Iceland which had been officially permitted by the Hansetag since the 1490s. And punishment for breach of the restrictions was very harsh, including expulsion from the Hansa or loss of ships and goods. It seems that there was no other way of controlling the Shetland trade, in the hope of keeping its increasing size and importance within bounds. The complaints from Bergen only go to underline that the trade was sizeable and continuing; and other sources confirm its growth. One thing is noticeable because it seems surprising to us—in the council acts which restrained direct trading, the Orkney Islands are frequently not mentioned. The reason for this lies in the fact that the Hansa merchants did not make direct contact with them as often as they had done before.

In Shetland itself there was little change of a kind likely to enforce obedience to the Hanseatic-Danish staple system. Especially after the pledging of the islands to Scotland, there was little reason to try to force Hansa merchants to accept orders from royal officials such as those in Iceland. And no check was made by strong merchant corporations like that existing in Bergen. In this matter Shetland was very similar to Faroe. Restrictions were also placed on direct trade with Faroe by the Hansa in this same period, but neither of the two island-groups could be effectively dealt with because of the local conditions. What is clear is that there was a steady increase in the Hanseatic trade with Shetland in the fifteenth and sixteenth centuries, and the pattern of trading changed from one which used the Bergen staple system to one of direct contact. The trading records of the Hanseatic towns show this very clearly: thus we find merchants from Danzig in Shetland from 1487 onwards, from Bremen after 1498, from Hamburg after 1547, from Lübeck after 1562, from Rostock after 1599, from Stralsund after 1601, and perhaps also from the so-called Zuider-Zee cities of Kampen and Deventer after 1498. Lübeck merchants took part in direct trade with Shetland until 1645, longer than any other of the Baltic ports. Hamburg merchants, indeed, at first concentrated on trade with Faroe, but the trade policy of the Danish crown imposing licences within a regimented system since 1553 drove them into a new trade with Shetland. As early as 1498 Bremen merchants were visiting Shetland in regular annual trips, sometimes with several ships. Bremen merchants were very active in the Bergen Kontor of the Hansa and returned home via Bergen, often adding dried fish from that city to their freight. A decree of the Hansa towns in 1446 made the purchase of fish in Bergen dependent on the import of corn from Lübeck so as to lead the dried fish trade to Lübeck, but the Bremen merchants took their dried fish direct to the consumer towns of their own area like Herford, Osnabrück and Stade as well as to Bremen itself. At one of the Hansetag, when they were accused of this, they retorted by divorcing their Shetland trade completely from Bergen. The Hansa meeting which permitted them to trade directly with Shetland in 1525 actually restated the requirement to use the Bergen staple, a paradox which reflected the difficulties of dismantling the old staple laws. Danzig, Kampen and Deventer too wanted freedom to expand their trade and, from this time onwards, merchants from North Sea towns sailed directly, along the English and Scottish coasts, to Shetland and back again.

The development and organisation of the direct trade with Shetland can be best studied from the Hamburg sources. Visits by Hamburg merchants to Shetland began very slowly about 1547 but by 1588 one or two ships were leaving annually for the islands. After 1600 the number rose to between two and five, after 1617 to between four and nine: in 1647 fourteen ships were trading with Shetland from Hamburg and by 1779 this had risen to twenty-six. The earlier skippers, threatened by a crisis in the later 1540s, changed from trading with England to trading with Shetland. Their ships were of average size—30 to 40 last, or 60 to 80 tons—each carrying between five and eighteen in their crews.[1]

These boats trading to Shetland did not appear to differentiate between sailors and merchants: all on the ship, the merchant and the skipper, the mate, the bosun, the cook, the cooper and the boy, were all part of the same 'maschup', a corporation with the aim of successful sea trade. This kind of group gives us an insight into Hanseatic society. The crew were built up according to the purpose of the undertaking. A skipper and a merchant gave continuity but the other members of the crew changed frequently. A sum was settled at the beginning for the keep of the crew and for all other expenses: any money which remained at the end of the voyage was given to charity—to the old, the sick and the bereaved at home.

Bremen sources provide especially valuable evidence about the conduct of such voyages to Shetland. The Bremen ships usually left in the early spring, one ship in 1562 reaching Baltasound as early as April. And the return trip was usually begun in the last days of August or early September. Given normal weather, the voyage from the Weser to north Shetland, the favourite trading area of Bremen merchants, took over two weeks. Pilots were employed to help ships enter or leave harbour, especially in Whalsay Sound. In one instance, however, in 1697, having a pilot aboard did not prevent the loss of the ship—in a case with a definite international flavour, for it concerned an English ship with a Scottish captain and a Danish certificate, which was insured in Bremen but had left from Hamburg and which had been taken by French pirates before being released after ransom; the boat was then lost on the rocks with a 'lodman' (pilot) aboard, about half a mile off the coast of Shetland.

We have seen that Bremen merchants chose to trade with north Shetland. What we know of one family, called Detken, underlines this. In 1659 this family provided skipper, mate and another deck officer (the three were brothers) in a ship visiting Shetland. About a hundred years earlier an ancestor of theirs had already brought his 'maschup' of three or four ships to the harbour of Baltasound, to Burravoe and Cullivoe on Yell and to the sound between Unst and Uyea, and he had controlled the export trade of Unst, Yell and Fetlar. When in 1560 or 1561 another Bremen ship tried to trade in Baltasound the Scottish foud (Olaf Sinclair) intervened, attempting to bring part at least of the Bremen import-trade to the mainland. But the intruder was apparently not content with the mainland substitutes offered to him, of harbours in Laxfirth, Scalloway and Bressay Sound.

It seems as if, at this time, there were at least seven ships from Hamburg and Bremen in Shetland harbours: and if each one of these demanded, as was the usual practice, a bay for itself then someone like the intruder just mentioned may well have come to the conclusion 'that there were more ships than frogs in Shetland'. While they were in Shetland the crews lived on board ship, but the merchants stayed at least part of the time on dry land. While the ships also carried all the food and other necessities required for the time spent in the islands, the crew of each vessel was also allowed—after special payment to the foud—to build a hut or several huts on land. These were usually stockrooms but may have also been used as general accommodation by those engaged over a period of many years in the Shetland trade.

The Hansa merchants offered the Shetlanders their imports of beer, meal and salt and probably also of textiles. These goods were exchanged with farmers and fishermen—even in 1649 with a minister of the church. Since the beginning of the direct Shetland trade in the second decade of the sixteenth century the Hansa merchants had increasingly bought butter, fat, wool and feathers in the islands, but their special interest was in fish. Here, quite clearly, the demand outran supply, for there were frequent quarrels among the Hansers about the right to conduct the fish trade in this or that bay. The merchants sometimes stayed in the island over winter; and, while this was not strictly forbidden, it was against the usual practice because those who stayed could gain an advantage over their competitors in arranging purchases for the following season. Even small crews carried a cooper for the breaking of barrels and for the cooping of fish; and the merchant-boats carried fishing gear, as we can see in the records for 1653 and 1679. But the cash balance which they may have had on hand from payments for fish was required for the feeding of the crew which, after all, stayed for four months of the year in the islands. Frequently the seventeenth-century Hansa ships bought from the islands only their own food and the salt which they required for preserving their catches of fish—salt which had often come from Scotland, had been sold by Scots in Bremen and then had returned on Bremen-Shetland ships almost to its point of origin. It is therefore understandable that the Bremen merchants were annoyed when in 1671 they were required to pay import duty for the salt they brought to Shetland.

There were advantages to Shetland in these prolonged visits by Bremen and other merchants, but there were disadvantages too. One stemmed from the so-called 'ausreedesystem', a procedure frequently applied in the Scandinavian economic area. This meant that goods supplied to customers by the Hansa would be accounted as debits and these debits had to be erased in the following year by the provision of goods traded on the basis of a moneyless exchange. Thus in good times there was very little opportunity for the Shetlander to make a living by exporting because the annual production of the islands was already committed for the payment of old debts. The non-arrival of the foreign merchants' ships was no solution, however: for if they did not come, for some reason or other, then there could be serious want of provisions. Under this system there could be no easy adjustment of export levels to changes in either production or consumption.

And the restriction of the licensed trading only to certain bays led to confusions too. It was never clear whether a licence was given by a foud for one year or more, whether the skipper just had to accept the situation if he found that 'his' bay on a subsequent year was already occupied or whether he was allowed to drive away the intruder. Some merchants certainly believed that, even if they had no current licence, they had a right to come for goods still due to them from the year before. Sometimes, too, there was some difficulty about who the licence-holder actually was. The close connections within a 'maschup' could make it unclear whether a ship had been licensed or whether the licence had been given only to the leading merchant: and so it could happen that two parties—that is, the old skipper and his crew or the old merchant on a new ship—would oppose each other in the year after they had sailed together.

If the Hansers only came to catch fish for their own supply, then, reasonably enough, there grew up a tendency among the fouds to demand harbour dues since no import duties could be levied. At the beginning of the seventeenth century the right to enter a particular harbour would usually cost an annual duty of six englotten or one taler. But the more popular Shetland herring became, the more these charges increased. In addition to the sums mentioned, merchants had to give annually per ship four tons of beer, two tons of malt, one side of bacon, fifteen ells of linen and a gilded gun with fine inlaid decoration.[2] Furthermore, the royal foud demanded a five per cent import duty and a five per cent export duty, while a duty of four per cent went to the customs officer. The Bremen merchants objected to these impositions but with very little result. Nonetheless, the very close connections which the Hanseatic merchants built up with the Shetland producers had one important economic result: to the great chagrin of merchants in Bergen, Shetland fish was very cheap and was therefore much in demand. Shetland became well-known, and remained so, in the northern European ports.

Shetland fish, its oldest export, was known in the Hansa as early as the fifteenth century. It was not to be sold like Bergen fish 'runt for Rothscher', but was to be 'gevlacket'—i.e. opened, spread out and dried on the rocks. The usual treatment of round fish, tying together two fish by the tail and drying them on special stands, or of Rotscher, splitting the fish from the tail-end and drying them on stands, was forbidden. The main reason for this was probably to prevent Shetland fish being mixed up with Bergen fish. There is evidence that Shetland fish was hard dried; that is, it was particularly valuable as a durable albuminous food and was favoured in the provisioning of ships for long voyages.

Using the figures we have for the trade between Hamburg and Shetland and Hamburg and Iceland, that with Shetland was about a fifth of the Iceland trade. If we also take account of the trade with Lübeck, it can be estimated that Shetland had between five and ten per cent of the trade which went through Bergen. To this we can add the trade conducted by Shetlanders themselves; and then exports to Holland, especially to Amsterdam. With this addition it can be assumed to have exceeded ten per cent. But this still does not take into account the increase in Shetland trade from herring, which took place in the early seventeenth century in a change which gradually diminished the importance of the earlier trade in dried fish.

The records for Hamburg allow us to make a direct analysis of the impact of this herring trade. In the years 1629–1633, the Shetland Islands took third or fourth place in providing herring to Hamburg with about 270 tons annually. Much more, however, was imported by the Dutch who were the largest suppliers of herring to the Hamburgers (40,000 tons per annum), but some of this Dutch herring had come in the first instance from Shetland. (Meat and fish oil were exported only in small amounts.) The heyday of the Shetland herring fishing and herring trade was still to come, and had to wait for the Dutch. By the early eighteenth century the Bremen and Hamburg merchants were still trading with Shetland but not any longer as members of the old merchant-corporations. And when the lexicographer Johann Heinrich Zedler described the conditions he found in Shetland in 1742 and the characteristics of its inhabitants, Shetland's place in the economic history of the Hansa towns had already been forgotten in continental Europe. Zedler wrote that 'the first inhabitants of Shetland seem to have been Germans which can be seen from the mixture of the German and the old Gothic languages as well as in their measures, their way of counting and of weighing'. Zedler's amazing theory seems to have been based on Norn, which must have still been spoken in the islands then. Yet this curious statement about the German origins of the Shetland inhabitants is perhaps a very weak echo of those earlier times when German Hansa merchants had spent as much as a third of their sea-faring life in Shetland.

NOTE

1 These were small ships compared to those trading with Iceland, which averaged 60 last and had as many as 77 persons on board, with perhaps 19 sailors and as many as 58 merchants.
2 The language of the Bremen source describes the latter as 'ein vorguldeten gereiffelten langen und mit eingelegter laden gefertigen rhor oder buchsen'.

CHAPTER VII

The Netherland Fisheries and the Shetland Islands

H. A. H. BOELMANS KRANENBURG

THE MUSEUM of Dutch Sea-Fisheries, although it is located in Vlaardingen and not in the Dutch capital, is nonetheless a national museum. Vlaardingen itself has played an outstanding part in the history of the Dutch herring fishing industry upon which our connections with the Shetland Islands are mainly based and therefore it is particularly appropriate for the museum to send a representative to this congress. So it is that I, a member of the board of the museum in Vlaardingen, am here to speak on the relationship between the Netherlands and Shetland, with particular regard to the fishing industry during the past five centuries.

Five hundred years is a long time, and this means that I will have to confine myself to the main facts. I should also explain that the sources for this study, at least in the Netherlands, are very scarce. In the case of merchant and passenger shipping a good deal of data would be available in ships' journals; but the skippers of fishing vessels, while they may carry out their jobs very well, are not good writers. This was so in the past, and it is still the same now. If such journal material from fishing vessels once existed, then it seems to have been lost; at least I have not been able to recover any material of this nature. Fortunately there are other sources and these give us some clues about the subject in question. Even so, the data are very scattered and cannot be said to afford us a complete picture.

What about the Dutch fishing industry at the time when the Shetland Islands came under Scottish rule? It was a time of relative prosperity for the fishing industry in the Low Countries under the reign of Charles the Bold of Burgundy (1467–1477). The Burgundians tried to bring as many as possible of the duchies and counties in the territory of the Netherlands under their authority and wanted a stronger central power in the countries they governed. One can discern in arrangements for the protection of the fishing industry and the merchant navy, in the endeavour to build up a Netherlandic navy, and in the appointment of its own admirals to it, this striving after more centralised control. However, in 1469 this lay still some way in the future, at least as regards formal structure, since the history of the admirality and councils of admirality in the Netherlands actually begins with a decree of 1488.

Protection of the fishing industry in those days was an important matter. There was a continuous conflict between the French kings and the Burgundian dukes, as a result of which Louis XI of France promoted the commerce of France and England and boycotted the commerce of the Dutch provinces, in particular that of Flanders. The French therefore tried to hamper the herring-fishing industry of Flanders, Zeeland, and Holland as much as possible. Next to corn, fish was the most important food of these areas and was accordingly of decisive importance for the populous and industrialized province of Flanders. The centre of the fishing industry was at that time along the Flemish coast in the North Sea and the Westernscheldt and, as is well-known, the fishing industry of Zeeland and Holland resulted from the radiating pressures from the Flemish market, in which Bruges occupied a dominating place.

In the late Middle Ages salted herring was imported from the land of Skåne in the south of Sweden (then part of Denmark) and was sold in Bruges and its suburb Damme. The salted herring was landed by Hanseatic, by Zeeland, and by Dutch merchants. About 1400 a partial termination of the herring catches along the coast of Skåne and the interruption of its commerce with Bruges led to the fishermen on the North Sea beginning to salt herring aboard their ships. This development was of course resisted by the Bruges importers but, once started, it could not be stopped; and gradually the landings of North Sea salted herring outmatched those from Skåne. This change had been completed by 1469 and, for this very reason, French attacks had begun on the fishing industry in the Burgundian provinces. During Charles the Bold's reign the French were not very successful; the landings of salted herring increased rather than decreased, mainly because the trade-routes to the east began to run via Cologne and Neurenberg and there were increased opportunities for sales along the canals. But it was not long after Charles' death before the French were more successful. For instance, an enquiry about taxation in 1494 shows that, in the case of Beets in the neighbourhood of Hoorn, the herring fishing industry had been reduced by half since the end of Duke Charles' reign. The situation in Vlaardingen was even worse according to the same enquiry. Not a single vessel was left out of the ten or twelve well-equipped herring boats which had used Vlaardingen as their home-port before the war with France. Ships and fishing gear had been stolen; the mates had been taken prisoner and those fishermen who had returned home had had to find other jobs elsewhere. In 1514, when another similar enquiry was made, it can be seen that the situation had not improved.

By 1469, however, the Netherlands fishing industry was developing and Dutch fishermen were sailing to fish off the Shetland Islands. About that time, throughout Europe, fishing mainly took place in coastal waters; in other words, fishing was intimately connected with the neighbouring shore. Even Schonen's was a coastal fishery whose catch had to be salted ashore as quickly as possible. Indeed, the only country where deep-sea fishing began to develop (using a type of ship which will be discussed later on) was the Netherlands.

There was, of course, coastal fishing on the Flemish banks, and from this developed the main and more important North Sea fishing. The Flemish called this 'North-over', the Dutch referred to it as 'deep-water' and the British named it 'East-Anglia' fishing. The season of fishing the North Sea in the time of Burgundian ascendancy lasted from the feast of St Bartholomew till that of St Martin, in other words from 24 August to 11 November. It was a time of year during which there were no thoughts of fishing off the Shetland Islands.

Yet there are clues which nonetheless point to extension northwards. In 1482 we know that the tariff for a convoy of herring busses was twice the usual rate when the vessels fished to the north. And this double tariff was related to the larger type of ship which was employed in the more distant grounds. Also, the northern season started earlier; in the time of Emperor Charles V it began on 25 July and, later in the sixteenth century, on St John's Day. The decision to begin on St John's Day (24 June) is important as this was to be the fixed date for about three centuries; and with its establishment the fishing grounds off the Shetland Islands began to be used by men from the Low Countries. So we can assume that about the year 1500 the Dutch came to Shetland, although that cannot be taken to mean that they did not fish off the Scottish coast or north of it beforehand.

THE NETHERLAND FISHERIES

For example, in 1410 the Dutch Count complained that his country's fishermen were attacked by the Scots while engaged in honest fishing; these fishermen were surely, therefore, closer to the Scottish coast than to the Dutch coast. The Count took immediate action, authorising the inhabitants of Brouwershaven to inflict losses on the Scots. It is unlikely that Shetlanders were involved, however. But this situation was to change in 1540, when James V wrote to the cities of Holland, Friesland and Flanders, and particularly to Schiedam and Rotterdam, that their inhabitants—just like the people of Bremen in those years—having started to fish closer to Orkney, Shetland, and the northern coast of Scotland, had violated Scottish fishing rights. The Scottish king therefore had his admiral warn the Dutch fishermen concerned that they must refrain from such criminal acts.

Did foreign fishermen meet a warm welcome on other coasts in the time of the development of coastal fisheries to deep sea fisheries? Generally not, and this is by and large unchanged to the present day. Coastal fishermen consider foreign fishermen competitiors both in catching the fish and also in selling it. If possible, national coastal fishermen try to limit freedom of fishery. Yet this was not always the case everywhere. While the Danish kings have always assumed their sovereignty over the northern seas, the English about 1500 are to be found defending a very lenient point of view. The Shetland people may have been rather suspicious of foreigners when they came under Scottish rule. The Scottish attitude towards foreign fishermen was probably much more restrictive than that seen in English policy. It must be remembered that the Scots mostly fished in bays and therefore had only little contact with the real deep sea fishermen. Nevertheless fishing was of more importance to the Scots than it was to the English, not least because it provided an important income for the Scottish crown. It is understandable that the Scots were not very friendly towards foreign fishermen. In spite of commerical treaties in 1541 and 1550 no agreement about the freedom of the seas was ever signed by the Stewarts: and after 1603 they introduced their protective policy to England and tried to put it into practice.

The change in the Netherlands from coastal fishing to deep sea fishing was closely connected with the development of a type of vessel which was able to stay at sea longer, carrying a more numerous crew and with storage space for barrels and salt. The ship which met these requirements was the herring buss, a type of vessel which was to be the backbone of the Dutch herring fishing industry for almost five centuries and which first appears in documents written in 1405. It was used both in fishing and as a merchantman—quite a common combination in those days. It has generally been assumed that it was of Dutch origin, but there is now reason to doubt that: for the Norwegian king, Håkon V, sent a ship called the *Kingbussen* from Trondheim to Kings Lynn in the fourteenth century; and in the same period we find that Sigurd Skallerud, the richest merchant in Trondheim, possessed three ships, called *Hjelp*, *Olavsbussen* and *Kallrudbussen*.

Since it was not at all strange in the Middle Ages to incorporate in a ship's name an indication of the type of the ship, it may well be that these Norwegian 'bussen' are very similar to the later Dutch 'buis'. In that case the buss is not of Dutch origin but a Norwegian type of ship adapted to the requirements of fishing by constructing a fixed deck, holds for the driftnets and for the barrels and salt, and the setting up of a work classification which made the herring buss the modest forerunner of the factory vessel.

The herring buss was a widely-known type of vessel and it is the Norwegian version which is to be recalled when James IV of Scotland (1488–1513), in his efforts to strengthen the national fishing industry, ordered that herring busses must be ships of at least twenty tons. By that time, however, the Dutch herring buss had experienced a century-long specialized development, variations in driftnets bringing alterations in vessel-type which in turn stimulated improvements in fishing gear, and so on. In addition to the herring buss the barge came to the north; and from this barge there developed later the Scheveningen and Katwijk bluff, i.e. bowed fishing-boats. These were the boats which were so frequently found in the port of Lerwick around 1890.

The herring industry of the Netherlands reached its peak of importance in the seventeenth century. By then the Flemish and the Zeeland fishing industries had greatly declined and the salt-herring fishing was concentrated in the province of Holland. Amsterdam was then the staple-market of the world and was a focal point for the herring fishing industry. From Amsterdam salt fish was exported to Hamburg and elsewhere in the Baltic, up the river Rhine, and to France, for here was one of the few processed foods of an age without knowledge of deep-freezing. In the main, the herring came from busses which sailed out of Rotterdam, Schiedam, Delfshaven, Vlaardingen and Maassluis in the south, and from Enkhuizen, Hoorn and De Rijp in the north. In the most prosperous period of this fishery, some five hundred vessels were engaged in the trade. At first some coastal ships took part but their importance dwindled through time. In those days Scheveningen and Katwijk played a relatively unimportant part in the trade. Not until the second half of the nineteenth century do these towns with Vlaardingen, come to dominate the Bay of Lerwick by the number of their boats. A few sources from much earlier times give additional information. A fish auctioneer from Scheveningen, Adriaan Coenenzoon, at the end of the sixteenth century tells us that the herring busses, as well as the pinks, started the fishing season off 'Hitland' and 'Orckeney'. We learn that it was on St John's Day that herring-nets were shot for the first time off 'Hitland', 'Phayrillt' and 'Boekenes' (Shetland, Fair Isle, Brough Ness). By St James's Day (25 July) the boats had moved more to the south and finally finished the season off the coast of East Anglia. Around 1670, a century after Coenenzoon's story, Pomponne—the ambassador of the French King Louis XIV in The Hague—reported to his king that the Dutch started fishing for herring after the month of May in the vast areas between Norway and Scotland, and then sailed south along the eastern coasts of Scotland and England. It became the custom that, on average, a buss made three trips—one to the north for the matties and full herring, a second to the Dogger Banks and thereabout, and a third to the East Anglian coast. The records of the city of Schiedam indicate that the first voyage was normally the most successful one, and it may therefore be assumed that some 35 to 40 per cent of all the herring to be sold in Holland were caught in Shetland fishing grounds.

In the same report in which Pomponne refers to the herring fishing industry, he also mentions another source of income for the Dutch: this was the whale fishing industry, particularly as it was carried out in the neighbourhood of Greenland. Although the Dutch did not chase whales in the vicinity of Shetland, the islands still played a great part in this form of fishing.

While the catching of whales might be based on places as different as Spitzbergen and Jan Mayen Island (Mauritius), the fleets bound in both directions, remarkably enough, sailed together from ports in Holland or Zeeland, and separated in the neighbourhood of the Shetland Islands for their different destinations. This we know from notes in the log-book of a young mate, 'M. A. de Ruyter', who sailed from Flushing on 8 May 1633 on board the whaler *de Groene Leeuw*.[1]

For Michel Adriaarszoon de Ruyter it seems that sailing in the waters off the Shetland Islands formed part of his seaman's training. De Ruyter confirms the religious attentiveness of Dutch seamen and fishermen. When they were to be on the fishing-grounds on a Sunday, the herring-nets were not shot on a Saturday. If there was a port or bay nearby, then they would call there and put out to sea in the earliest hours of Monday. It is clear that they were likely to have called in at the Sound of Bressay. The landings they made would be a welcome change for crews who might have to spend months on board ship at a stretch. There would be good opportunities for the exchange of news, the possibility of taking in new provisions and fresh drinking water; and Bressay Sound could provide shelter for the transfer of herring catches to herring-carriers which then transported the fish to Holland. In this way there came to be a lasting contact between the Dutch fishermen and the local Shetland population: but it was a contact which also might bring its troubles—as in the disastrous year of 1703, when there was a state of war between the Republic of the United Netherlands and France and the French navy went out of its way to inflict losses on the Dutch fishing-fleet.

Drift-net vessels usually fished in groups and, as we have seen, it was customary for them to gather together at weekends in some convenient port. The French knew this very well. Thus they sent men-of-war to the north, and located part of the Dutch herring fleet in the 'Bay of Hitland'. According to Dutch reports, it was the fishing fleet from Enkhuizen which suffered especially from the French action. In what was no more than a short battle many fishermen were killed; in all, about a hundred herring-busses from Enkhuizen were set on fire and the crews of the ships which were destroyed crowded into the remaining vessels and sailed for home. Beggared by the French attack, the fishermen had to apply for poor relief while the local authorities took care of the widows and the orphans of those who were killed. It appears that the Dutch fishing industry never recovered from this blow; the high point of the herring fishery in the biggest maritime province of the Netherlands had been reached. During the rest of the eighteenth century the Dutch herring fleet was destined to number no more than two hundred and fifty vessels, of which by the end of the century some fifty per cent originated from Vlaardingen. For the time being, Vlaardingen replaced Enkhuizen as the centre of the Dutch herring trade.

Even then the troubles of the Dutch fishing industry were not at an end; for in 1795, after the outbreak of the French revolution, the Netherlands were occupied. No fishing could take place before 1815 because of the war with England, and twenty years of practical stagnation were devastating both for the fleet and for the crews.

Whereas the Dutch market had been the centre of the herring fishing industry in the past, this position was occupied in the first half of the nineteenth century by London, a change from which Scottish and English herring fisheries gained most benefit. The Dutch monopoly of the German market also ended, and the people of the Netherlandic fishing-ports lived on in the shadow of a grand past.

In a community like that of the Shetland Islands it hardly needs to be said that the fishing industry is notable for its successive periods of ups and downs. The decline of the early nineteenth century was to be followed in Holland by a new period of prosperity, a prosperity closely related to the introduction of a new type of vessel—the herring-lugger. After all the misery which the Dutch fishing industry had suffered from France over a span of many centuries, the French now came to contribute positively to its success: for the lugger-type of boat originated from Boulogne. At the same time fishing nets manufactured from hemp were replaced by cotton nets and it was the combination of luggers and cotton nets which put the Dutch herring fishing industry on its feet again.

The fishing-villages along the coast, Katwijk as well as Scheveningen, became active again in the salt-herring trade with their herring busses: and the older bonds with Shetland were renewed. Indeed the relations between the Dutch and the islesmen were to be as intensive as they had been two centuries before: and, in particular, strong contacts were forged with the burgh of Lerwick. Names such as those of Van der Toorn and Den Dulk from Scheveningen and Parlevliet from Katwijk became as well-known in the months of June and July in the streets of Lerwick as were older and more familiar Vlaardingen names. A photograph take in 1892 shows us a fleet of at least one hundred Dutch herring busses in the bay at Lerwick, one-third of the total number of vessels possessed by Dutch fishers in that decade. And if we add to that the two hundred sailing luggers (the greater part of them based on Vlaardingen) which also came to Shetland, the comparison with an older period in the history of the herring fishery is evident. As before, big catches were made in the neighbourhood of the Shetland Islands, in the fishing-grounds off Lerwick, Bressay, Fair Isle and close to Balta Sound. This revival continued until the First World War broke out.

With this war we come to another milestone in development, for the old type of bluff-bowed fishing vessel did not outlive the period 1914–1918. It was now to be entirely pushed aside by the sailing lugger (of which in 1919 there were already about six hundred) and by the steam lugger (of which sixty-six were in operation by the end of the war). Together they formed a fleet of enormous capacity which must have been a spectacular sight when it sailed north. Part of it regularly called in at Lerwick in spring-time, perhaps accompanied by the hospital-church ship *De Hoop* which took care of both the religious and the physical welfare of the Dutch fishermen when they were at sea and away from home waters. Even before the First World War, it would have been usual to find Dutch nurses and ministers ashore in Lerwick, ready to serve the needs of the visiting fleets. It is notable that when Dutch fishermen talked about Lerwick at home they tended to speak of the 'Island', as if the whole of Shetland was to be identified with Lerwick and its environs.

But, once more, good times gave way to bad. Between 1920 and 1930 the sailing lugger disappeared as these vessels were equipped with engines. The number of luggers constantly decreased and the economic crisis in the years after 1930 was taken as a reason for cutting down the Dutch herring-fleet year by year. Where once the aim had been to catch as much herring as possible, in these years of crisis supply had to be adapted to demand. The most distant fishing-grounds were avoided and the fishermen preferred to be home with their families at weekends rather than in the distant Bay of Lerwick. The advances in technology and management therefore greatly reduced the annual contacts between the Netherlands and Shetland: and what contact there was became more incidental.

With the Second World War came yet further change in the pattern of Dutch fishing. With the fleet still mainly consisting of engine-powered vessels for drift-net fishing, attention was in general directed towards southern areas more than in the past and Dutch boats only rarely appeared in the waters off Shetland. These vessels landed enormous catches until the mid-fifties, and the herring-grounds off the Shetland Islands were more and more ignored. With the later 1950s came the decline in the herring catches from the North Sea grounds: a fact first noticed on Dogger Bank, then off the East Anglian coast. Soon it became impossible for the drift-net vessel to cover its expenses. Within a few years the entire drift-net fleet had practically disappeared, only about ten vessels being left.

The typical Dutch herring-fishing industry, with its accent on salted herring, is a thing of the past. Shipowners have changed to trawl-fishing, preferring to trawl for herring and, if possible, to cure and salt part of the catch aboard. Trawl-fishing is thus of a quite different character: it is, moreover, a continuous rather than a seasonal matter. As stocks declined, so landings of herring grew less and less important and by 1968 all landings amounted to less than 25 per cent of landings made during the mid-fifties—a situation made even worse since, with the extension of its fishing-limits by Great Britain.

The old contacts between the Netherlands and Shetland have faded away but in the Netherlands there is an older generation of shipowners and fishermen who still remember Lerwick as a good berth for their vessels and as a hospitable place for them at the weekends. There they encountered cordial sympathy for their welfare while they were away from home. They probaably brought to it something of their own way of living. And from Lerwick they also took home souvenirs which still decorate the homes of many of our older fishermen. On Marken, once an island where many inhabitants were employed in the Dutch herring-fleet, there are many reminders of an age now long past: in 1915 G. J. Bloes Kzn, an expert on Marken folklore, wrote:

> Plates with 'Greetings from Lerwick', the picture of Queen Victoria or of King Edward, prove that the fishermen of Marken often went shopping in the ports with the intention of taking home souvenirs for their families when they were fishing in the Bay or along the coasts of Scotland and England. Hitland pottery also testifies to that, pottery which we can see in their cupboards; brown milk-jugs, coffee-pots, tea-pots and sugar-basins all decorated with highly coloured flowers, as well as Hitland night-caps with their bright brims.
>
> It's a pity that this pottery, as a consequence of legal division of properties, has been scattered in such a way that one finds here the coffee-pot, elsewhere the milk-jug and again in another place the sugar-basin, all parts of a set which formerly surely must have been complete and which decorated the table in times of festivities and on Sundays when the housewives had visitors. They would not have liked to do without these things, even if they could have got nickel or silver for them.

I should like to testify now to the fact that his old affection remains. Where the direct tie has disappeared, history replaces it: museums take the place of the active trade and industry. Hence the readiness with which the National Fishing Industry Museum in Vlaardingen agreed to be represented at this conference. May this contact renew a bond of friendship between Lerwick and Vlaardingen such as existed in the past between the fishermen of our two communities.

NOTE

1 'The nineteenth of May; we got the bearing of 59 degrees and 48 minutes and guessed our position to be about nine or ten miles off Hitland, West by North from us and we drifted in Western direction the whole day until the evening having fair weather and a North wind.
   Then it became very quiet until two o'clock in the morning of the twentieth of May. The wind blew from the East and we sailed four degrees North North-West. Later the wind changed to North-East and North-East to East. Then we saw Hitland the "Fraenhock" (Frangisvaag on the Far Oer?). In the afternoon on the twenty-first of May, we determined the position of the red-end of Hitland at seven to eight miles. On board the ship of "Klaas Cornelissen" skipper "Barend van Haar" held a farewell sermon which was taken from the gospel according to Sint Matthew the fifth chapter and the sixth verse. So we said goodbye in the name of the Lord. Two ships went to Spitzbergen and two to Mauritius.'

SOURCES CONSULTED

A. Beaujon, *Overzicht van de Geschiedenis van de Nederlandsche Zeevisscherijen* (Leiden, 1885).
D. Brouwer, *Tweede Vervolg van de Historie van Enkhuizen* (Enkhuizen, 1938).
A. Bijl Mzn, *De Nederlandse Convooidienst, 1300–1800* ('s. Gravenhage, 1951).
R. Degrijse, *Vlaanderen Haringbedrijf in de Middeleeuwen* (Antwerpen, 1944).
Enqueste en de informatie upt stuck van der reductie van den schiltaelen, voertijtd getaxeert en de gestelt geweest over de landen van Holland en-de Vrieslant, gedaen in den jaere MCCCCXCIIII (bewerkt door R. Fruin) (Leiden, 1876).
F. W. Fulton, *The Sovereignity of the Sea* (London, 1911).
S. P. L'Honofe Naber, *Walvisvaarten Overwinteringen en Jachtbedrijven in het hoge Noorden (1633–1635)* (Utrecht, 1930).
Informacie gedaen in den jaere MDXIV: met voorbericht van R. Fruin (Leiden, 1866).
H. A. H. Kranenburg, *De Zeevisscherij van Holland in den Tijd der Republiek* (Amsterdam, 1946).
H. A. H. (Boelmans) Kranenburg, 'Zeescheepvaart in Zuid-Holland 1400–1500' in 'Zuid Hollandse 1400–1500' in *Zuid Hollandse Studien*, deel XI (Voorburg, 1965).
Pomponne's Relation de mon ambassade en Hollande 1669–1671, H. H. Rowen (ed.) (Utrecht, 1955).
J. van Reygersbergh, *De oude chronycke ende Historiën van Zeelandt* (Middelburg, 1634).
H. Rösock, *Trondheims Historie* (Trondheim, 1939).
H. J. Smit, *Bronnen Tot de Geschiedenis van den Handel met Engeland, Schotland en Ierland* ('s-Gravenhage, 1928).
J. C. Vermaas, *Geschiedenis van Scheveningen* ('s-Gravenhage, 1926).

CHAPTER VIII

Five Centuries of Shetland Fisheries

ALISTAIR GOODLAD

THE LAND resources of Shetland are marginal: in temperature and sunshine the islands only approach the limits needed for crop-growing, and if animal rearing is not impossible it can at times be difficult. But if we turn to the resources of the sea the picture is quite different, for it has proved to be a bountiful supplier of food and of goods for trading in return for those things which could not be or were not produced within the islands.

The five hundred years of fishing between 1469 and 1969 can be divided into phases distinguished from each other in time and in character. Shetland has historically been at the centre of the European fishing world, not on the fringe; and because of this it has been most strongly influenced at different periods by the fishing nation which happened to have an ascendancy (in terms of quantity and value of fish caught) in the area. The interaction of social, political and economic factors within the islands has also been important. But the interplay of these factors has been governed, in one way or another, by the physical basis of the fishery. It is therefore necessary to establish some guide lines as to what fish have been and are available in the seas around Shetland.

The so-called boreal sea zone seems to provide good conditions for the proliferation of the common commercial species of fish such as cod, haddock and herring; and Shetland seems to be well within the limits of tolerance of temperature and salinity acceptable to a large number of these species, including herring, cod, haddock, whiting, mackerel, ling and cusk as well as such shellfish as lobster, crab and scallop. Moreover, Shetland is particularly well located in relation to the North Atlantic Drift and the North Sea. It lies at the juncture of those water masses on the relatively shallow, northerly angle of the North Sea platform, which together provide extraordinarily good feeding conditions in the immediate area of the islands.

The water on this platform usually varies between 50 and 90 fathoms to the edge of the Continental shelf where it dips sharply to 500 fathoms or more. Within the 100-fathom line are the areas of easiest harvest, a fact confirmed by the way that, throughout history, the major fishing fleets of almost every nation around the North Sea have come to Shetland. The Shetland fishery, therefore, has not been locally developed, stimulated by the material or cultural requirements of the islands. The influences on the fishing industry have been, and now are, as varied as the people who fish in the seas around this land. So great have been the innovations in technology and organization, brought into the islands from outside, that relatively little is now left of the original fishery of Norse times. The little that is left is apparent in language, small-boat type and a few peculiarities of inshore gear.

During the fifteenth century Shetland seems to have still been part of the Scandinavian province. The system of fishing was that found in the preceding five (or more) centuries and was almost identical with that existing at that time in Norway. Trade was mainly carried on through Bergen. It is from this Norse period that Shetland took the boat-type and technology which were in large measure to govern the scope and range of the later fishery based on the islands. The boat-type then in use is perhaps most similar to the Ness yål of the present day. The boats were relatively shallow and narrow: they were long, with a pronounced sheer and a low freeboard amidships from which the four oars could be easily worked. They were probably very like the small tenders found with the Gokstad ship. Their range was probably little more than one to three miles offshore, but at that time there was likely to have been no need to go further from land. The two sites of Jarlshof and Underhoull produced some evidence of fishing, mainly weights made of soap stone which seem to have been used for hand-line fishing. Bones found in middens associated with the sites of settlements show that cod, saithe, ling and cusk were the main types of fish caught: and these are fish which can still be caught in quantities adequate for subsistence close to land. There is no evidence of long-line fishing which, it seems, only came into the islands in the late sixteenth century from England or Holland. While most of the fish caught were probably eaten in Shetland, a surplus was probably exported through Bergen by local merchants in return for goods which were not produced in the islands.

The date 1469 is not itself vital in the history of the Shetland fishery, but Boece mentions a Bremen merchant in Yell in the late fifteenth century—and this is very significant, being the first known appearance of a Hansa merchant. The coming of these merchants to the islands seems to be associated with a relaxation in the system whereby all trade was channelled through one of the 'kontors', e.g. Bergen: some kind of decentralisation had taken place. Merchants who had been based in Bergen now appeared in areas which were the sources of the raw materials in which they traded. To the evidence for these in literary sources, we can add place-names on old maps: Sandwick Bay, for instance, is often called 'Hamburgh Haven' or 'Bremen Haven', and until very recently there was also the 'Bremen Strasse' in Whalsay.

On arriving in the islands in May, the merchants generally set up booths which they normally rented from landowners. In these booths were stored such goods as lines and hooks, tobacco and alcohol, which were exchanged for fish, skins, butter and oil. The expansion of direct Hanseatic influence in Shetland brought with it the first real sign of commercialism in Shetland fisheries, for a surplus was produced and made possible the importing of more than the simple material necessities of life. A greater intensity of fishing in turn led to greater surpluses with which Shetlanders bought such luxuries as spirits, linen, soap and candles. Goudie says of the preceding era that 'the peasant was just a farmer and thereafter, as occasion or necessity required, a fisherman'. But by 1700 Brand reported that 'Here are many who follow no trade but their fishing'. Such marginal activities as corn growing were often abandoned and, by 1711, only enough corn could be grown to provide for five months of the year.

There was not much change in fishing until the late seventeenth century although the long-line had been introduced by c.1570, possibly by English or Dutch fishermen active in the area. By the late seventeenth century some environmental change had caused a lack of fish inshore: 'small Norway Yoals adventure far out into the sea and oft endure hard weather'. By 1700 Brand was writing that 'they put some leagues into the sea and sink the land . . . they stay out for several days'. By this time, however, the influence of the Hanseatic merchants was beginning to decline, largely because of increased Scottish and later British influence—most obviously in the increased pressure on the merchants to pay customs. By 1708 the Calendar of Treasury Papers records that 'Since the Union the few Hollanders or Bremers that used to come here were so discouraged by the duties that they gave over their trading'; by 1708 the day of the Hanse had passed and the salt tax of 1712 ensured that it would not come again. The common belief that the imposition of the salt tax suddenly stopped the trade of the Hanseatic merchants is quite wrong.

It is beyond the scope of this paper to say much about the foreign fisheries around the islands. It is well known that, from the early sixteenth century onwards, the English were fishing for ling and cod, usually en route for the Icelandic grounds. In the seventeenth century, Scots, usually from the Fife area, were also active around the islands and a few were granted concessions for the drying and hauling up of their boats. These Scots fishers also caught cod and ling. According to the records, however, the main activities of these foreign fishermen lay rather in sheep stealing, goose-shooting and in generally putting the islanders in a state of fear and alarm. The Hollanders had meanwhile been visiting the area since c.1500, fishing for herring and also using long lines—as Dr Kranenburg's paper shows. But it is worth while to point out here, however, that this long-line (or demersal) fishing by the Dutch fluctuated less violently than did their herring fishing and receives significant mention towards the end of the eighteenth century. Once again, however, there was no pronounced impact on the Shetland fishery; the Dutch did not influence the fishing technology of the islanders beyond the use of the long-line. And they affected the social pattern little in their buying of locally-produced articles for money, spirits or tobacco.

The so-called haaf or ocean-fishing period in Shetland is generally regarded in a heroic light. It occupied the last three-quarters of the eighteenth century and most of the nineteenth. At its peak men ventured 40 to 50 miles from shore in open boats, 25 feet to 30 feet long, to catch ling and cod by long-line in the months between May and August. It was distinctive not only by the range and the technology which accompanied the fishery but also in the social and economic system upon which it was based.

One of the prime tenets of the haaf fishing system was that the fisherman was a tenant-farmer who fished on behalf of a landowner (usually a Scot) under conditions which are normally regarded as being oppressive. Today we often take a kind of perverse pleasure in looking back on this period, taking the opportunity it offers to revile the landowner-merchants. It is not well enough known that the landlords were no more willing subjects of the conditions of the time than were the tenants. In the early eighteenth century the landmasters were forced into fishing by the banishment of the Hanseatic merchants. Later, they were ready to take full advantage of the strong position they had unwillingly created and it is difficult to find excuses for them: they simply wished to take as much economic gain from the social and economic environment as they could. With the departure of the Hanseatic merchants the Shetland tenantry were cut off from the supply of money on which they had been dependent. As a result, they were no longer able to pay cash rents. Furthermore the landlords could not market the produce they received in rental and, at the same time, lost the rents they had taken for the bøds (or 'booths') of the Hansa merchants. The only course open to the landowners was to enter the trade as middle men. Limited knowledge of markets, small capital resources and obstruction by the Germans in the traditional European markets, all led to difficulties and even to cases of bankruptcy in the earlier part of the period. And occasional gluts of imported fish from Newfoundland only added to the difficulties. The first half of the eighteenth century is therefore one of trial and change. By the late 1730s Gifford of Busta had begun to establish a market in Spain with hard-dried, light-salted fish, a market which was later to stimulate the haaf fishery for, during the later half of the eighteenth and throughout the nineteenth centuries, Shetland continued to rely heavily on a trade in dried salt fish to Spain and the Mediterranean countries. The fishery experienced a considerable growth as early as the 1740s.

After 1750 marketing was improved when London merchants began to buy fish from the landowners in the islands, became the new middle men in the trade and eliminated the risks (which the land-masters had previously run) associated with distant, fluctuating markets and the hazards of eighteenth-century transport. The new organization helped to raise prices to the fishermen and also to encourage investment in boats and equipment, especially by the land-masters who gave out vessels and gear to the tenant-fishermen. The situation had changed. Originally the land-masters had been forced to take over the trade in fish for the good of their tenants as well as themselves. Now they could maximise their profits by having as many tenants, and therefore as much fish and as much rent, as possible. The result was an intensified truck-system, a system which provided the necessities of life to the tenant in return for the right to buy his catch at the end of the fishing season. Subdivision of farms produced for the landlords more fishermen and more rents: but it also meant that more tenants were now unable to provide sufficient food for themselves from their holdings and it increased their dependence on fishing, which alone could give them a cash or credit surplus and thus maintain them in the remainder of the year.

The new fishery- and truck-systems were at their height in the early years of the nineteenth century when 400–500 boats were in use and about 3,000 men employed in them. The location of permanent and temporary fishing settlements now changed and by the late eighteenth century the largest fishing stations were those at the extremities of the islands—chosen to cut down on the travelling time to and from the fishing grounds. Such places as Fethaland, Stenness, Gloup and Haf Grøney were now the main locations. In the 1730s only a very few six-oared boats (sexaerings) were available. These then greatly increased in number and were increased in size, up to about 30 feet overall, as well as in depth and in beam. Sail came into more common use after 1800. In Faroe and in Lofoten where the same economic and social pressures were not apparent in the fishing industry, we do not find a similar development in the boat type.

In the later half of the nineteenth century the social and economic situation changed again in Shetland and led eventually to the end of the era of the haaf fishing. One factor behind this was the apparent increasing inadequacy of the sexaering for the task it was expected to do. A fishing disaster in 1832 caused the loss of 105 men and led thereafter to the introduction of half-decked boats. In 1881 another disaster claimed the lives of fifty-eight men and gave the final blow to the sexaering as the staple Shetland fishing craft. Also, during the latter half of the century, the haaf fishery had been overtaken by cod-fishing from smacks which were able to operate in more distant waters. And herring fishing from a Shetland base had also grown up in the same period. Competition for fishermen from these two sources, as well as the alternative employment in modern steamships of the British merchant fleet, led finally to the eventual demise of the haaf fishery.

During the late eighteenth century the dominance of the merchant land-masters was challenged by several small merchants who set up in business in Shetland and bought fish in competition with them. Often they had to do this clandestinely because of the pressures which the landlord-merchants could exert upon their tenants in order to sustain their monopoly. These outward-looking small merchants were very successful and, by the beginning of the second decade of the nineteenth century, were experimenting with decked sloops to fish for cod by hand-line on the banks around Shetland. With the discovery of the so-called Regents Banks to the west of Foula (now known as the Papa Bank and Otter Bank) the fishery developed quickly. During the 1820s a government bounty scheme stimulated its expansion as did the money gained by Shetlanders, either from prize money during the Napoleonic War or from whaling at Greenland, which became available for investment. Small decked vessels could operate at sea for up to two weeks at a time; the crews split the cod and salted them in the hold. It seems possible that by the mid- or late 1820s some vessels were operating outside immediate Shetland waters: in the crewing agreement of the sloop *Ann* in 1824, for example, there is a direct reference to smuggling, which would indicate that the vessel was operating in foreign waters—possibly Faroe, since this was the nearest to Shetland.

During the 1830s the cod fishery was challenged by the growth of herring fishing from Shetland. But in the 1840s the temporary herring boom ended and cod fishing was once again established as second in importance to the haaf fishing. During the 1840s trips were made as far away as to the Disko Bank off the west coast of Greenland and also close to the North Cape of Norway. The vessels which were used for this kind of fishing probably measured over 100 feet in length and constituted a fairly high capital investment. The period from 1840 to 1880 formed the peak era of cod fishing. It was then that it outpaced the haaf fishery in quantity of fish landed, range of fishing areas and capital invested. In the 1850s a pattern was established of making one trip to the home banks in February and March, then setting out in April for Faroe where two trips were made, and finally in late summer going to Iceland or Rockall according to the reports of the abundance of cod.

The cod fishery was an important influence in moving the focus of fishing activity in the islands. Previously, the needs of the haaf fishery had dictated the location of fishing settlements on or near the northern and southern extremities of Shetland. But the vessels fishing for cod were too large to haul up on exposed beaches and they required sheltered, deep water as harbours. The major fishing settlements, therefore, shifted towards the indentations on the south and west coasts, especially to Scalloway, Skeld, Whiteness and Weisdale. To the north Voe provided adequate facilities, and on the east side of the islands was Lerwick which offered not only a good harbour but also a base for merchants engaged in cod-fishing as owners and part-owners or simply as processors.

The era of the cod fishery, in my view, far surpasses the great period of the haaf. During the haaf fishery, men no doubt pitted themselves with great gallantry in small open boats against the sea and wind, but they were driven to do so by the whims of Scottish land-masters. During the cod fishery, on the other hand, the men not only ranged much further afield in their much more powerful boats, but they were also their own masters to a significantly greater extent. The crew and/or the skipper were more often owners of the vessel in which they sailed; if they were still, to some extent, economically dependent upon the merchant for buying, processing and selling the fish they caught, they still had much more economic independence than their counterparts during the haaf period. At any rate, after a relatively slow and steady growth towards a peak in the period between 1850 and 1880, the cod fishery then went into a very rapid decline. Several factors were at work here. Deteriorating weather in Iceland shortened the fishing season. There was increasing competition from the Faroese both on the fishing grounds and, after the breaking of the Danske monopoly in 1856, in the markets. The recruiting of crews became more difficult with the competition from alternative employments in the new steamships and the great iron clippers of the British merchant fleet: a young man was much more ready to undertake a voyage around the world in one of these vessels for an assured income than to face, year after year, the arduous conditions of hand-line cod fishing around Iceland and the unpredictable returns from it. But perhaps the most important reason for the decline of cod fishing was the growth of a home-based herring fishery. It did not require a fisherman to spend many hard weeks at sea: instead, with a berth on a herring-fishing lugger, he needed to be at sea only one night at a time and might look forward to returning to his home every weekend. By 1900, therefore, the cod fishery was almost at an end: but it has provided so high a point in the history of Shetland fisheries that it will be difficult ever to match or surpass it.

Until the late nineteenth century herring caught in Shetland waters by Shetlanders represented only a small part of the total catch of fish. Dr Kranenburg has pointed out that the Dutch fished Shetland waters for long periods with a fleet of up to 500 vessels. Shetlanders, by contrast, operated for only short periods with a few open boats and a few nets and caught very small quantities of fish. But a rapid expansion took place in the 1830s, only to end in a sudden decline: the markets deteriorated and in 1840 a great gale destroyed many boats and much gear. The short early boom had ended.

But by 1870 we find Scottish decked vessels of about 55 to 60 feet beginning to venture north, catching demersal fish in Shetland waters by long-line. They also used a few herring nets to catch bait for their long-line gear. And so successful were these bait nets that in 1872 a considerable herring fishery began to be established. In 1874, 1,100 barrels of fish were caught by 50 boats; by 1881, 59,586 barrels were caught by 276 boats. With this swift development of the herring fishery comes a new factor in the Shetland fishing industry, namely the stimulus of outside rather than home-based interests, in this case the skippers and curing interests from Scotland. But it was a fishing pattern which quickly attracted the participation of Shetlanders, so that by 1900 the native fishermen had largely given up haaf and cod fishing and concentrated entirely on herring during the summer months. In winter, however, they still fished inshore for demersal species as they had done previously.

For Shetlanders, indeed, this period of herring boom brought a much smaller degree of expansion than is normally thought to have been the case. The change to herring mainly meant a simple change of occupation or a change of emphasis in their normal occupations. It did not mean that more native fishermen were employed than previously. For instance, after 1900 the steam drifter was more and more used in the herring fishery. But only four of them were owned by Shetlanders: they were based in England or in Scotland, and only appeared in Shetland between May and August already fully manned. Steam drifters were too expensive for Shetlanders to buy themselves, a fact which was—rather curiously—to prove a blessing in disguise since they rapidly became uneconomic and obsolete. The local fishing vessels, frequently bought second-hand from Scots, were retained during this period; and, around the time of the First World War, many of them were given motor engines. They then were to form the backbone of a fleet which, technically, remained almost unchanged until the end of the Second World War. Shetland may have missed out on the steam phase to its ultimate advantage.

The change of emphasis to herring again brought a change in the geographical centres of Shetland fishing. The cod fishery, as we have seen, was largely focused towards the west and south-west of the islands. In its initial phases, the herring fishery was scattered around the islands but with more fishing stations to the east and north than elsewhere. But steam drifters and motorized vessels began to compose a large part of the fleet and these vessels required services which could only be given at larger centres. In 1906, the auctioning of herring began at Lerwick. The smaller outlying stations closed and fishing activity was concentrated on Balta Sound, Lerwick and (to a lesser extent and in the early spring only) on Scalloway. Increasing mechanization and the location of processing plants have since then made for centralization in Scalloway and Lerwick, and also in Whalsay and Burra.

The herring fishery stimulated the local development in Shetland of a large processing industry, mainly in the salting and packing of herring for export to European markets. It was an industry that depended largely upon the seasonal immigration of large numbers of workers, usually Scots, in the pay of Scottish curers. Up to 20,000 fishermen also came north each year. Some of these immigrants established themselves temporarily in Shetland for the season: a few married and settled down in the islands. Decennial censuses up to 1921 show a growing number of inhabitants born outwith Shetland, usually from the north-eastern counties of Scotland. The decline in the herring industry then brought a corresponding decline in the proportion of Shetlanders born outside the islands.

In and after the First World War the markets for salted herring in Germany and Russia disappeared: a drastic decline in the quantity produced is shown by Fishery Board records for Shetland. The native fishermen now had only the prospect of a return to the offshore cod fishery, but they no longer had the expertise nor the equipment necessary to prosecute this successfully. As a result many men emigrated from the islands during the 1920s and 1930s. Those who remained still fished for herring but on a greatly decreased scale, from motor boats 50 to 70 feet long, and used the same vessels in winter to fish with long-lines for haddock and whiting on the inshore grounds.

With this the Shetland fishing industry reached its final phase. From the late nineteenth century onwards, mainland Scotland provided an important market for fresh fish, particularly for haddock and whiting, with the opening of a regular steamship ferry between Shetland and Aberdeen. Since 1918, and more especially since 1945, the white fish industry of Shetland became largely dependent on this market. With the introduction of the Danish seine after the Second World War, there were greatly increased landings of haddock and whiting taken from grounds on which a rich stock developed in the late 1940s because they had been only lightly fished during the war. The success experienced in this period, when a small fleet supplied a fairly large market, led to some capital accumulation and thus to investment in new vessels which completed the dominance of Scottish influence in Shetland fisheries. These dual-purpose boats were of

Scottish type, almost all built in the north-east Scottish ports of Peterhead, Fraserburgh and Buckie. Equipped with diesel engines, echo sounders and radios, they had a potential range of well over 100 miles but in fact remained within waters some twenty miles off Shetland. During the summer months many sailed with catches to the market in Aberdeen; others landed their white fish in Shetland and had it taken by mail steamer to Aberdeen; the remainder, especially vessels under 50-feet, sold the fish to local buyers acting as dealers for merchants in Aberdeen and Glasgow. Fishing for herring was continued, using the vessels for their second purpose—and using the gear that had been used for centuries, the drift net. But now the herring was increasingly used fresh, or frozen, or was kippered, and there was a corresponding decline in the traditional salt-curing.

When in 1959 a fish plant was established in Scalloway for the filleting and freezing of haddock and whiting, there was another change in the sources of influence in Shetland fisheries. The preceding period had been characterized by the almost complete Scottish domination in their technology and economic structure. There was now a beginning to a new period in which local initiative began something of a 'Shetland' revival. Plants have been established in Lerwick and in Scalloway, more recently on the island of Yell (and there is the possibility of more in Whalsay and elsewhere on the Shetland mainland), for the processing of haddock, whiting, herring, crab, lobster and other shellfish. And these are prompting an increase in the number of multi-purpose vessels; vessels which can trawl, use seine nets, work lobster or crab pots, dredge for scallops and can also drift-net for herring.

Since 1965 there has been a very large Norwegian herring fishery, using purse seine around the Shetland Islands. The Norwegians land high volumes of herring which they sell at a relatively low price for processing for meal and oil. Shetlanders traditionally dislike low-value utilization of fish, for the older members of the fishing community recall the depression period between the wars when large catches were made and had to be dumped. Shetlanders have therefore been reluctant to enter the field of modern purse seine fishing. Now, however, it seems that fish caught by purse seine can be used in higher-value forms after processing. Although there may be over-fishing in general terms in the North Sea, the herring—being migratory—concentrate in the area of Shetland on their movement westward, staying immediately inside the 12-mile limit during the months of June, July and August. At this time, therefore, although the total quantity may be diminished, it seems likely that sufficient concentrations will remain within reach of Shetland or British fishermen to promote a viable efficient herring fishery.

Shetlanders are once again struggling to develop a degree of local industrial enterprise in the fishing industry, utilizing as well as they can all the fishing resources around the islands, and using the developments in technology, the capital and the expertise which are available, wherever they come from. Once again Scandinavia is becoming a major area of influence, with important investment by Norwegians and a substantial market link with Sweden. At the same time, the Highland and Islands Development Board has provided probably one of the greatest stimuli by substantial loans and grants for fisheries' development, given sufficient local initiative and expertise. From being a small community dominated by particular influences outside itself, Shetland is developing—with help but without domination—a great independence and self-reliance.

Editor's note—Since he delivered this lecture in 1969, Dr Goodlad has published an extended treatment of his theme, in his *Shetland Fishing Saga* (Lerwick, 1971). This book contains a full listing of sources, printed and manuscript, which the author used in his background researches for the lecture.

CHAPTER IX

Shetland History in the Scottish Records

MARGARET D. YOUNG

THE SCOTTISH Record Office is the central record repository for all Scotland and it houses, as well as the national records, other classes of record which in England and elsewhere would be deposited in local record offices. With such a concentration of material in one place, it follows that any account of record sources for Shetland history held there must be selective. The main purposes of this paper are to indicate the range of contents of the main record groups,[1] to illustrate the information which may be gained from them and, generally, to offer some guidance towards their use. All the sources dealt with below relate to the period after 1469 and I shall concentrate on those which are, for various reasons, less well-known—because they have been in private hands, as in the case of family and business muniments; or because modern archive practice has brought in new sources, as in the case of the transmission of departmental records to the Scottish Record Office; or because, quite simply, the material is being currently sorted and catalogued—for example, the exchequer records and the Register House plans.

We must, of course, start with the national records for they are, in each country, the essential framework for a study of that country's history. In the case of Scotland, this means by and large material before the Union of 1707: for after that date Scotland lost both her main legislative body (parliament) and her main administrative body (the privy council). One aspect of the Scottish records which must be borne in mind is the fact that Scotland has twice suffered heavy losses to her national records—once in the 1290s when Edward I of England carried off many of the records to London; and again at the Restoration when records, which had been taken south by Cromwell during the Commonwealth period and which were being returned to Scotland, were lost when the ship carrying them to Leith foundered in the North Sea. While the resultant scarcity of early material may not be of direct consequence for the study of Shetland history, it is the reason why so many of the most important series of our national records start so late. What, then, is there of Shetland interest in the national records? Among the State Papers (SP)[2] is a section containing treaties with Norway, Sweden and Denmark, 1312–1589, which includes the marriage contract of 1468 in which the Orkney Islands were pledged. The islands were among the jointure lands of Mary of Guise on her marriage to James V and there is a bond of manrent by Robert Carnegy of Kynnarde in 1548 whereby he binds himself to serve the queen as her man in consideration of £100 yearly furth of the rents of Orkney and Shetland. Repercussions of the war with Spain are illustrated by letters written in Latin and Norwegian, dated 18 September 1626, by the magistrates and council of Bergen concerning a complaint by the owners of the *Lam*, captured by a Scottish ship in Shetland waters while on a voyage from Bergen to Spain. In 1950 certain state papers were transmitted from the Public Record Office to the Scottish Record Office among which are 28 volumes of the warrant books of the Secretary for Scotland between 1670 and 1709. In Volume i is a precept of 1671 by the king for the payment, among other arrears, of profits from ships taken in the Dutch war including two prizes taken in Shetland, a warrant authorising payment for transport of hawks for the king from Orkney and Shetland in 1671 and a letter of the same year authorising the commissioners of the treasury to farm out royal revenues in the Islands.

The acts of the parliaments of Scotland are extant from 1466 to 1707 together with some rolls of the thirteenth and fourteenth centuries—all that remains of the original medieval records—but the series has been carried back to 1124 by using various MS collections and the whole has been printed in eleven volumes with a remarkably comprehensive index. This source contains intermittent references to matters which were of concern to Shetland and its people. Another invaluable source for general information is the Register of the Privy Council of Scotland (PC) which was the body responsible for the day-to-day government of the country up to the Union, in local as

1. Sixerns and Hanseatic bods at Fethaland, North Roe

2. A crofter's cottage

3. Haymaking at Benngirth, North Roe

4. Crofting community—alive

5. Crofting community—dead (Uyea, North Roe)

6. Lerwick from the south

7. The herring boom: Lerwick fishing station

8. John Brown (?) and his team of gutters: late 19th century

well as national affairs. The Register is extant from 1545 and is printed up to 1690, with later volumes to come. Here, for instance, is contained information on Denmark's various attempts to raise with Scotland the question of the redemption of the islands; in 1564 an embassy headed by William Douglas of Whittinghame, although largely concerned with trade, was instructed that, if any mention were made of Orkney and Shetland, they were to disclaim all knowledge of the question, saying they had never heard any controversy on this subject, and thus 'can gif na ansuer thairto'.

While parliament and privy council disappeared at the Union, the Scottish exchequer continued to exist, although remodelled on English lines in a simpler form with the separate Scottish treasury being abolished. The exchequer records (E) constitute a great mass of material which is in process of being arranged. The pre-Union exchequer records include the exchequer rolls from 1326 to 1708, printed so far from the beginning to 1600. Among various crown rentals there are to be found the rents and duties for Orkney and Shetland in 1612, a rental of Shetland for 1628 and, among the papers of the Auditor's Office, the declared accounts for 1697–1713 of George Mackenzie of Stonhyve[3] who was assignee to the crown rents of Shetland before 1703 in compensation for losses in his capacity as tacksman of the Northern Shires. Among the treasury vouchers are the accounts of the Shetland garrison, in what was later to be Fort Charlotte, for 1667–8 and these include payments for provisions brought from Leith, to sailors manning transports, to gunners at the Fort itself and to Robert Mylne, master mason, for his work there. Both pre- and post-Union exchequer records are important for the accounts of customs and excise they contain. There are customs books for Shetland for the years 1668–81 and port accounts for 1671–2. From 1742 to 1830 we have the quarterly customs accounts for Lerwick which show full copies of the merchants' entries of goods exported and imported. Also of value in this range of exchequer material are the returns for various assessed taxes including window and house tax for 1759–98, inhabited house tax for 1778–98 and the commutation tax for 1784–98 (an additional tax imposed on houses and windows): it is worth noting that these returns give the names and designations of the inhabitants as well as the duties payable by them.

Among the records of chancery (C) the most important is the register of charters issued under the great seal. Extant from 1306 and still in current use, it has been printed from the beginning to 1668 with indexes of persons, places and offices: and thereafter, there is available a typescript index of persons. Invaluable for information about lands and landowners, this register contains grants of lands and of major offices and the titles and confirmations of vassals' charters. The succession of an heir to his inheritance gave rise to another important source of information about lands and their owners in Shetland as elsewhere. Before the heir could obtain possession, the sheriff had to summon a jury to determine what lands the heir's predecessors had possessed, what they were worth, the terms on which they were held, and so forth. The sheriff reported their findings to chancery and his return was then entered in the Register of Retours. The first entry for Shetland is dated 1605. The Register has now been fully calendered up to 1699, with an index of persons and places; from 1700 the series continues under the title of the Services of Heirs, printed in decennial indexes under surnames. Crown grants were also made under the privy seal (PS) and that Register is extant from 1488 until 1898 when it was discontinued; it is in print from the beginning up to 1580, and there are further volumes in preparation. These grants cover a wide field including presentations to church livings, appointments to minor offices, and gifts of pensions and escheats, i.e. property forfeited to the crown; we find, for example, that in 1566 Sir William Murray of Tullibardine, comptroller of Scotland, had a grant of the office of foud of Shetland with the right of holding 'lawtyngis'.

The ownership of land in Scotland can in many cases be traced back continuously to the early seventeenth century, for in 1617 the Register of Sasines (RS), the land register of Scotland, was instituted by act of parliament. The original charter granting land contained a precept directing that real and actual possession be given to the grantee and this transaction was of such importance that it came to be written down by a notary who, in the presence of witnesses, had seen the giving of earth and stone on the actual ground as symbolising the change of ownership. These notarial instruments of sasine, along with other private transactions, were recorded in notarial protocol books (NP) which are an important source of information before the establishment of the Register itself, and one such exists for Orkney, Shetland, Forfar and Banff from 1576 to 1615. The act of 1617 established a General Register of Sasines which applied to lands anywhere in Scotland and also a Particular Register in respect of regions approximating to the counties: sasines could be registered in either. In 1868 one General Register in county divisions was instituted. The Particular Register for Shetland is extant from 1623, although not indexed until 1781, but minute books are available from 1661. It is certain that a study of the seventeenth-century Register would reveal a great deal of information about the possessors of land in the islands and would show too the change from udal to feudal holdings.

Before the institution in 1532 of the Court of Session, the supreme civil court in Scotland, the privy council, acted in a judicial as well as an administrative capacity and early legal material is contained in the Acts of the Lords of Council, 1478–1532, some part of this source being already in print.[4] After 1532 the proceedings of the court are available to researchers in the Acts of the Lords of Council and Session, 1532–59. A separate Register of Acts and Decreets is extant from 1542 with an index from 1810 and printed minute books from 1782; for the earlier period reference must be made to the MS minute books, extant for the years 1557–1659 and from 1661 onwards. These Registers are themselves only summaries of the processes (i.e. the files of papers relating to particular cases which provide us with a great mass of material): the Scottish Record Office is making steady progress in transferring their information to a card index. Among nineteenth-century processes is the appeal taken by Bruce of Sumburgh to the Court of Session following on his action in the Sheriff Court of Orkney and Shetland against the salvors of whales driven ashore at Hoswick Bay: Bruce had claimed a share of the profits.[5] These papers not only contain information on whale-killings generally—as for instance that three hundred and fourteen men and boys drove the whales ashore and that the profits of the sale were £450 and the expenses £166. 10s.—but also investigate Bruce's claim that the heritors of Shetland had a right to a share of all whales stranded and killed on the shores of their lands conform to the laws, usages and rights of the islands.

An important series connected with the civil courts are the Books of Council and Session or Register of Deeds (RD) wherein all transactions, except those relating to the transfer of property, might be registered for preservation and execution, the registration forming the basis on which legal action, if necessary, might follow. The Register is extant from 1554 and like the Register of Sasines is still in current use; but unlike the sasines, where the original writ was returned after registration, the original deed is retained in the Register House. These deeds cover a variety of transactions including bonds, marriage and other contracts, and wills and are an invaluable source of information on every class of society. Of special interest for Shetland history are the contracts for the freight of ships or charter parties. One such was drawn up at St Margaret's Hope on 27 June 1693 between the owners of the *Issbell* and certain merchants of Wick, to carry cargo to Lerwick and return with cargo to Wick or Staxigoe; in this case the cargo is not specified but such details are frequently given. The deeds have been calendared from 1554 to 1595, with an index from the beginning to 1588: there are indexes of persons only from 1661 to 1694, 1750 to 1752 and for 1770 onwards with work in progress to fill the gaps. Execution of a decreet of the court, once legal action had been taken, proceeded by various letters under the signet, known collectively as Diligence Records (DI). In these instances the first steps were the raising of letters of horning by which a debtor who failed to fulfil his obligations was publicly denounced rebel by a messenger-at-arms so that his estate could be attached for the debt; and the issue of letters of inhibition which prevented the debtor from alienating his property under threat of legal action. There are General Registers of Hornings from 1610 and of Inhibitions from 1602: a Particular Register of Hornings and Inhibitions for Shetland is available from 1685 to 1739 and from 1773 to 1869, the earlier volumes still being in the hands of the sheriff clerk.[6]

The records of criminal trials in Scotland in the High Court of Justiciary are extant from the late fifteenth century and cases have been printed by the Bannatyne Club,[7] the Stair Society[8] and the Scottish History Society.[9] There is particular Shetland interest in the full accounts of the trials of Earl Patrick and Robert Stewart, his son, and also in trials on charges of piracy which are of note for their information on shipping and cargoes. Relevant to this topic, and of particular importance for Shetland history, are the records of the High Court of Admiralty (AC) which dealt with civil actions relating to maritime contracts and wrecks and with criminal actions of piracy and mutiny: the jurisdiction of this court continued until 1830. There is one volume extant for sixteenth-century cases, entitled 'Acta Curiae Admirallatus Scotiae' and dating between September 1557 and March 1562.[10] Among other records of this court are 107 volumes of decreets (1627–1830) and the first volume for 1627 provides examples which illustrate the kind of information available. Ships taken during the war with Spain included the *St Peter*, going from 'Danskein' to Spain and apprehended in Shetland waters, whose cargo consisted of wax, two 'shreud' of sail, 600 lbs of cheese, 85 sides of bacon, 16 barrels of bread and 55,000 pipe-staves for making puncheons. In the same year the *St Lawrence* of Lübeck was taken carrying a cargo of salt and timber for Spain and also documents, including bonds in the 'Dutch' language, which were translated for the court by Andrew Bruce of Muness and by Robert Bruce, fiar of Symbister. There are also eight volumes of criminal records from 1781 to 1792, one of which includes the case of Wilson Potts, master of the *Dreadnought* of Newcastle: he was charged with rape, theft, robbery and piracy in that he was alleged to have abducted a young woman from the Faroes, stolen a cow from there, captured the *White Swan* of Copenhagen, taken her into Baltasound and then stolen money and other goods from the ship. It is hardly surprising to learn that he was hanged on the shore at Leith.

In the context of legal records I should mention the various court books which are so important for the study of local conditions; especially in a remote area like Shetland, with strong Scandinavian traditions which were being gradually ousted by Scottish influence during the seventeenth century, the information they provide is invaluable. It is fortunate that there exist a court book for 1602–1604, when the old order under the personal rule of Earl Patrick was still in force, and volumes for 1612–13 and 1614–15 which cover the period of the abolition of the old laws in 1611 and the promulgation of the Country Acts in 1615. It is even more fortunate that these three volumes have now been printed.[11] The later court books for Shetland, those for 1615–28 and 1630–65, while they have gaps, nonetheless show this process of continuing change and would repay detailed study. The Scottish Record Office also holds the Bailie Court Book of Dunrossness, Sandwick and Cunningsburgh for 1731–35 (RH11), which gives some indication of conditions in the earlier eighteenth century. Justice was still administered very much according to the Country Acts and the cases were mostly concerned with the theft of sheep, peat and corn, with the keeping of unlicensed sheepdogs and with the committing of 'High Riot . . . under silence of night'. Other local courts which must be mentioned are the Commissary Courts (CC), the successors of the pre-Reformation bishop's courts, which took cognizance of matrimonial causes, administered intestate, moveable estates, and confirmed testaments. This last aspect of their work is of most help to historians since, in confirming a testament, the court drew up an inventory of the moveable goods of the deceased: these confirmations contain therefore a great deal of information about household furniture, clothing, livestock and crops belonging to persons in all classes of society and much genealogical information as well. For instance, a testament dative of James Sinclair of Mael in the parish of Burray, who died on 23 May 1622, tells us that his goods included horses, oxen, sheep and pigs, crops of bere and oats, an old 'four arring bot' and six old worn silver spoons; we learn too that money was due to him by two Kirkwall merchants and that among his debts were payments of landmaill and umboths[12] and wages to three servants, two men and a woman.

These classes of records have been generated by government action of one sort or another. I would now like to move on to consider various classes of record which have been deposited by outside bodies in the Scottish Record Office, both for their preservation and for easier access to them by the general public. In 1960 the Church of Scotland records, until then preserved in the General Assembly Tolbooth Library, were deposited on indefinite loan and subsequent accessions have been deposited in the Scottish Record Office since that date. These records (CH) comprise the older records of the general assembly, records of synods, presbyteries and kirk sessions, where they are not still held locally, and records of former Free, United Presbyterian, United Free, and other churches which united with the Church of Scotland in this century. For Shetland there are Established Church session minutes for the parishes of Delting from 1709, Unst from 1720, Northmavine from 1729, Walls from 1735, Sandsting and Aithsting from 1736, Fetlar from 1754, Sandwick from 1755, Dunrossness from 1764, Fair Isle from 1828 and Whalsay from 1847; and minutes of the presbytery of Olnafirth from 1848 to 1929. These records are important not only for information on religious matters but also as a source for social history since the church was much concerned with education and charitable work such as poor relief. A few examples must suffice to indicate the range of data which these records allow us. In 1729 a case of slander was transferred from the local bailie court to be dealt with by the kirk session of Northmavine; in 1828 the kirk session minutes of Fetlar took note of the parochial library there, which was open from 1 p.m. to 5 p.m. on the first Saturday of each month, and included a list of books available; the session clerk for Fair Isle recorded in 1829 that at communion there were seventy-nine communicants (of whom eleven were new) and noted that three of the elders had left to join the Methodists. Among the records of the Free Churches in Shetland are the kirk session minutes of Dunrossness from 1858 and

Uyeasound from 1881 and the Shetland presbytery minutes from 1843.

Also important as a source for church and general social history are the Heritors' Records (HR), mostly of the nineteenth century. Heritors, as the landowners in the parish, were responsible for the upkeep, among other things, of manses and churches and schools. Prior to 1925 these heritors' minutes include assessment rolls and lists of inhabitants, while the names of the poor of the parish are regularly entered before 1855. That the drift from the landward areas in Shetland to the towns is no new phenomenon can be seen in an entry in the Lerwick heritors' records for 1824 which indicate a serious falling-off of collections for poor relief as a result of the establishment of two dissenting meeting houses and also of an unusual influx of 'destitute and indolent families from country to town'. Information on parochial education is frequently found. Thus there were eighteen applications for the appointment of a new schoolmaster in Unst in 1867 at a salary of £50 a year, the subjects to be taught and their relevant fees being set out in full—reading, grammar and composition at 1s. 6d., plus writing at 6d. extra; arithmetic and geography at 6d.; book-keeping at 1s.; geometry and algebra at 3s.; classics at 4s.; navigation at 7s. 6d. Among other church records transmitted to the Scottish Record Office are those of the Teind Court (TE). These are largely post-1700, and have been added to pre-1700 papers already in the Record Office. The earliest Shetland records among these are for Fetlar and Yell in 1709 and for Tingwall, Unst and Lerwick in 1722. They are mainly concerned with the allocation and adjustment of ministers' stipends.

The work done by the Records Liaison Section in the Scottish Record Office is the result of recent developments directed toward the location and preservation of record material held by private or departmental bodies in Scotland and has resulted in large accessions of important groups of material. Since 1946 the National Register of Archives (Scotland), with its headquarters in the Register House, has been surveying family muniments held in private hands, or by law firms, and other collections such as business papers. Most of Scotland has now been covered. The Register also acts as a clearing-house for information about the record-groups which come under its surveillance. The dangers of the loss and dispersal of such privately-held material is obvious while its importance to the historian is great: it is, apart from anything else, one source from which gaps in the earlier public records may be filled. Such collections have special characteristics not found among the more formal administrative records and they are, of course, invaluable for the study of particular localities. Owners may deposit their papers with the Scottish Record Office either outright or on permanent loan; if the latter, the office cares for and inventories the collection and makes it available to the public while the owner retains the right of possession, on the understanding that the collection will not be withdrawn except in exceptional circumstances. In May 1968 a survey was carried out in Shetland and seven collections were inspected. Four were of papers in the custody of the local library comprising the muniments of Bruce of Sumburgh and Hay of Laxfirth, the Lawrence Williamson MSS and miscellaneous items including presbytery records from 1700 to 1808. Three collections survyed *in situ* were the Gardie House, Neven of Windhouse and Edmonston of Buness muniments. These contain material of great local interest; for example, among the Gardie House papers are sixteenth-century writs, a court book of Unst for 1731–3 and Admiralty Court papers. Copies of all seven surveys have been deposited in the Lerwick Library and may be consulted there. The Register has also carried out a preliminary survey of some of the Marquis of Zetland's papers which contain some material relating to Orkney and include papers concerning the vice-admiralty of Orkney and Shetland from 1765 to 1834 (GD173/236).

These deposited collections are classified as Gifts and Deposits and among the miscellaneous series is a skatt book of Zetland, undated but of the sixteenth century (GD1/366), and the 'Complaint of the Shetlanders against Bruce of Cultmalindie' in February 1576/7 (GD1/368) which has been printed by the Maitland Club. The Douglas Collection (GD98) came to the Record Office in the 1930s as the bequest of an Edinburgh bookseller. One of the items it contains is an inventory of 1591, giving details of the goods taken from a great ship of 'Danskene' lying in Shetland: these included a barrel containing certain books of 'ane historie . . . of the cuntreis of polonia, Muscovia, prussia and utheris thairto adiacent' and pieces of ordnance with their equipment. The records of the British Fishery Society (GD9) contain a great deal of information on Scottish fisheries in general and include a letter of 1773 to the Duke of Argyll from an inspector of the society who had recently completed a tour of Shetland, commenting on twenty-five different experiments in fishing by new methods. The papers of the Society in Scotland for Propagating Christian Knowledge (GD95) contain a journal of a visit to the society's schools in Shetland made by two of its members in

July and August 1835: like many travellers to Shetland before (and since) they found getting there the most difficult part: thus, on arriving in Peterhead to catch the packet, they found that 'on its return from Shetland a few days before . . . [it] had been much damaged in a gale of wind and had lost its mast, rigging and sails'. It was not until 28 July that they arrived in Lerwick having left Edinburgh on 13 July, but they proceeded nonetheless to visit every school in the islands except Fair Isle and Foula, and even included the schools run by the General Assembly Education Committee. As a result, their journal contains many general observations on the state of education and on teachers' qualifications, with a detailed description of each school, the number of its pupils, sometimes the population of the village and remarks about the condition of the schools. They also comment how the heritors in Shetland had been remiss in establishing parochial schools in the eighteenth century, with the result that the provision of education had been left to the church and the society.

The two most important private collections for Shetland history in the Scottish Record Office are the muniments of Bruce of Symbister (GD144), comprising 29 boxes which have not yet been inventoried, and those of the Earls of Morton (GD150) in some 156 boxes. The islands were granted to Morton on 15 June 1643 under redemption for £30,000 sterling; in 1742 they were granted outright to the same family which sold them in 1766 to Sir Laurence Dundas, ancestor of the Earls of Zetland, for £63,000. Understandably, the Morton papers contain a great deal of material relevant to Shetland, accumulated during the years of the family's administration: here I can give only a few examples of the wide variety of topics they cover. Whales were highly valued by the inhabitants of the islands and conflict frequently arose between the latter and the landowners who claimed a share in the products of a whale-killing; in a letter of 1716 John Scott of Scotshall informs Morton that a hundred whales had been taken at Haroldswick in Unst and promises to secure his lordship's share. Other papers deal with wrecks, also a possible source of trouble between those who salvaged the cargoes and the authorities. This series starts in 1665 with a report to the Earl of Morton about the wreck of the *Carmerlane* of Amsterdam on the Skerries in December 1664, 'which sad Accident was keeped up from the knowledge of any except such as live in the said Remote place for the space of Twentie four dayes or therby'. The authorities finally salvaged three little chests containing 'hollander money', which is listed in the papers. Four more ships, three from Amsterdam and one from Hamburg are noted in this group which ends with the wreck of the *Wendela* of the Danish East India Company in 1738. Among other items of interest in the Morton papers are rentals for the period 1652 to 1765, which include a suit roll of the heritors, udallers and liferenters of udal lands in Yell for 1709, a petition of the same year by the inhabitants of Orkney and Shetland for the repair of the fort [Fort Charlotte] and the establishment of a military force ('the Inhabitants being extraordinarily opprest by the french privateers'), an indenture of 1709 between Morton and a company formed to smelt lead with pit or sea coal, a customs report of 1737 commenting on an increase in smuggling resulting from there being no military forces available to control it, and letters from the earl's factor in the 1740s and 1750s, John Craigie, which give valuable day-to-day accounts of the running of the estates. There are also many ecclesiastical papers which throw light on local conditions as, for example, reports on the parish of Nesting in 1731 where the minister had had no manse for twenty-eight years and on the establishment of a school by the heritors of Sandsting and Aithsting in 1758.

Another function of the Records Liaison Section is to review, and to select for preservation, the records of the four Scottish government departments—Development, Home and Health, Agriculture and Fisheries, and Education. When the Liaison Section has completed that task, the records are transmitted for preservation to the Scottish Record Office, where many of them are now available to readers and are in use. The bulk of these records relate to the nineteenth century and the detailed information they contain on local matters is invaluable to historians; they will no doubt be more used as time goes on and new fields are found in them for the social and economic historian. Some examples from the records of each department may be given in order to illustrate the information they make available. The 'roads and bridges' file of the Development Department (DD) for the 1890s contains notes on the effect of the Crofters' Act of 1886 on the ability of landlords to keep up roads on their lands: among these we find evidence of the lack of suitable roads and footpaths in Yell where an exceptionally large number of schools were therefore required in relation to the size of the population—eleven schools in all for 2,500 inhabitants of all ages in 1895. Among the records of the Education Department (ED) are those of the Endowed Institutions Commission of 1879 which include returns from the parish schools in Shetland as to the number of their scholars and the subjects they studied. The Royal Commission on Religious Instruction, to be found among the records of the Home and Health Department (HH), received returns made by parish ministers in 1835–6 which note the population of each parish, the religion professed by the inhabitants, the type of work carried on by the parishioners—often with the complaint that the increase in population and difficulty of communications made the ministerial charge too onerous for one man—and details of the building and re-building of parish churches.

But the most important departmental records for Shetland history are those of the Department of Agriculture and Fisheries (AF) since it had responsibility in the nineteenth century for the development of the Highlands and Islands. The series of 'crofting files' contain much general information and include complaints made in 1889 about insufficient communications with mainland Scotland and absence of harbours and lighthouses, while in 1893 we have reports of destitution due to the failure not only of the corn and potato crops but also of the fishing. The Lerwick Fishery Office records, available from 1822 onwards, contain reports on the different kinds of fishings and the number of vessels engaged therein, with letters, curing books and also weekly reports in a tabular lay-out after 1854. Among the Fishery Board's miscellaneous papers are reports of the 1890s relating to harbours in Shetland: these contain general tables, giving accounts of harbours, piers, natural landings, the numbers of fishermen and boats employed; there are also reports on individual piers, some with sketches. The 'fishery files' for 1892 have references to the oldest herring curing station in Shetland—at Sandsair—and the introduction of large-decked fishing boats. The Congested Districts Board was set up in 1897 to aid agriculture and fisheries, to provide lighthouses, piers, harbours and home industries and to encourage the migration of crofters to other parts of Scotland from the over-populated crofting areas. The reasons given by various Shetland parishes in their applications for assistance illustrate well the conditions of the period. In addition the 'emigration files' give a great deal of information about general crofting conditions, and include a proposal by the minister of Unst in 1887 for the emigration of local crofters to Canada. Some of these more modern records are still currently in use, e.g. the parish summaries of the agriculture census taken annually in Scotland. The first series of these runs from 1866 to 1911 and covers holdings of various sizes; the second series runs from 1912 to the present and covers holdings of one acre and above. These agricultural statistics give easy access to information on crops, livestock and horticulture and they are much used, especially by school-children and students working on local projects.

As well as having responsibilities for these Scottish departmental records, the Records Liaison Section is concerned with records of certain English governmental departments which had and have their headquarters in Scotland such as the Board of Customs and Excise (CE). The Scottish Board of Customs was established after the Union and continued to exist separately until 1723 when a single Board was formed with England, certain commissioners being deputed to reside in Edinburgh in order to deal with Scottish business. Likewise the Board of Excise was established after the Union and became a single U.K. board, but with a Scottish off-shoot, in 1823. Among the records here which relate to Shetland there are customs minute books, (1723–1828), excise minute books (1799–1830), and letter books of the eighteenth and nineteenth centuries. An entry in the customs minute book for 1777 relates how the sloop *Betsay* of Philadelphia was taken as a prize in the war with America by the customs officers of Shetland, with a cargo of 4 puncheons of rum and 27 barrels of flour. In a memorial by the commander of the sloop *Princess Caroline*, stationed in Orkney, expenses of £21 were claimed for hiring another sloop to allow the mate and some of the crew to go to Shetland and investigate the smuggling of spirits, on the grounds that his own ship was too well-known to the Shetlanders: he was allowed expenses, not least since he had captured 61½ ankers of spirits and 3 boxes of tobacco. Other papers show the Board considering the case of Mr. William Balfour, collector at Lerwick, who had been absent without leave for two hundred and thirty-one days between November 1775 and August 1777: they decided to pay his salary only for the days he actually worked, remarking that 'the Collector be acquainted that, though the Board have no objection to make to his honesty and integrity, yet the Revenue may have suffered by his absence'.

A brief mention is all that can be made of some miscellaneous collections which contain material relating to Shetland. The Register House series of deposits includes a collection of charters and other writs (RH6) of which most of those relative to Shetland have already been printed in the Viking Society's *Records of Orkney and Shetland*, vol. i; they include a charter of 1465 in Norse by which Andrew Williamson transferred lands in Unst to Symon Hognason. Another Register House collection, called Orkney and Shetland Papers

(RH9/15), contains a Deed of Upgestry of 1582 by Halya Turbeinsdochter in Unst and Manss Ollasonne, her husband; and, among various rentals, an abbreviate of the land and other duties of Shetland c.1585–90; a photostat copy of a rental of the lordship of Zetland for 1656 to 1672; a skatt rental for 1716–17 (the holograph of Thomas Gifford of Busta) and a rental for the years 1830–40. Also in this collection is a testimonal of 1610 in favour of Edward Sinclair of Marrasetter as heir of his brother Oliver, one of the four sons of Henry Sinclair of Brugh, having right by udal law to a fourth part of certain lands in Shetland, and also papers relating to the offices of lawrightmen and ranselmen in Shetland in the eighteenth and nineteenth centuries.

Also in this group of miscellaneous collections are the records of the Board of Trustees for Fisheries, Manufactures and Improvements in Scotland (NG), established by act of parliament in 1726. Entries in the board's minute books show the kind of help which it was able to give: in 1765 the distribution of lint seed was authorized in Shetland and £50 was granted to Lady Mitchell for having introduced linen manufacture there, and in 1768 a grant of £30 was made to 'the adventurers in the cod and ling fishing in Zetland'. The Highland Destitution Records (RH21) are concerned with relief work in the 1840s and 1850s throughout the Highlands and Islands. They include registers of relief work carried out in Shetland parishes between 1847 and 1850, which give the name of the head of the family relieved, his occupation, etc., and worksheets which repeat this information but add the number in the family and details of the stock it owned. Most information is to be gained, however, from the correspondence addressed to the Committee of Relief by their officer in Shetland, in which he reports on the state of the country, the diseases of grain crops and potatoes, and the public works which were being organised.

Lastly, I must draw attention to the collection of Register House plans which is being currently arranged: more than 10,000 plans have already been listed, thus opening up a new field for the study of historical geography and allied subjects. The plans fall into two groups: one consists of sheriff court plans of the nineteenth century relating to various public utilities including railways; the other is a more varied collection of plans, most of which were withdrawn from Court of Session processes on their re-arrangement in 1849, but with additions from departmental records and from private muniments and other sources. A few of the plans were drawn up in the early eighteenth century but most are dated between 1750 and 1850, the crucial period of change in Scottish agriculture.[13] They are largely topographical, but include some architectural, industrial and railway plans. The first volumes of a series of descriptive lists of the collection have now been produced in the Record Office and have been published.[14]

Two examples must suffice to illustrate the kind of material which this source makes available. An engraved map of about 1780 relating to fishings shows the draught of the north part of Northmavine from Uyea to Brebister (including the settlements of Uyea, Sandvoe, Flugarth, Isbister, Houll and others) with the landing places, the location of the fishermen's summer huts (called lodges) and the courses of the boats to the fishing grounds, while there is also an inset plan of Fethaland and Brebister (RHP685). The other plan shows the common or skattald of Fitful Head and adjacent 'rooms' in the parish of Dunrossness in 1818 (RHP4003), and it is the earliest Shetland plan for the division of a commonty held in the Register House. The division of skattald and run-rig in Shetland was permitted under an act of parliament of 1695 which laid down the procedure for dividing commonities in Scotland generally, although the skattald differed from commonties elsewhere in Scotland in three respects: its origin lay in the land system of udal law; it was closely integrated with the room-land system and the township; and it covered, in general, very large areas. In a period of subsistence agriculture the skattald was essential, since it provided not only pasturage but peat for fuel and turf and divots for building. But encroachments on this common land went on everywhere so that, with the changes which took place in agriculture in the second half of the eighteenth century, it became necessary to make clear the division of the lands among those landowners who shared the commonty. The procedure laid down by the act of 1695 was quite simple: an action had to be raised in the Court of Session in which the pursuer declared evidence for his claim to a share in the commonty—evidence which had to be documentary since no plea of custom or of common usage would stand in court. If the claim was allowed, the court appointed a commissioner who had power in turn to appoint necessary persons, such as a valuator and a surveyor, to draw up a plan of the commonty and work out a scheme of division based on the valuation of the heritors' lands. The process for the division of the skattald of Fitful Head,[15] which amounted in all to 1,365 acres, was raised by Robert Bruce of Symbister against Andrew Grierson of Quendale in 1815 and contains much information of local interest in the depositions made by witnesses as to past

SHETLAND HISTORY IN THE SCOTTISH RECORDS 135

uses of the commonty, including one by an eighty-year-old man who had been a tenant as early as 1772: also among the papers is the scheme of division finally settled on in 1826.

It should be remarked that the Directory of the Commonties[16] in the Record Office lists as many as 107 divisions of skattald and run-rig in Shetland. Actions were raised in eleven parishes, in the following numbers—Delting, 11; Dunrossness, 17; Fetlar, 9; Lerwick, 7; Nesting, 5; Northmavine, 5; Sandsting, 11; Tingwall, 11; Unst, 23; Walls and Sandness, 1; Yell, 7. The processes for these divisions constitute an important and barely-used source for the social and economic history of the islands' communities.

NOTES

1 Some of these groups are available in print, either as official publications or in editions printed by learned societies.
2 Letters in brackets are Scottish Record Office class references.
3 I.e. Stonehaven in Kincardineshire.
4 *Acts of the Lords of Council in Civil Causes, 1478–95, 1496–1501* and *Acts of the Lords of Council in Public Affairs, 1501–1554* (both published by the H.M.S.O.); *Acta Dominorum Concilii, 1501–1503* (published by the Stair Society).
5 Bruce *v.* Smith and others (EP86/July 1890).
6 With the establishment of a local archives office and the appointment of a professional archivist, many of the locally held collections of manuscripts referred to in this lecture have since been deposited in the archives in Lerwick; also more collections have been surveyed, e.g. the papers of Hay & Company of Lerwick (*Editor's note*).
7 R. Pitcairn (ed.), *Criminal Trials in Scotland, 1488–1624* (Edinburgh, 1833).
8 Stair A. Gillon (ed.), *Selected Justiciary Cases, 1624–1650* (Stair Society, 1953).
9 W. G. Scott-Moncrieff (ed.), *Proceedings of the Justiciary Court, 1661–1678* (Edinburgh, 1905).
10 This consists of a series of Acts and Decreets and has been printed by the Stair Society.
11 G. Donaldson (ed.), *The Court Book of Shetland, 1602–1604* (Scot. Record Soc. 1954); R. S. Barclay (ed.), *The Court Book of Orkney and Shetland, 1612–1613* (Kirkwall, 1962) and *The Court Book of Orkney and Shetland, 1614–1615* (Scot. Hist. Soc., 1967).
12 'Umboth' or 'ombod' in Norn means the vicar's tithe; that is the smaller teind, not the corn teind.
13 After 1850 the Ordnance Survey becomes the main source of information.
14 I. H. Adams, *Descriptive List of Plans in the Scottish Record Office* (H.M.S.O., 1966), i.
15 Bruce *v.* Grierson (EP11/7/1826).
16 I. J. Adams, 'A Directory of Former Commonties in Scotland', appendix to 'Division of Commonty in Scotland', unpublished Ph.D. thesis, University of Edinburgh, 1967.

CHAPTER X

The Discovery of Shetland from 'The Pirate' to the Tourist Board

JOHN M. SIMPSON*

BY THE 'discovery of Shetland' I do not mean to suggest that in Sir Walter Scott's time or earlier Shetland was in any sense undiscovered. But, as a visitor to Shetland myself, I want to show how earlier visitors discovered the islands for themselves, and which of their discoveries each regarded as most important. I have not attempted a full survey of the development of tourism in Shetland which would, I believe, be a large undertaking. It is with the various individual visitors that I am most concerned; and some of them were very far from being tourists in the normal sense of the word.

Many visitors must be omitted. Other papers delivered to this conference refer to the fishermen, from many lands, who came here over the centuries. The impact of their coming, particularly in the years just before 1914, on Lerwick and even more on Baltasound, must have been very considerable. I think especially of the Swedes at Baltasound, with their own chapel and their pastor, and their purchases of sweeties, in particular of conversation lozenges.[1] The brave Norwegians who came during the Second World War appear in another paper. Some German prisoners found their way here too, of course. And in that war, as in earlier ones, there were the British forces stationed in the islands. The soldiers who guarded Shetland against Hitler, just like those who came in Napoleon's day, settled in rather well. For men who did not choose to come, and who frequently came from backgrounds very different from Shetland, they seem often to have been very happy. In 1814 Scott noted that the officers of the veteran regiment who garrisoned Fort Charlotte enjoyed their life in Lerwick: the general lack of ostentation there meant that they could keep up appearances on a pay that would have been inadequate elsewhere.[2] In Andrew Cluness's account of the good relations between Shetlanders and servicemen in the last war, there is the sort of tribute rarely accorded to soldiers stationed far from home.[3] One large group of 'visitors by accident', as it were, was constituted by those whose ships were wrecked on the shores of the islands. Perhaps the most celebrated modern wreck of this sort was the German ship *Lessing* which foundered off Fair Isle in 1868. The four hundred and fifty emigrants on board, as well as the crew, were all rescued and cared for by the islanders.[4]

In turning to individual visitors, I must omit the eighteenth-century travellers in Shetland, but certainly not because they are wholly unimportant. An example of their interests can be found in the Rev. George Low, an Angus man: he was a keen naturalist and antiquary, tutor to a Stromness family and, later, parish minister of Birsay and Harray. He visited Shetland from his Orkney base in 1774, and left an account of his trip which was not fully published till 1879.[5] This contains a drawing of the Broch of Mousa—'the greatest antique curiosity in these isles', as he called it—of which he also gave a careful description.

For Shetland as for many other places, the starting point for a discussion of modern travel and tourism is Sir Walter Scott. Scott could well be called the first tourist. If he went somewhere and later used the scenery of that place as the backdrop to one of his novels, then the scenery there became suffused for his readers with the same romance and drama as the novels, and the readers wanted to go and see it for themselves. Scott visited Orkney and Shetland about 1814, and used his idea of the islands as they had been about the year 1700 as the setting for *The Pirate*, published in 1821. From 29 July 1814 Scott was for six weeks a guest of the Commissioners of the Northern Lights on board their yacht. The main purpose of their trip round Scotland was an inspection of their lighthouses, but for Scott the occasion was a pleasant jaunt, occupying his mind during an anxious time until it could be seen if his recently published first novel, *Waverley*, was to be a commercial and critical success.[6] Its success was swift and great, and Scott embarked on his series of Waverley novels, exploiting Scotland's most glamorous scenes and epochs. *The Pirate* was the fourteenth of these. Like others, it inspired stage plays, again helping to publicise Shetland and its scenery and customs. Scott's knowledge of Shetland had been gathered during only six days, and that visit preceded his novel by seven years. But his keen eye for customs and scenery alike, his abiding interest in the structure of society wherever he went, and the diary that he kept during his visit, all helped him to fill *The Pirate* with circumstantial details of Shetland life. Both his diary and his novel betray some of the misapprehensions to which visitors anywhere are prone. His hosts were the lairds, and it was therefore unlikely that he would perceive how far the sufferings of ordinary Shetlanders were the result of the landlord system that had evolved. But he admitted in his diary that 'I cannot get a distinct account of the nature of the land rights.'[7] And while Scott saw the paternalist landlord as crucial to the type of society he himself most admired, he never made the mistake in Shetland or elsewhere of supposing that landlords were either all-wise or always virtuous. Of Shetland conditions he wrote perceptively: 'the proprietors are already upon the alert, studying the means of gradual improvement, and no humane person would wish them to drive it on too rapidly, to the distress and perhaps destruction of the numerous tenants who have been bred under a different system.'[8]

Recently, critics have been busy raising again the stock of Scott as a novelist. *The Pirate* has not usually been much used in this enterprise. Ever since its publication, the very feature that brings it into this paper, namely its social and topographical detail, has been held against it. The *Gentleman's Magazine* in 1821 grumbled that 'it partakes more of the nature of an essay on the topography of the island of Zetland and the manners and customs of the inhabitants' than of a novel.[9] The *Scotsman* thought that some boring characters had been thrust into the novel simply in order to illustrate facets of the 'nationality' of the Shetlanders ('nationality' being a word that Shetlanders themselves might well relish in this context).[10] Agnes Mure Mackenzie revived the old libel on the novel in 1932 by writing 'It is a good guide book, but pure tushery as fiction.'[11] Let me merely say here that there seems to me much more than this to *The Pirate* as a novel. While friends of Shetland will read it, those seeking a good story ought to too, for the principal characters should hold the interest of all readers. I mention only the Troil sisters, and Clement Cleveland the pirate (modelled remotely on John Gow who had been executed in 1725), and the great Norna of the Fitful Head, the 'Reimkennar'. As far as Norna is concerned, we know that in Shetland as elsewhere women were in the past sometimes credited by themselves and by others with magical powers, including control over the wind. Norna, as Scott drew her, was such a woman. He clearly wished us to see her as basically a self-deluded, and hence in one sense a pitiable, creature. But—and here he is surely in tune with Shetland folklore—he knew that his readers would rightly give no thanks to an artist who dealt with the supernatural and yet sought to provide a rational and debunking explanation for every last detail. As he says in his introduction to *The Pirate*: '... the professed explanation of a tale, where appearances or incidents of a supernatural character are explained on natural causes, has often, in the winding up of the story, a degree of improbability almost equal to an absolute goblin tale.'[12] Hence he leaves hanging over his Norna an atmosphere of something not quite canny.

If *The Pirate* is some way below Scott's best novels, it still shows a great writer dealing with a worthy subject.[13] Let William Hazlitt in the *London Magazine* sum the matter up:[14]

> Of the execution of these volumes we need hardly speak. It is inferior, but it is only inferior to some of his former works. Whatever he touches, we see the hand of a master. He has only to describe action, thoughts, scenes, and they everywhere speak, breathe, and live. It matters not whether it be a calm sea-shore, a mountain tempest, a drunken brawl, the 'Cathedral's choir and gloom', the Sybil's watchtower, or the smuggler's cave, the things are immediately there that we should see, hear, and feel. He is Nature's Secretary. He neither adds to, nor takes away from her book; and that makes him what he is, the most popular writer living.

The illustrations for the splendid Abbotsford edition of Scott's novels provide a pictorial counterpart of the romantic image of Shetland that Scott created in words. Some of the illustrations concentrated more on figures than on landscape. The moonlight meeting of Brenda Troil with the hero, Mordaunt Mertoun, for instance, was depicted but the scenery in it was clearly not unique to Shetland, and could well be described as a rocky coast almost anywhere during the Romantic Movement. The famous Cradle of Noss is shown complete with little figures climbing for seafowl, amid weather so bad as to make the enterprise rather unlikely. This view of the Cradle by William Dickes, which goes all out for dramatic effect, may reasonably be compared with the sober and factual drawing in a book by Dr Robert Cowie a quarter-century later,[15] to which later reference will be made. Some of the best illustrations in the Abbotsford edition are by William Collins, R.A., an Englishman who was specially commissioned by the publisher Cadell to go to Shetland in 1842. He was accompanied by his son, later to be his biographer but better known for his novels, since he was the William

Wilkie Collins of *The Woman in White*.[16] This artist traversed Shetland by pony, and in the picture 'Triptolemus Yellowley and party depart for Burgh Westra' shows characters in the novel similarly travelling on their ponies. They are actually seen passing a Shetland corn-mill of which Triptolemus, an agricultural improver, is scornful: '. . . it's just one degree better than a hand-quern—it has neither wheel nor trindle—neither cog nor happer'.[17] William Collins was greatly taken with Sumburgh Head, and in another drawing makes it the setting for the rescue after a shipwreck of the pirate Cleveland by the hero Mordaunt Mertoun.

Why has *The Pirate* not prompted a greater flood of imaginative writing or created a greater tourist boom in the Northern Isles than it has? Neither any supposed demerits of the book nor, I believe, any other simple or single explanation will help us altogether. The relative inaccessibility of Shetland, as compared with, say, Loch Lomond or the Trossachs is one obvious point. I will suggest also a more intangible but perhaps quite an important consideration. For two centuries in Britain the Celtic twilight has had a great vogue. With the Western Isles we may, if we choose, associate an atmosphere of charming melancholy and of wistful mourning over dead loves and battles long ago. This is a tawdry caricature of the spirit of the inhabitants of the Western Isles but it is one that has stirred many people's imaginations. Fewer people seem enamoured of the courage and the laconic toughness of the inhabitants of the Northern Isles from Norse-times onwards.[18]

Among the long-standing reasons for visiting Shetland has been the study of its rocks and plants, its bird and animal life. I must omit the pioneer scholars of Shetland flora and fauna, but there is an excellent short account of them readily available.[19] The pioneer geologists are very interesting too, and the first notable one of these was Robert Jameson. Jameson, a Leith man with Shetland forebears, became professor of Natural History at Edinburgh University in 1804, in his thirtieth year. Ten years before this, he had spent three months in diligent scientific work in Shetland. *An Outline of Mineralogy of the Shetland Islands and of the Island of Arran* was his first major work and was published in 1798. Jameson was an influential teacher, but not because of any showy gifts in lecturing: he was, said a pupil, 'plain, practical, not to say prosaic, but accurate, painstaking, and diligent as an observer . . . he so rarely ventures on figures of speech that the one or two metaphors in which during the whole session he indulged were well known, and waited for, and when produced were welcomed with annual rounds of applause.'[20] His lectures had the distinction of boring Charles Darwin among others: his great influence stemmed from the period he spent studying with Abraham Gottlob Werner in Freiburg, a brilliant but, in some ways, a profoundly mistaken geologist.[21] For many years Jameson used the weight of his prestige to advance Werner's theories, and the members of his school were particularly associated with Shetland; hence so were the Wernerian theories.

The Rev. John Fleming was a West Lothian man, an Edinburgh graduate, and an associate of Jameson's.[22] It was Sir John Sinclair of Ulbster who commissioned Fleming to survey the minerals of the Northern Isles, which resulted in 'The Economical Mineralogy of the Orkney and Zetland Islands' published some years later as part of John Shirreff's *General View of the Agriculture of the Shetland Islands*.[23] Among Fleming's other Shetland studies was a paper on the narwhal or sea unicorn.[24]

But Fleming's Shetland visit yielded him more than simply publications. He had been far-sighted enough to get from Sir John Sinclair introductions to the ministers of Shetland. When the parish of Bressay fell vacant, the patron—Thomas, Lord Dundas—failed to exercise his right to present a new minister, which then passed to the members of Lerwick presbytery. In 1808 they unanimously nominated their new friend, the Rev. John Fleming, at a time when, by then too late, Dundas decided that he wanted to present someone else. Fleming refused to budge 'on the ground', says his biographer, 'that it would be uncourteous both to the Presbytery and the people'. But, we are told, 'the patron seemed to be won by the manly frankness and decision of the young minister. He became his firm friend, and was ever afterwards ready to promote his interests'.[25] And so it seems, for it was Lord Dundas who in 1810 presented Fleming to the parish of Flisk in Fife, a parish small enough to leave him ample time to study natural history.[26]

Also under Jameson's aegis was one of the best known of all visitors to Shetland, Samuel Hibbert, M.D. Hibbert dedicated his book *A Description of the Shetland Islands*, published in 1822, to the Wernerian Society of Edinburgh: and it was Jameson who convinced Hibbert of the importance of the latter's discovery of deposits of chromite, which led ultimately to the mining industry in Unst.[27] Hibbert's book was intended as a geological treatise, but he was persuaded to include material on the scenery, antiquities and superstitions of Shetland. With his book appearing just after *The*

Pirate, he was resigned to being seen 'as a mere foil to the greatest of all modern masters of description'.[28] In this he was too modest, for the non-geological portions of his book have been twice republished, most recently in 1931 in an edition containing a valuable sketch of Hibbert's life by Dr T. M. Y. Manson.[29] The illustrations in Hibbert's book, from his own drawings, are very attractive and include one of Shetland fishermen used in the Abbotsford edition of *The Pirate*. This was not Hibbert's only literary connection with Scott: he shared Scott's interest in the supernatural, and the novelist was to draw on some of his later work in that field.

A pleasant feature of natural history studies in Shetland is the way that the cairn of knowledge has been built up from rocks placed on it by visitor and by native alike. Of later geologists I have space to mention only Professor Heddle of St Andrews, a noted mineralogist,[30] and Dr Finlay, a son of Shetland, who among other discoveries found at the ness of Sound a fossil fish which was named after him.[31] Notable among native pioneers in the study of flora and fauna were the members of the remarkable Edmonston family.[32] I may mention here that it was at the Edmonstons' home of Buness in Unst that in 1817 the French scientist M. Biot conducted experiments with the pendulum. Biot was struck by the peace of the island. 'During the twenty-five years in which Europe was devouring herself', he wrote, 'the sound of a drum had not been heard in Unst, scarcely in Lerwick; during twenty-five years the door of the house I inhabited had remained open day and night.'[33]

In more recent times, ornithologists and other naturalists have become very frequent visitors. As James M. M. Fisher says in his 1952 study of *The Fulmar* (or the maley, as one should say in Shetland): 'A list of the early visitors to the Herma Ness area who made notes on the fulmars is, indeed, a list of some of the pioneers of British field ornithology.'[34] The natives have continued to make their contribution, and Fisher acknowledges the help given him by reports from his friend James W. Jamieson, for many years shepherd of Noss. Less than native to Shetland, but surely more than mere visitors, are L. S. V. and Ursula Venables. They spent eight years in Shetland in compiling material for their book *Birds and Mammals of Shetland*. They had a cottage in another Noss, the township near Loch Spiggie on the western seaboard, and Mrs Venables has written on their life there in *Tempestuous Eden* (1952) and *Life in Shetland* (1956).

I've mentioned one clergyman coming from the south, and they were a breed of whom the Shetlanders were not always greatly enamoured. But there were some honourable exceptions. The evangelists James Haldane and William Innes made a thorough four-week tour of Shetland in 1799, reaching as far as Fair Isle, Foula and the Out Skerries. The Rev. John Mill of Dunrossness was impressed by these men, and unimpressed by the General Assembly's criticisms of them. He wrote of them: 'that such men would undertake such a vast circuit, and waste their persons and properties with an eye only to a shadow of vain glory, is ridiculous to suppose'.[35] Sir Walter Scott's host at Tingwall was the Rev. John Turnbull, whom Scott described as 'a Jedburgh man by birth, but a Zetlander by settlement and inclination'.[36] Tragically, Mr Turnbull's wife, son and daughter, and their maidservant, were drowned on a frozen loch in the winter of 1837–8.[37] A brief visit was paid to Shetland in 1822 by the Rev. Daniel McAllum, a Methodist minister who was sent to find out if his church could usefully appoint a missionary in Shetland. Like Scott he recorded the honour accorded to an islander who had died the brave death of falling from the crags; he listened to a sermon of Mr Turnbull of Tingwall, and was grudging in his praise; and he suffered as he voyaged home—'July 11th. Our course was through the trackless sea, out of sight of land—Sickness and qualmishness nearly all this day unfitted me for everything—It was existence and not life'.[38]

An important visitor came to Shetland, as well as to Orkney and to mainland Scotland, in 1839. He was Christian Ployen, Danish amtmand[39] and commandant in Faroe. The *Reminiscences* of Ployen's voyage were published in Copenhagen in 1840, and in Lerwick in translation in 1894.[40] As he says, 'I had become convinced that there is a great similarity of soil and climate in the two groups [of islands], though Shetland has reached a higher state of development. I therefore judged that it might be advantageous to visit Shetland, accompanied by two or three intelligent Faroese, and endeavour to become acquainted with such improvements as might be available here.'[41] His account of Shetland, especially of the fishing industry, shows how good he himself was at learning improvements, and I think we know what excellent improvers the Faroese people have remained.

Another visitor to Shetland was the distinguished Faroese scholar Jakob Jakobsen, cand. mag. of the University of Copenhagen and researching in Shetland in 1893–95 for his doctorate.[42] He studied the place-names and the Norse language of Shetland, the Norn. Ultimately his books about Shetland appeared both in Danish and in English, his great work on Shetland being, in its English version, the *Etymological Dictionary of the Norn Language in Shetland*, published in two volumes in 1928 and 1932.[43] In his preface to this book, he scrupulously lists his informants, including, in Foula, David Henry of Guttorm, descendant of William Henry who had recited a Norn ballad to the Rev. George Low in 1774. Jakobsen is a figure of major importance. At first sight he might seem to be simply and quietly engaged with the past. The Shetland Norn that he so carefully investigated had ceased to be a living language, and he was of course much concerned with the past literature and antiquities of his own country too. But his work has to be seen as a whole. He was associated, in his own country, with a very great scholarly achievement, the establishment of Faroese as a modern literary language. Faroese was, and is, of course, a very live language, but it was necessary to establish an agreed orthography. Orthographies were hammered out by Venceslaus Hammershaimb and by Jakobsen, who offered different systems. It was Hammershaimb's that was adopted, but Jakobsen's part in the movement was a very important one too. Shetlanders are right to venerate him: perhaps they will never again have their own separate language, but they do well to see Jakobsen as a symbol of the abiding place of the Shetlanders with the Faroese and the others in the Scandinavian cousinhood. The advance of the Faroese language and Faroese material progress can't be wholly coincidental happenings. No small land today, nor perhaps any big one, can prosper while lacking cultural self-respect and pride in its own traditions.

From the mid-nineteenth century onwards have appeared a number of publications of the sort that visitors, as well as sometimes Shetlanders themselves, would find useful. In and after the 1860s there were various editions of reference books like the *Zetland Directory and Guide, with Road Map* from W. R. Duncan of Aberdeen, and the publications of W. Peace and Son of Kirkwall, such as their *Orkney and Shetland Almanac and County Directory* and their *Handbook to the Shetland Islands*. At least four editions over a twenty-five year period was the achievement of Dr Robert Cowie's *Shetland: Descriptive and Historical*, which first appeared in 1871. Mention has already been made of the picture of the Cradle of Noss in this two-part book, the second part being a useful guide book. Even the most selective booklist on Shetland ought to include John R. Tudor's *The Orkneys and Shetland; their Past and Present*

State, published in London in 1883. Tudor got specialists to deal with the natural history, and wrote about a myriad of other topics himself.[44] He was an indefatigable and resourceful traveller throughout the islands: the drawings in his book are neutral and factual, for example one of rock formations seen from Hillswick Ness, and present a contrast to the romantic pictures in books published earlier in the century.

More guide books about Shetland are largely what one might expect. Nelson's *Thorough Guide to Orkney and Shetland*, for instance, published in 1908, did not belie its name. But the *Guide to Shetland* published by T. & J. Manson of Lerwick in 1932, and republished several times up till 1942, was something rather special. Apart from specialist sections on natural history and antiquities, and a list of relevant books, it is notable for its attempt to restore placenames to an etymologically-correct form. As the *Guide* trenchantly puts it: 'The official and therefore prevalent spellings of several Shetland place-names err for many reasons, but principally, it seems, on account of mistaken interpretation on the part of lairds, ministers, officials and others.'

From the mid-nineteenth century too, improved sea communications with mainland Scotland made feasible the growth of tourism. Here, clearly, I draw my material from Professor Gordon Donaldson's *Northwards by Sea*. A regular summer steamship service to Lerwick began in 1836, and in 1838 the Aberdeen, Leith and Clyde Shipping Company (later the North of Scotland line) obtained a government contract to convey mails to Shetland once a week in summer—an early passenger from Lerwick to Aberdeen on this run being Christian Ployen. An additional weekly sailing in summer was begun in 1866, and in 1881 a third weekly summer run to Scalloway and the minor ports amid the tricky waters of the west side of Shetland. Before the First World War there were as many as five sailings a week. In 1937, one hundred and one years after the steamship, an air service came to Shetland: but, even in face of this competition and of other difficulties, it is notable that passenger-ship runs have continued thrice weekly.

Some of the North of Scotland line's most interesting ships should be mentioned. The first *St Magnus*, supposedly designed as a blockade runner during the American Civil War, ran speedily between Leith and Lerwick from 1867 till 1901. The first *Earl of Zetland* was used on runs within Shetland from 1877 till 1946.[45] The first *St Rognvald* was used, starting in 1886, for Norwegian cruises, and was given a promenade deck for this purpose. The first *St Sunniva*, named after an Irish princess who went to Norway, cruised to Norway from 1887 onwards: modified in 1908, she ran regularly from Leith to Lerwick till she broke up on Mousa in 1930.[46]

The North of Scotland line were pioneers of Scandinavian cruises: these began in 1886 but it was only from the 1890s that there were tours among the Shetland Islands themselves, tours which have now lapsed. 'The weather was the unpredictable factor', Professor Donaldson says ominously.[47] But the North of Scotland line had meanwhile developed another type of holiday service with sailings on a regular route combined with a stay at a hotel: this side of their enterprise began with the erection of their own hotel at Hillswick, first advertised in 1902.

Another intriguing hotel of the same period was at Cloosta, a fairly remote township in the parish of Sandsting and Aithsting. The design was commissioned in 1895 from Robert Lorimer, then a rather new Scots architect but later a rather famous one. At some time between 1908 and the First World War, the hotel was burned down. It seems to have been quite a grand place, catering for those who could pay high rates in order to enjoy their fishing, and it is said that, on occasion, a hundred people would sit down to dinner there.

Tourism today is a tricky subject to discuss, but perhaps everyone will agree that there is room for advance in Shetland. I expect the Shetlanders will advance by themselves as they always have done: but one hopes that in future such self-help will be supplemented by adequate government assistance. In the fourth century B.C., Xenophon pointed out the value to Athens of the tourist trade and recommended that hotels be built by the state from public funds. Now British pragmatism often needs more time than Xenophon has given us so far to chew over such a radical idea. It is therefore particularly good to see the building of the new Lerwick Hotel and to learn that the Highlands and Islands Development Board has backed it.

Tourism is often economically vital for a community, but while the local people's interest in tourists has to be sustained and businesslike, the average tourist has perhaps only the vaguest interest in the people among whom he stays so briefly. The best sort of visitor, on the other hand, comes to see and maybe to enter a little into the whole life of a living community. Such a visitor was Roland Svensen, whose beautiful book on St Kilda, Foula, Fair Isle and the Out Skerries was published in English in 1955 with the title *Lonely Isles*. Svensen warns, in connection with the Out Skerries, that it is sometimes easier for a community to preserve a simple and sound life when the tourists leave it alone.[48] Of his island communities he says: 'Deep down there is a burning desire to keep and care for such places for coming generations',[49] and this is a feeling that he himself clearly shares. Another visitor, quite different, was Hugh MacDiarmid who lived with his wife Valda in Whalsay from 1933 to 1942. These nine years gave him more time to sense the people and his surroundings than those to whom the word visitor is usually applied. But as early as 1934, in his essay on 'Life in the Shetland Islands', he wrote well, I believe, on Shetland scenery and 'the treasures and rich lessons of a certain asceticism [that] the Shetlanders provide'.[50] It would be presumptuous for me to say whether he writes well on the Shetlanders, and I fear some of his views may have been distasteful to them. But in showing them to be moulded by their centuries of privation he strikes the same note as does Andrew Cluness, and he writes very impressively of the Shetlanders' 'quiet puissance of character which is apt to seem incredible to the outsider discerning enough to catch a glimpse of it'.

NOTES

* The author wishes to thank four Shetlanders for their help to him in preparing his paper: Miss Laurenson, Mrs Sinclair, Professor Donaldson and Dr Manson.
1 Charles Sandison, *Unst: My Island Home and Its Story* (Lerwick, 1968), 65.
2 'It was singular to hear natives of merry England herself regretting their approaching departure from the melancholy isles of Ultima Thule.' (Sir Walter Scott, *Waverley Novels*, vi, 319. References to Scott's novels are to the Abbotsford Edition published by Robert Cadell in 1842–7).
3 E.g. 'The Green Howards were universally liked': Andrew T. Cluness, *The Shetland Isles* (London, 1951), 87.
4 Roland Svensson, *Lonely Isles* (Stockholm, 1955), 99.
5 Rev. George Low, *A Tour Through the Islands of Orkney and Schetland* (Kirkwall, 1879).
6 J. G. Lockhart, *Memoirs of the Life of Sir Walter Scott, Bart.* (Edinburgh, 1837), iii, 129–178: R. Stevenson, 'Scott's Voyage in the Lighthouse Yacht', *Scribner's Magazine*, xiv (1893), 492–502.
7 J. G. Lockhart, *Memoirs of Scott*, iii, 145.
8 *Ibid.*, 154–5.
9 *Gentleman's Magazine*, xci (1821), pt. 2, 541–2, and suppl. (1822), 607–13. For a list of reviews of *The Pirate* see J. C. Corson, *A Bibliography of Sir Walter Scott* (Edinburgh, 1943), 245–7.
10 *Scotsman*, 29 Dec. 1821.
11 Agnes Mure Mackenzie, 'The Survival of Scott', *London Mercury*, xxv (1932), 270–8.
12 *Waverley Novels*, vi, 319.

13 An interesting recent discussion of *The Pirate* occurs in A. O. J. Cockshut, *The Achievement of Walter Scott* (London, 1969).
14 *London Magazine*, v (1822), 80–90, reprinted in P. P. Howe (ed.), *The Complete Works of William Hazlitt* (London, 1830–4), xix, 85–94.
15 Robert Cowie, *Shetland: Descriptive and Historical* (2nd edn., 1874), frontispiece.
16 William Wilkie Collins, *Memoirs of the Life of William Collins, with selections from his journals and correspondence* (London, 1848), ii, 209–225.
17 *Waverley Novels*, vi, 399.
18 In the discussion following the paper, Dr R. G. Popperwell claimed that it was Norway and the other Scandinavian countries, rather than Orkney and Shetland, that came to have a romantic Norse aura in the minds of nineteenth-century Britons.
19 L.S.V. and U. M. Venables, *Birds and Mammals of Shetland* (Edinburgh, 1955), ch. i.
20 J. Ritchie, 'A Double Centenary—two notable naturalists, Robert Jameson and Edward Forbes', *Proceedings of the Royal Society of Edinburgh*, Sect. B, lxvi, 29–58: Jessie M. Sweet, 'Robert Jameson and Shetland: a family history', *Scottish Genealogist*, xvi, 1–18.
21 C.L. and M. A. Fenton, *Giants of Geology* (New York, 1952), ch. iv.
22 Rev. J. Duns (ed.), *The Lithology of Edinburgh; by the late Rev. John Fleming ... with a Memoir* (Edinburgh, 1859).
23 John Shirreff, *General View of the Agriculture of the Shetland Isles* (Edinburgh, 1814), 105–135.
24 Rev. J. Fleming, 'Description of a small-headed Narwal, cast ashore in Zetland', *Memoirs of the Wernerian Natural History Society*, i (1811), 131–148.
25 Duns, *Lithology*, pp. vi–vii.
26 Fleming's subsequent career is interesting. Ultimately he became professor of Natural Science at New College, Edinburgh, in 1845 after having been a professor at Aberdeen University. Having joined the Free Church at the Disruption of 1843, he had moved in order to ensure that the trainee ministers of the new and young Church were equipped to defend the Christian faith from a standpoint of proper scientific knowledge.
27 See Sandison, *Unst*, 41–4, 90–6.
28 Samuel Hibbert, *A Description of the Shetland Islands* (Edinburgh, 1822), xiii.
29 The 1891 and 1931 republications of Hibbert were both by T. and J. Manson of Lerwick, and the latter contains a biographical sketch of Hibbert by Dr T. M. Y. Manson.
30 M. F. Heddle, *The Mineralogy of Scotland*, ed. J. G. Goodchild (Edinburgh, 1901).
31 Andrew T. Cluness, *Shetland Isles*, 253.
32 L.S.V. and U. M. Venables, *Birds and Mammals*, ch. i.
33 John R. Tudor, *The Orkneys and Shetland: Their Past and Present State* (London, 1883), 558–61.
34 *The Fulmar* (London, 1952), 157.
35 Rev. John Willcock, *A Shetland Minister of the Eighteenth Century, being passages in the life of the Rev. John Mill* (Kirkwall, 1897), 123.
36 Lockhart, *Memoirs of Scott*, iii, 158.
37 G. M. Nelson, *The Story of Tingwall Kirk* (Lerwick, 1965), 47–8.
38 Rev. Daniel McAllum, *Remains of the late D. McAllum ... with a memoir* (by J. Crowther) (London, 1829), 85–116. H. R. Bowes, 'The launching of Methodism in Shetland, 1822', *Proceedings of the Wesley Historical Society*, xxxviii (1971–2), 136–46, gives the background to McAllum's visit.
40 Christian Ployen, *Reminiscences of a Voyage to Shetland, Orkney and Scotland in ... 1839*, trans. by Catherine Spence (Lerwick, 1894; 2nd edn., 1896).
41 *Ibid.* (1896), xiii.

42 For Jakobsen see C. Matras, 'Jakob Jakobsen', *New Shetlander*, lxxiv, 13–16: T. M. Y. Manson, 'The personal impact of Jakobsen in Shetland and Orkney', *Fróð-skaparrit* (Annal. Societ. Scient. Faeroensis), 13 bók. (Tórshavn, 1964), 9–13.
43 Jakob Jakobsen, *An Etymological Dictionary of the Norn Language in Shetland* (London, 1928, 1932).
44 Some of the material he used here had previously been published in *The Field* under his pseudonym, 'Old Wick'.
45 In her last years this lady was honourably employed running illegal immigrants into Palestine.
46 G. Donaldson, *Northwards by Sea* (Edinburgh, 1966), 75–105.
47 *Ibid.*, 71.
48 Roland Svensson, *Lonely Isles*, 121.
49 *Ibid.*, 11.
50 Hugh MacDiarmid, 'Life in the Shetland Islands', first published in *At the Sign of the Thistle* (London, 1934), 148–163, repr. in *The Uncanny Scot* (London, 1968), 80–92; see also his *The Islands of Scotland* (London, 1939).

CHAPTER XI

Population and Depopulation

WILLIAM P. L. THOMSON

IN SHETLAND one is very much aware that demographic characteristics help to determine the kind of society which exists and limit the ways in which that society may develop. Shetland's population in 1969 was small and, as a result of a century of decline, had a predominantly elderly age structure. Economic development and the provision of satisfactory services depend so much on these characteristics that the measure of Shetland's success as a twentieth-century community is its ability to retain population. Population is not just a passive factor, the response to economic change, but also operates as an active factor affecting the ways in which economy and society may develop. As well as trying to establish the general trend of the population total, which before mid-eighteenth century is quite unusually obscure, this paper attempts to examine this inter-relationship of population and economy.

Population trends: increase

The table on page 151, of Shetland's population, shows a rapid increase in numbers in the late eighteenth and early nineteenth centuries, interrupted by a definite step during the period of the Napoleonic Wars. Following 1831 there was a marked deceleration in the rate of increase until the maximum population was reached in the census of 1861. Thereafter the decline was continuous for more than a century. Initially the decline was rapid, but levelled off at the end of the nineteenth century, only to slide disastrously in the period between the wars. Since 1945 the decline has continued, but at a diminished rate; and in 1966 the population stood at 17,245.

TABLE I
POPULATION TRENDS, C. 1600–1966

Date	Popln.	Date	Popln.
1600[1]	9,750–12,000	1861	31,670
1632[2]	12,000	1871	31,608
1700[3]	20,000	1881	29,705
1755[4]	15,210	1891	28,711
1784[5]	18,350	1901	28,166
1796[6]	20,186	1911	27,911
1801[7]	22,379	1921	25,520
1811	22,915	1931	21,420
1821	26,415	1941	No census
1831	29,392	1951	19,352
1841	30,558	1961	17,809
1851	31,078	1966	17,245

Notes:
[1] estimate by Donaldson
[2] estimate by Bruce
[3] Campbell
[4] Webster
[5] *Edinburgh Courant*
[6] *Old Statistical Account*
[7] Census returns hereafter

From 1801 onwards, the basic source of information is the census, held every ten years with the exception of 1941. A census was also held in 1966 when Shetland was a special study area, and so had a full census instead of the ten per cent sample census held in most parts of Britain. Although in the census period one is on reasonably sure ground, census information sometimes requires careful handling. Some writers believe that the 1801 census was up to five per cent deficient in England, although more accurate in Scotland. In Shetland such evidence as there is suggests that it was fairly accurate. In recent censuses allowance must be made for merchant navy men temporarily absent, herring workers temporarily present and the concentration of secondary school pupils in Lerwick.[1]

Before the censuses there exists evidence of three kinds: lists, calculations, and estimates. Before 1600 the population is almost completely unknown. The extent of the arable land always imposed certain limits, and evidence of place names and rentals suggest that the settlement pattern has always been of much the same extent, but the actual numbers within this pattern are unknown. Calculations based on the number of brochs and other structures have been attempted, but are subject to such an enormous margin of error that they may be discounted. Brøgger estimated a population of 20,000–22,000 for the early middle ages.[2] This too must be subject to a large margin of error and may be an over estimate.

A list of the numbers of communicants for each parish exists for about 1600, and from this Donaldson has calculated the population of each parish, and estimates the total population of the islands to be 10,000 to 12,000.[3] A similar list exists for the parish of Nesting in 1627 when the number of communicants was less than it had been in 1600.[4] Thus one might prefer a lower figure as an estimate of the population in the early seventeenth century. Bruce writing in 1784 stated that the population in 1632 was 'not two thirds of the present 20,000'.[5] Confidence in this estimate is shaken by the fact that he had somewhat overestimated the population of his own day, but nevertheless this agrees reasonably well with Donaldson's figure.

Campbell estimated a population of 20,000 in 1700, his information apparently based on Sir Robert Sibbald.[6] There is no reason to suppose that this estimate is particularly accurate. It would imply a rate of increase as great as from 1750 to 1850, and also a considerable decline in the early eighteenth century before Dr Alexander Webster's count of 1755, when the population was 15,210.[7] But a decline in the first half of the eighteenth century does seem possible. Edmondston,[8] without quoting sources, believed the population was greater in 1733 than it was in 1755. Between these dates the population of the parish of Aithsting and Sandsting fell from 987 to 911, and there was believed to have been a decline in the Unst[9] and Fetlar.[10]. Figures are also available for the parish of Northmavine where, in 1722, there were 1100 to 1200 'indigent people',[11] presumably the total population, but by Webster's count in 1755 that total had dropped to 1009. Such a decrease, it will be argued, could be the result of smallpox epidemics, and Northmavine was not an area which was badly affected compared to some other places.

A total is also available for the 1790s from the *Statistical Account*, like Webster's, based on information supplied by the parish ministers. These may sometimes represent incomplete counts—Shetlanders were apparently unwilling to be enumerated—but may, more often, over-estimate the resident population by including those who were temporarily absent in the navy or at sea. Other lists exist for 1802 and 1804, drawn up for the distribution of famine relief, and are useful as a check on the early censuses.

Records of births, deaths and marriages in the eighteenth century were ill-kept and fragmentary. They are very discouraging material for demographic study. A further source of information which might repay investigation are the skat rentals, particularly the rental of 1716–17. A striking feature of the rental is the very large number of ley farms in some parts of Shetland. There are few in the south of

Shetland, and considerable numbers in Whiteness, Weisdale and the west, but very large numbers indeed in Unst and in Fetlar where twenty-six per cent of the merks were ley. It is apparent from the rental that the term 'ley' does not imply that these crofts had been annexed to larger farms as grazing. Only rarely is a complete 'toun' in ley, and normally it is the case that there are one or more vacancies among the group of tenants.

One may also dispose of the suggestion that this land was not genuinely tenantless and that the ley lands were a device for the avoidance of the payment of skat, skat not being required from lands which were ley. The rental of 1716–17 permits the distinguishing of udal land, land feued and 'propertie land' which is earldom land let to tenants. The proportion of 'propertie land' which is ley is very high and on earldom land there can be no question of the estate conniving at skat avoidance.[12] In any case the economic circumstances of the early eighteenth century make wholesale skat avoidance improbable. One must conclude that considerable areas were genuinely without tenants.

There are three possible causes in the immediate past to which these ley lands may be attributed—the smallpox epidemic of 1700, the scarcity caused by disastrous harvests in the 1680s and the rapacious management of the earldom estates whereby exactions were so heavy that the land was left without tenants. But ley lands also existed at a rather earlier period. There is a rental of ley lands in 1650 and in 1664 Alexander Douglas of Spynie was unable to feu lands which were then 'still ley'.[13] The evidence of the rentals is elusive, but one can perhaps conclude that the amount of land under cultivation had been greater at some unspecified period in the past; that there was no great pressure of population on land in the seventeenth century; and that the evidence is consistent with a declining population at the beginning of the eighteenth century, a decline which we have seen is indicated by certain other meagre sources.

Following Webster's count of 1755, one is on much surer ground; and from then until 1841 the population was increasing rapidly. This increase is not, of course, peculiar to Shetland, and therefore one must be careful not to explain it entirely in isolated local terms. In recent years there has been a continuing debate about the causes of increasing population during this period. Some of the causes postulated, such as improved standards of housing or hospitals, are obviously inapplicable to Shetland where there would appear to be two possible explanations; firstly, that the increase was attributable to a declining death rate due to the conquest of smallpox and the provision of famine relief; secondly, that the increase was due to a rise in the birth rate as a response to the changing economy with the greatly increased scale of commercial fishing. Both of these possibilities will now be examined.

(A) *That the population increase was due to a falling death rate.*

Smallpox was not the only killer disease. Many deaths were caused by scarlet fever, whooping cough, typhus and particularly measles, but in the eighteenth century smallpox was the most important disease of the epidemic type. In urban Scotland the mortality was between one in four and one in six of those affected, but it appears to have been higher in Shetland, probably because of a lack of initial immunity. The remote islands such as Fair Isle and Foula were particularly vulnerable, as they were to other epidemical diseases. The method of treatment of smallpox presumably also contributed to the high mortality. Until 1770 the so-called 'hot method' was followed with plenty of gin, blankets and roaring fires.

Smallpox first appeared in Scotland in the seventeenth century but the first known outbreak in Shetland was in 1700 when infection was introduced, apparently by a young gentleman returning from the south. The smallpox 'seized upon many, old and young, and was so universal, that upon one Lord's Day there were ninety prayed for in the church in Lerwick'. This represents about one in seven of the town's population and Brand believed that one third of the population died in many districts.[14]

The smallpox then recurred in a twenty-year cycle. It returned in 1720. One in eight of Lerwick's population died; Fetlar was badly affected; and according to tradition the island of Foula was depopulated, leaving barely enough men to crew a boat. Many of the present Foula population are descended from a recolonisation which followed this disaster. The epidemic of 1740 was particularly severe in the north isles of Unst and Fetlar. In Unst some land went out of cultivation and fifteen years later crofters sometimes held several crofts. In Fetlar the churchyard was filled in every corner, and during the unusually severe winter corpses remained six weeks unburied.[15]

From 1740 to 1761, when it next flared up, smallpox seems to have smouldered on. In the 1761 outbreak inoculation was first practised but, as the charge for it was one to five guineas and the results uncertain, understandably only ten or twelve people were inoculated. But in the epidemic of 1769 several hundred were inoculated by a surgeon, and in the following years inoculation quickly gained acceptance.[16] There seems to have been little of that opposition to it, often religious, which was found in Central Scotland. Sometimes inoculation was performed by a qualified doctor, sometimes by ministers such as the Rev. W. Mitchell of Tingwall who inoculated 994 persons between 1774 and 1793 (a total representing a majority of his parishioners), sometimes by 'gentlemen' and sometimes by 'common peasants' such as the remarkable folk hero, Johnny Notions.[17] He was John Williamson of Hillswick and he practised what was basically the 'Suttonian method' developed in England in the 1760s: the matter he used he dried in peat reek, buried underground with camphor for seven or eight years and inserted by breaking the surface of the skin only; in this way he inoculated several thousand persons and is reputed to have had the remarkable record of never having lost a patient. Other practitioners were not always so successful. For example, when smallpox returned in 1791, there were twenty people who died of the disease in Aithsting and Sandsting and another ten who died of the effects of inoculation.[18] Mortality on this occasion was fairly light and McKeown and Record have argued that declining smallpox mortality may be due to an alteration in the character of the disease,[19] but it may also be significant that in Aithsting and Sandsting 80 per cent of the population had been inoculated. Further outbreaks occurred in 1802 and 1804 by which time inoculation was almost universal. Inoculation was replaced by vaccination in the early nineteenth century, with the use of cowpox instead of smallpox matter; but the absence of the disease led to neglect and considerable mortality when smallpox returned in 1830 for what was the last major outbreak. Smallpox deaths were reduced to only about one per year by the mid-nineteenth century.[20]

Given the unsatisfactory nature of statistics relating to mortality, it is difficult to estimate the effects of smallpox, but the following tables does give some indication of its severity in Shetland:

Date	Area	Approx. Mortality	Source
'frequently'	Yell	20%	OSA
1700	Many districts	33%	Brand[21]
1700	Shetland	25%	Edmondston[22]
1700	Fetlar	15%	Bruce of Urie[23]
1720	Shetland	25%	Edmondston
1720	Fetlar	13%	Bruce of Urie
1720	Lerwick	12%	Spence[24]

Date	Area	Approx. Mortality	Source
1740	Unst	33%	Ross[25]
1740	Fetlar	20%	Bruce of Urie
1740	Aithsting/Sandsting	12%	OSA
1761	Shetland	25%	Edmondston
1761	Fetlar	15%	Bruce of Urie
1791	Aithsting/Sandsting	2%	OSA

One might put only little reliance on the figures of Brand, often a source of dubious information, and of Edmondston who wrote at the beginning of the following century, but there is no particular reason to doubt that the remaining figures are substantially correct. When one considers the very heavy losses in Fetlar—15 per cent in 1700; 13 in 1720; 20 per cent in 1740; and 15 in 1761—all in a span of sixty-one years, it seems clear that smallpox alone was sufficient, not only to prevent an increase but to cause that actual decline in numbers which Bruce of Urie reported had actually taken place. With the decline in such smallpox mortality, a rapid increase of population is possible. The theory that the eighteenth-century population increase in England was the result of inoculation has recently been advanced by Razzel,[26] and his argument applies even more strongly in Shetland, because of the particularly high mortality followed by an unusually complete acceptance of inoculation. But recognition of this as a major factor does not necessarily imply that it was the only factor at work.

The other natural check on population expansion was famine, before the provision of famine relief in bad years. The climate of Shetland is cool, damp, windy and uncertain; it is a climate particularly unsuited to the growing of grain. There was never enough grain for Shetland to be self-sufficient even in a good year. Bad years, the result usually of a rainy summer or an early snowfall before the harvest was in, could bring hardship; and if this were combined with a failure of the fishing there was complete destitution. Before the introduction of the potato, food supply must have been very precarious. Potatoes were first grown about 1730 and, being more certain than corn in a cool climate, they quickly became a main item in the diet.

Possibly the worst years were from about 1630 to 1636 when there were disastrous harvests, still remembered 150 years later. Four thousand people were reputed to have perished in Orkney.[27] The years 1661 to 1663 were also years of great scarcity of fish, particularly herring; the corn was blasted; and there were heavy losses of animals.[28] The 1680s and 1690s appear to have been disastrous in Orkney;[29] evidence for these decades in Shetland is, however, lacking. From 1737 to 1743 there was again a period of great scarcity, particularly in 1740, a year in which there was a smallpox epidemic and which also had a long and particularly severe winter. Spring was late and the harvest poor, with scarcity that year and the next. The inhabitants of Northmavine were reduced to eating the flesh of whales[30] which, unlike the Faroese, they would never do in normal circumstances. Few died of absolute want, but such hardship must have contributed to mortality from other causes, particularly smallpox.

There were years of scarcity again around 1766,[31] but the worst period in the eighteenth century was from 1782 to 1786 when there was a series of unusually wet summers followed in most years by early snowfalls. In 1782 the snow came in October before the harvest was complete; 1783 was wet and the harvest poor; 1784 was again wet, the harvest again poor, with snow in November before it was completed in most districts. In 1785 the summer was again wet and the corn appears to have been largely uncut when snow came in November. In 1786 the spring and autumn were wet, but a mild spell in October and November allowed a tolerable crop to be harvested, the best for five years.

In contrast to earlier periods of scarcity, famine relief arrived on a considerable scale in these years. Government supplies arrived during the second bad harvest and were distributed in October and December 1783. Dundas sent meal to his tenants, forty tons of biscuits were distributed *gratis* by the government and, by the end of 1784, meal and potatoes were available at subsidised prices.[32] In 1785 charity subscriptions amounted to £308 16s in Hull and £1,049 8s 7d in Edinburgh. Further subscription lists were opened in York, Newcastle, Bristol, Leeds and other places, and the charity distributed through the clergy.[33]

During the Napoleonic Wars there was a general disruption of the economy with large numbers of men in the navy and traditional trade links broken. Wet summers caused destitution in 1802 and 1804 and there was an early snowfall in 1807.[34] Government relief was again provided and some believed the distress to be worse than 1784.[35] But the years following the Napoleonic Wars were fairly prosperous. Trade flourished and weather conditions appear to have been reasonably good until 1835 when there began a series of six bad harvests, accompanied by a failure of fishing and whaling and also by the financial distress caused by the bankruptcy of Hay & Ogilvie in which many people lost their savings. In 1836 the corn crop was sufficient for four months only, and the situation was about the same the following year. In March 1837 there were said to be forty-two families in the parish of Walls with insufficient food for the next six days and very few had sufficient for three months—and even that was still some way short of the next harvest. This situation was typical of all of Shetland, apart from one parish, unnamed, where the situation was said to be even worse.[36] Yet at this stage no relief had been distributed although money was being collected. The first relief to arrive was on 19 May 1837, a cargo from Aberdeen subscribers to a charitable list, and another from the Society of Friends. But charity relief was not only slow to arrive, it came through uncertain channels. The Aberdeen meal, which had been carried by the schooner *Ardent* to Fladdabister, was distributed on the basis that one half of the price had to be paid in cash and the other half in labour to the proprietor or minister, an improper distribution which led to acrimonious exchanges between the proprietors and Arthur Anderson's *Shetland Journal*.[37] Meal was similarly distributed in Nesting, and it is from this period that we can date Shetland's first roads, the meal roads.

Following this series of bad harvests, Shetland was affected by potato blight between 1846 and 1849. With the subdivision of crofts, the potato was playing a more and more important part in the economy; yet, because of the importance of fish in the diet, there was never that total reliance on the potato that there was in Ireland and the effects of the blight were consequently less severe. Since 1849 there have, of course, been hard times, but there has never been a period of comparable scarcity.

It remains to be seen now what was the effect of these periods of destitution on population patterns. They operated indirectly as a cause of emigration (and this will be discussed later) and directly by affecting the numbers of deaths, marriages and births. Apart perhaps from the 1630s, few individuals died of absolute want; yet the combination of hunger, a fish diet and the slow and inadequate relief, had a measurable effect. The following table indicates the record for the parish of Walls in the later eighteenth century:

WALLS, 1787–92[38]

	Baptisms	Marriages	Deaths	Harvest conditions etc.
1787	?	?	?	Good
1788	24	15	20	Very good
1789	29	10	19	Good

WALLS, 1787–92—*continued*

	Baptisms	Marriages	Deaths	Harvest conditions etc.
1790	48	12	26	Good
1791	44	17	23	Poor; mild smallpox
1792	28	6	38	Rather poor

These figures cover four good years and a period of minor scarcity in 1791–2, and show certain characteristic features. The number of baptisms is higher after successive good harvests, perhaps not only because the number of births has been greater, but also because there was a reduction in infant mortality before baptism, something which increased considerably in times of scarcity. There is an increase in the number of deaths after successive poor harvests, and also a decrease in the number of marriages. Mill in Dunrossness[39] notes this relationship between harvest returns and the number of marriages in the same period. At an earlier time of scarcity, we find there were no marriages in Aithsting and Sandsting parish in 1740 and none in Whiteness and Weisdale the following year.

(B) *That the population increase was due to a rising birth rate.*

Was the increase in population due to changes in the economy operating through an increase in the birth rate rather than a decreasing death rate? Following the decline of the German-controlled trade, fishing passed into the hands of the proprietors who were able to operate on a greatly increased scale. Although this process began in the early eighteenth century, the changes were not very common until about mid-century, that is at approximately the same date as the population graph begins its rapid upward trend. But that is not to say that they are necessarily related, although many contemporaries believed this to be the case and, indeed, some like Fea believed that the proprietors operated a deliberate population policy—increasing the numbers of tenants on their property with a view to increasing the numbers of fishermen.[40] Such an increase was particularly easy to accommodate in a system of 'rigga rendal' agriculture where land was reallocated at intervals, where an extra tenant meant only a slightly smaller share for everyone and brought a change that was relatively painless—although, when it was too frequently repeated, one which resulted in the very small crofts of the early nineteenth century. Outsets, where new hill land was broken in, could also be created, as in Aithsting and Sandsting:[41]

> There is one farm possessed by seven tenants and three outsets, which in 1742 had only two tenants. There are many others where the number of families is tripled. Formerly the landlords of this parish had little concern with the ling fishing.

But it is important to establish whether this subdivision was the cause of the population increase, or simply the effect. It is important, too, to see how changes in the economy might influence the population characteristics. Rather than affecting the death rate through increasing the total means of subsistence, changes in the economy were believed to have affected the birth rate through a lowering of the age of marriage. A *prima facie* case for this hypothesis can easily be developed. Crofts, although they had once been larger, can never have been sizable agricultural units. Before the introduction of the haaf fishing they would be able to support one family only, as they do at the present day, and this would lead to a postponement of marriage and perhaps to a significant number of people who never married. But with the expansion of commercial fishing, boys of eighteen or nineteen went to the summer fishing where they earned £16 to £28 Scots; they were men, and were perhaps encouraged to marry by the proprietor, anxious to bind a good fisherman with a family and debt.[42] (An early age of marriage is characteristic of Shetland fishing communities even today.) Marriage, too, was apparently almost universal in the 1790s, and in Yell a bachelor was 'a very rare phenomenon'.[43] It is interesting that the ministers of the *Statistical Account*, writing only a few years before Malthus's *Essay on Population*, are almost obsessed by the early marriages and the improvident breeding of the poor, to which they not unnaturally attributed the increasing population.

But were they right? Two explanations have been suggested; firstly, that the increase was reflected in a fall in the death rate due to inoculation and perhaps the introduction of famine relief; and, secondly, that the increase was due to an increase in the birth rate, due in turn to earlier marriages following the introduction of commercial fishing. Both theories fit so far as dates are concerned; as we have seen, smallpox inoculation was introduced in 1769, famine relief in 1783 and haaf fishing about the middle of the century. But such evidence as there is suggests that the two hypotheses are not equally true.

So far as can be determined, birth rates do not seem to have been particularly high in the 1790s. The following figures show approximate birth rates derived from the *Statistical Account*:

BIRTH RATES IN THE 1790s (PER 1000)

Delting	20	Bressay	34
Yell	24	Unst	39
Lerwick	23	Fair Isle	37
Sandsting	22		

POPULATION AND DEPOPULATION

These figures must be hedged around by so many cautions that they may be of little value. They are mostly based on baptisms rather than on births and, by not taking into account infant mortality before baptism, they underestimate the number of births. Calculations are in some cases based on quite short periods, drawn from church records which were fragmentary and ill-kept. The average of these figures is 28.4 per 1000 and this may be compared to 28.2 per 1000 in 1862, by which time the Registrar General's figures are available. Neither of these figures is particularly high. In north European countries in the eighteenth century the birth rate was usually in the low 30s, and in under-developed countries at the present day it is of the order of 40 per 1000. Thus the evidence tends to suggest that the birth rate was not high, and therefore it seems unlikely that it determined the increase in population.

But not only is there evidence to show that the birth rate was probably low, there is also some evidence to show that it was probably decreasing at the time of the population expansion, as in Delting:

DELTING, 1755–1789[44]

	No. of Baptisms	No. of Marriages	Baptisms per 1000	Marriages per 1000	Population (date)
1755–59	150	43	30	9	956 (1752)
1760–64	156	55	30	10	
1765–69	183	51	30	9	
1770–74	–	–			
1775–79	–	–			
1780–84	170	45	24	6	1417 (1785)
1785–89	154	46	20	6	1504 (1790)

These figures show a very definite fall in the apparent crude birth rate, which in the period 1780–84 may be a response to the extreme scarcity of these years. It could also be partly a secondary effect in a time when the population had already started to increase and when the structure of the community was such that a large proportion of the population was below marriageable age.

It seems clear that the population increase was due to a decline in the death rate rather than to an increase in the birth rate. Smallpox mortality alone seems to have been sufficient to prevent any increase in population and perhaps to cause an actual decrease. The birth rate does not appear to have been particularly high, and may actually have been dropping due to the pressure of the population on resources. If we accept this, it follows that the subdivision of crofts was simply a matter of population pressure, and not the result of any deliberate population policy on the part of the landlords.

Population trends: decrease

But if there is doubt about the causes of the population increase we have investigated, there can be no doubt about the causes of the eventual decline—emigration. An increasing volume of emigration slowed the rate of increase and after 1861 turned it into a decrease, with particular consequences for the population structure and birth and death rates in Shetland.

In the eighteenth century there was little emigration from Shetland on an organised basis. There was certainly emigration of individuals—such as John Harrower, the destitute Lerwick shopkeeper who left in December 1773, his capital consisting of a supply of stockings which he gradually sold to finance his journey. It is interesting that his first intention was to make his way to Holland but, failing to obtain a passage, he was eventually forced to become an indentured servant to Virginia.[45] There had always been foreign travel for the sons of gentlemen, not only to Shetland's trading partners but, for example, on Dutch ships to both the East and West Indies.[46] Shetlanders, too, had served the Hudson Bay Company prior to 1741.[47] But Shetland had little part in that epidemical fury of emigration which swept eighteenth-century Scotland, especially from 1773 to 1775. Poverty and hardship were such that many were willing to emigrate, but they lacked the means to transport themselves;[48] yet these years saw the first organised local emigration, of 280 persons from Caithness and Shetland, perhaps to North Carolina.[49] In the destitution period in the 1780s Nova Scotia agents were active and persuaded some to emigrate, but the scale was again limited; in the 1790s there had still been no organised emigration from some parishes such as Delting.[50]

If the response to destitution in the eighteenth century had been to stay and suffer rather than to emigrate, there was a quite different response in the nineteenth century. The reason for change was a growing contact with the outside world and a loosening of certain ties which bound its inhabitants to Shetland.

The first of these factors was naval service. This in Shetland is often equated with the press gang, but initially Shetlanders were keen to serve and were in much demand for their sea-going skills. Large numbers served in the Seven Years War; on the termination of those hostilities in 1763, some 9000 Shetlanders were paid off.[51] There were large numbers, too, in the American War of Independence, especially after the involvement of the maritime powers of Holland and France. But by far the largest numbers served in the Napoleonic Wars. In the early 1790s the quota of seamen asked of Shetland was one hundred but soon recruitment was on a much greater scale, largely this time as a result of the arbitrary activities of the press gang. Between 1793 and 1801, indeed, 1100 were enlisted in the navy and the number had grown to over 3000 by 1809.[52] Many of these seamen never returned to Shetland but perished, particularly in the West Indies. The scale of these operations is clearly seen in the table of Shetland's population (page 151), which in this same period is also affected by the fact that as many as 600 men went to the Greenland whaling.

A second factor, tending to loosen older ties, was the abandonment of fishing tenures on many estates. The arrangement by which the tenant was obliged to fish for the proprietor had developed in the early eighteenth century, and by the second half of that century was the normal arrangement. But in Unst, for example, many fishing tenures appear to have been abandoned between 1820 and 1830; and by the 1840s fishing tenures existed on only a few estates.

Yet emigration must be seen not entirely from the point of view of the impulse to leave Scotland. The attraction of the destination and the means of transport are also important. In the nineteenth century we have the development of English-speaking countries overseas, an important difference between the Shetland and Faroese situations; also the establishment of the first regular steamer service to mainland Scotland in 1832, and a fortnightly service by the summer of 1836.

These factors create a pre-emigration situation, so that when destitution returned the response was rather to leave than to stay. Between 1815 and 1835 there was a period of prosperity, and during this time little emigration occurred. But in the hard years from 1835 to 1849, for the first time there was emigration on a very large scale—to an extent unknown in earlier famine periods. The effect of this can also be seen in the direction of the population graph. The Rev. George Clarke, the Methodist minister of Walls wrote of these years that

> I find it difficult to give you anything like a desciption of the deplorable state of affairs in these islands. A number of persons have within the last two months left our shores. Every vessel has taken more or less, and some have

been crowded. Men, women and children flying from starvation, some emigrating to America, others to places of which they know nothing.[53]

More would have left if they had had the means to do so, for emigrants are not usually the poorest and most helpless. But rather than America, it was probably the merchant navy which was the commonest destination. Many seamen, once abroad, drifted elsewhere never to be heard of again.[54] There had been quite large numbers of Shetlanders who became merchant seamen at earlier dates, for example in the scarcity period of the 1770s, but the 1830s is perhaps the start of the main 'merchant navy period'. An examination of the numbers gaining masters' and mates' certificates suggests the main flow began about 1835 and reached its maximum in the 1860s, although there were still 3000 Shetland seamen in the period between the two world wars.[55] By the late 1960s the number had been very much diminished.

But if those leaving in the 1830s were seldom heard of again, this was not true of those emigrating after the introduction of the penny post; news of others' success became one of the main stimuli to emigration. News from the new lands, the United States, Canada, Australia and New Zealand, introduced a climate of emigration fever. In a single issue of the *Shetland Advertiser* in 1863 we can find an advertisement by the Hudson Bay Company, announcing that labourers and sloopers were required, the pay £22 per annum plus keep, with at the end of a three-year engagement an option on a 25-acre site in the Red River Settlement in Canada; there is a letter from a successful emigrant to Quebec, giving news of other Shetlanders there; a long article, one of a series, on gold finds in Otago, New Zealand; an advertisement for four lads and a female servant, required in New Zealand; and, finally, a note that the fare from Lerwick to Aberdeen was 8s. steerage.

During the intercensal period 1861-71 there was a net loss through emigration of 3557 persons, and in the succeeding ten years a further loss of 4567.[56] These decades formed the period of greatest emigration, which declined thereafter because of the greater security of landholding in Shetland following the passing of the Crofters' Act, the relative prosperity during the herring fishing boom, and the curtailment of free passages to New Zealand. But Shetlanders were by then to be found in the American west, the Canadian prairies, Vancouver, Nova Scotia, Quebec, the goldfields of Victoria and Western Australia, and above all in New Zealand. New Zealand emigration agents 'stumped' through Shetland in 1874-75.[57] Again the emigrants tended to be from among the moderately prosperous: twenty families from the Melby estate received compensation for improvements to their holdings before emigration, and in Unst it was estimated that the emigrants were each taking with them between £30 and £200 each.

Emigration is selective and the effects of this can be seen in the numbers of males and females in the population. Whereas the numbers of males reached a maximum in the census of 1831 and thereafter remained very stable during the remainder of the nineteenth century, the female numbers follow a very different pattern; there was little emigration of single women until about 1870. For example, there had been a steady emigration from Foula since 1800, but by 1870 only one woman had left.[58] This process produced a very unbalanced sex ratio in most parts of Shetland, but from 1870 increasing numbers of women and girls went into domestic service, many in mainland Britain, some overseas. With the sex ratio in the local population as it was, and with the opposite situation existing in the colonies, Shetland girls may well have been more than interested to read in the *Shetland Advertiser* of the girl who had had six offers of marriage as soon as she had disembarked in New Zealand.

The population decline in the 1860s and 1870s is also partly due to clearance policy. This is a neglected aspect of Shetland's history, although the effects on the economy and on the population were considerable. The clearances were certainly less spectacular than in the Highlands, for few districts were thoroughly cleared; and there are few records of burning thatch or the enforced emigration of whole communities. Clearances tended to be piecemeal, with people initially displaced only quite short distances.

Nineteenth-century clearance policies did not create the first large farms, but they did introduce sheep as an important item in the economy. Previously there had been remarkably few sheep considering that 94 per cent of Shetland consists of rough hill land. Donaldson has calculated that the ratio of sheep to cattle in the early seventeenth century was only 2:1 in contrast to the current 34:1.[59] But it is interesting to see that the ratio of crofters giving evidence to the Napier Commission was exactly the same as Donaldson's: the large sheep farm was an alien creation.

As long as proprietors maintained their interest in fishing, it was to their benefit to maintain rather than disperse the population; but, as we have seen, fishing tenure was being abandoned in the first half of the nineteenth century. Land rents in Shetland were low and profits to the proprietor had come largely in the form of fishing activities, and when these were abandoned it was necessary to turn to another form of estate management. High prices for wool, before the advent of sizable imports from Australia, and increased prices for carcasses when communication was making their export possible, made sheep farming an attractive proposition.

There was already interest in improved farming at the beginning of the nineteenth century and some evidence of improvements in most parishes by the 1840s, but it was only from the 1860s that clearance policy got under way. There was thus only a short period before the process was largely halted by the passing of the Crofters' Act of 1886 which saved Shetland from certain further clearance. Certainly improvement was necessary. A typical croft might be about three acres in extent, the in-bye land lying runrig, undrained and exhausted by successive crops of bere. Beyond the hill dyke the skattald lay undivided and unregulated so that in 1814 it could be said that

> Landowners and tacksmen put as little value on a sheep as, in Great Britain, is put on a hare.[60]

Improvement was certainly necessary, but did agricultural improvement have to bring hardship, injustice and disposal of the population?

The process of clearance was not altogether straightforward, although a decrease in the number of proprietors in the first half of the nineteenth century made it easier. Hill land was undivided, not just in the sense that it was unfenced, but also because the boundaries of the various properties were not established. Any one proprietor could, however, force a division of the commonty, and land was then allocated on the basis of the number of merks held. In-bye land which was lying in run-rig and belonged to various proprietors could be similarly divided, and blocks of holdings could also be created by the process of excambion. All these preliminaries to improvement are common in Shetland in the first half of the century. It may be worth while to take one important example to show how the piecemeal clearance process might be worked and to see also, in detail, the effect on the population.

Tingwall, where bands of limestone create some of the most fertile farm land in Shetland, had seen some of the earliest agricultural experiments in Shetland. The Rev. John Turnbull for long managed a large and successful farm and, in 1809, had grown the first turnips in Shetland. By 1861, the 440-acre farm of Veensgarth had been created, including not only a large central section of the Tingwall valley but also all of the parallel and agriculturally less attractive valley of Dale.[61]

The Veensgarth property belonged to the Hay family who, owning property in Scalloway and throughout Tingwall, were the leading proprietors in the parish. Like most estates it was somewhat fragmented, but there was sufficient in their hands in the Veensgarth area to create a large block. The eventual farm was constituted by acquiring, by process of excambion, two merks at South Lea and two merks at Dale from the earldom estates, and the purchase of three merks at Fitch owned and occupied by a navy pensioner, Walter Halcrow. The farm came into existence through a series of well-defined stages. In 1804 Veensgarth itself was occupied by four tenants, and was indistinguishable from the other places it was to absorb; but before 1841 it had become a single farm—with 24 merks of valued land it was already quite large and it employed a farm labourer. The second stage had been accomplished before the first valuation roll was compiled in 1856, by which time the farm had been more than doubled in size to 50½ merks: it was now occupied by the proprietor himself and included the part of the adjacent farm of Uresland which he owned, and also Walster owned by George Hay, the son and eventual successor, but then occupied by his father, William Hay. The third stage was in 1861 when George, who had by then succeeded to the estate, incorporated into his holding Fraccafield, Dale, Fitch, South Lea, North Lea and Burra, producing a new farm of 4402 acres which was let to George Bruce, an Aberdeenshire farmer, for £314 per annum, almost exactly double the 1856 valuation. Initially Bruce cultivated 250 acres, but finger-and-toe disease in turnips led him to lay down most of the arable to grass. Holding the farm on a nineteen-year lease, he built substantial cattle courts, squared off fields, planted hawthorn hedges, drained meadow land and improved the hill pasture. His farm carried a flock of 600 blackface ewes and 600 Cheviots and was said to compare favourably with the farms of his native Aberdeenshire. On the termination of the lease, Bruce was reputed to have amassed not far short of £20,000, a figure which presumably includes compensation for improvements.[62]

Possibly there was no great hardship involved in the Veensgarth clearances. No family, except the Halcrows, the owners and occupiers of Fitch, had held the same crofts from 1804 to 1856; and, of the seventeen tenants who occupied the eventual farm, only three families remained on the same croft between 1841 and 1856. The population of the whole parish was a very unsettled one, and in other areas as well as this one the presumption that a croft usually remained in the same family for generations is incorrect. Yet the effect on population was still considerable, for the Veensgarth farm had once supported 21 families and about 120 people; and similar changes were repeated on other farms in the Tingwall valley and in Weisdale about the same date. To complete the story of Veensgarth, the farm was acquired by the Department of Agriculture in 1923 and divided to make holdings for service-men returning after the war. Nineteen holdings were created, about the same number as in the nineteenth century, and in this case the process of clearance was reversed.

It is possible to see the extent of clearance policy from the following table, and on this basis to estimate the overall effect on population:

AGRICULTURAL HOLDINGS BY SIZE, 1875 AND 1880 (IN ACRES)

Date	Under 50	50–99	100–1000	Over 1000	Total Holdings	Total Acres
1875	3765	64	9	1	3839	52256
1880	3529	66	6	3	3604	58357

This illustrates the kind of changes which were taking place on the very eve of the Crofters' Act. In these five years the number of holdings decreased by 235 and the big farms were tending to become bigger. Thirty per cent more land was in 1880 in holdings of over 50 acres. Note too the increase of 6101 acres in the total number of acres, which represents land which had been removed from the common grazings—one of the crofters' most frequent complaints to the Napier Commission in 1882–4. On the basis of the decreased number of crofts, it may be estimated that 1200 people had been displaced, a very large number within a five-year period.

Often those displaced were crowded on to poorer land when the better had been cleared and there are few examples of community emigration. When parts of the Garth estate were cleared in the south Mainland in 1874, the estate helped to arrange assisted passages to New Zealand. In Fair Isle, where a high birth rate had led to overcrowding there was also organised group-emigration. Some islanders had gone to Orkney in the 1830s; in March 1862 no fewer than 148 left to sail via Greenock to St John in New Brunswick, where they arrived in July.

The later pattern of emigration has been of a movement largely to central Scotland, with also fairly large numbers in the north-east: the cities of Aberdeen and Edinburgh are important attractions. Relatively few settle in the crofting counties, with which Shetland has difficult communications and few other contacts. Overseas the largest numbers continue to go to English-speaking countries, with Australia and New Zealand still the most important. There is hardly a Shetland family without close relatives in these countries. Canada and the United States are also frequently chosen, but the numbers going to southern Africa have been small. Small numbers are to be found too in many European countries, particularly Norway, mainly because Shetland girls marry seamen from these countries.

The volume of emigration until the late 1960s was much greater than the extent of immigration into Shetland, although from the time of the Earl Patrick immigrants have often had an effect disproportionate to their numbers. As immigration in the period before 1969 has already been dealt with by Professor Donaldson, it is sufficient to notice that its pattern has been quite different from that of emigration. Of those born outside Shetland, the largest numbers originated in the fishing communities along the Moray Firth coast with smaller numbers from central Scotland. This pattern is changing, and many of the newer immigrants belong to rather transitory professional groups. Again, links with the crofting counties are few, with the exception of Orkney. Of the total population in the later 1960s, 13 per cent had not been born in Shetland, a proportion slowly increasing, but still the lowest proportion of any British county except Orkney.

Population trends: variations within Shetland

So far we have been concerned only with trends for the total population in the islands, but within this general pattern there is a great deal of variation. The most exceptional locality is Lerwick. From small beginnings in the early sixteenth century, Lerwick grew in the látter part of the century to have a population of about 700 in 1700. In the seventeenth century the population apparently remained fairly steady, but at the beginning of the nineteenth century the town entered a remarkable period of growth. This increase, combined with a decline in the landward population, has resulted in a notable degree of urbanisation in Shetland. In 1800 one-twentieth of the population lived in the town, but in 1969 it contained over one-third of the total population of the islands. Its growth has been particularly connected

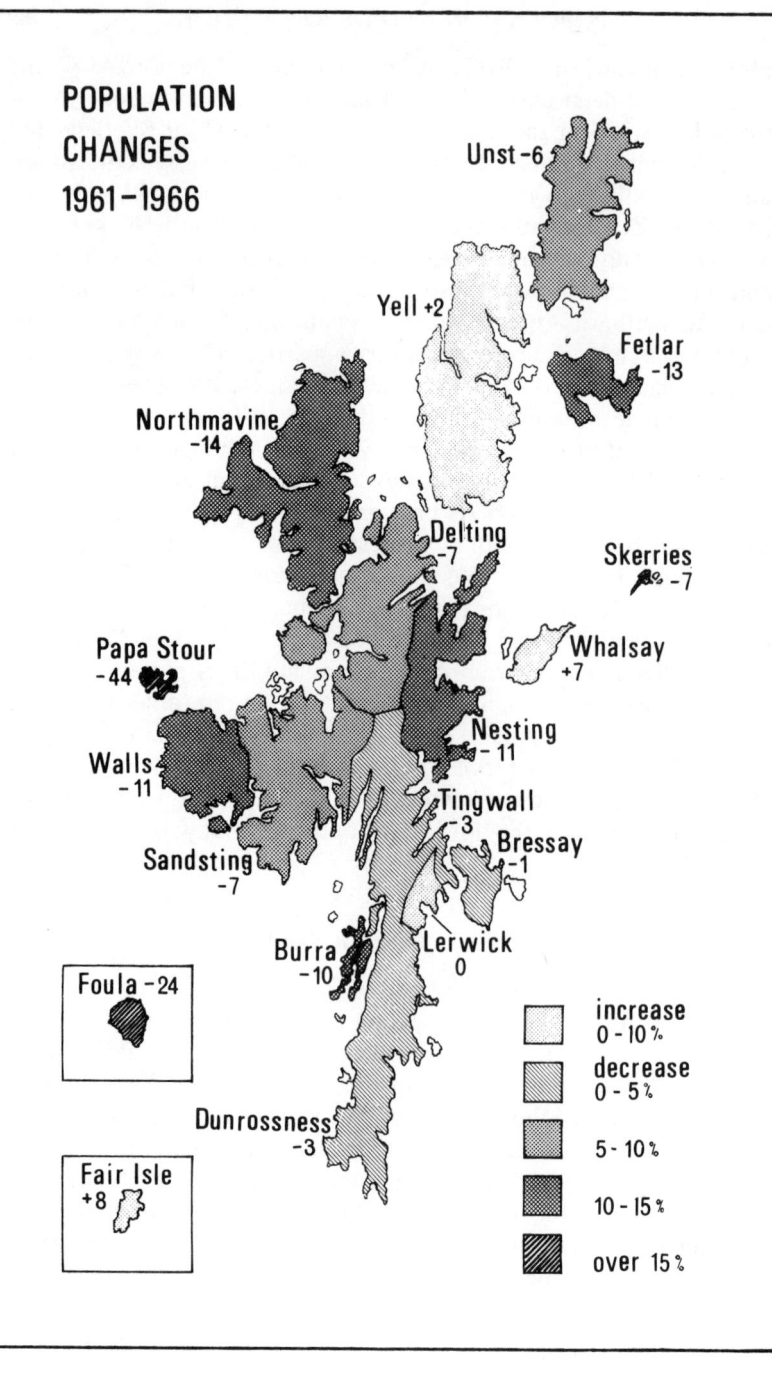

POPULATION CHANGES 1961–1966

- Unst −6
- Yell +2
- Fetlar −13
- Northmavine −14
- Delting −7
- Skerries −7
- Papa Stour −44
- Whalsay +7
- Walls −11
- Nesting −11
- Tingwall −3
- Bressay −1
- Sandsting −7
- Burra −10
- Lerwick 0
- Foula −24
- Dunrossness −3
- Fair Isle +8

Legend:
- increase 0–10%
- decrease 0–5%
- 5–10%
- 10–15%
- over 15%

1961 POPULATION AS % OF MAXIMUM

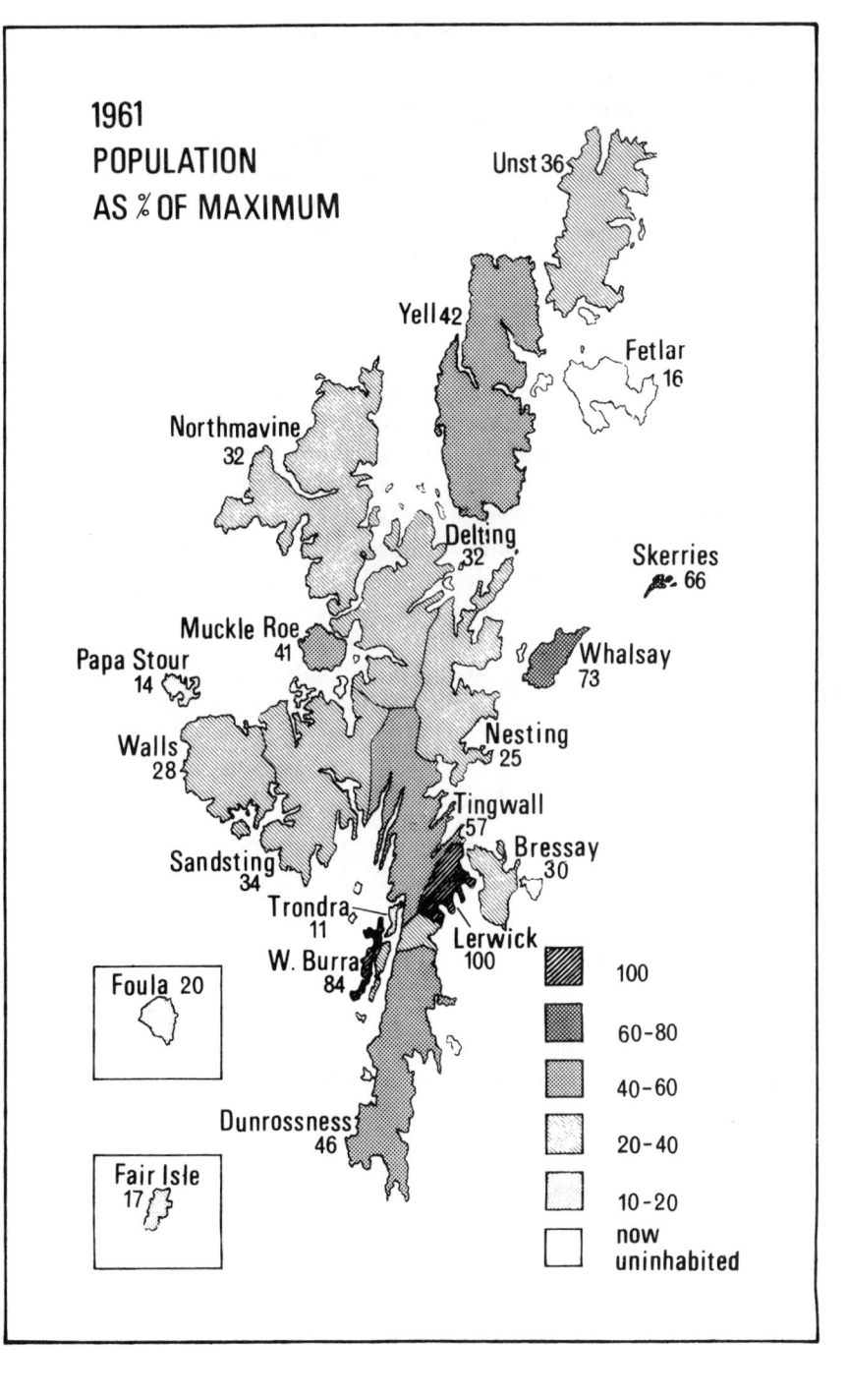

- Unst 36
- Yell 42
- Fetlar 16
- Northmavine 32
- Delting 32
- Skerries 66
- Muckle Roe 41
- Papa Stour 14
- Whalsay 73
- Walls 28
- Nesting 25
- Tingwall 57
- Sandsting 34
- Bressay 30
- Trondra 11
- W. Burra 84
- Lerwick 100
- Foula 20
- Dunrossness 46
- Fair Isle 17

Legend:
- 100
- 60–80
- 40–60
- 20–40
- 10–20
- now uninhabited

with the expansion of road transport, and the growth of service functions; at present its fishing fleet is much smaller and older than the fleets of Whalsay and Burra Isle. Further growth seems likely, and has only been prevented by housing difficulties, partly imposed by the peninsular site which the town occupies.

There is an important difference between agricultural and fishing communities. Even the best agricultural districts like Dunrossness and Tingwall (excluding Scalloway) retained in the later 1960s less than half their maximum nineteenth-century population. As croft sizes are small, an average of seven acres, and the drift from the land a general phenomenon, a continuing decline may be expected unless the population can be directed into other occupations. As service functions become concentrated more and more in Lerwick this is not easy, but the establishment of small knitwear and fish processing units in the 1960s have helped to retain the population in some areas. Meanwhile, fishing communities have been much more successful in retaining their population in that decade. Burra has retained 84 per cent of its maximum, Whalsay 73 per cent and even Skerries, one of the remotest communities, has retained 66 per cent. The contrast between Whalsay and Fetlar is a remarkable one. Fetlar is twice as large as Whalsay and much more fertile—the 'garden of Shetland'.

TABLE 2
POPULATION: WHALSEY AND FETLAR, 1793–1961

Date	Whalsey	Fetlar	Date	Whalsey	Fetlar
1793	500	796	1901	975	347
1841	628	761	1911	1042	279
1851	679	658	1921	921	224
1861	728	548	1931	897	217
1871	854	517	1941	–	–
1881	870	431	1951	859	161
1891	927	363	1961	764	127

Fishing was important there in the early nineteenth century, for it had one of Shetland's most important haaf stations and was a pioneer in the early days of the herring fishing. Yet, losing these fishing traditions and suffering disruption from clearance, it was the first district to suffer a population decline. Once the population was over 800, but in 1966 it had dropped to only 111 and in 1969 was even less. It illustrates the type of community which has reached that crisis point where economic measures are no longer sufficient to save the community. All the major recommendations of a report of only a few years ago have been implemented, an unusual outcome, yet the situation in Fetlar continued to deteriorate until 1969, and only the immigration of a number of marriageable individuals was likely to save the community. Whalsay was less important for fishing in the early nineteenth century and Hibbert,[63] who visited the islands, could describe it without mentioning fish—something which would be impossible today The change had already taken place by 1861, when Whalsay was the only area in Shetland with more men than women. Whalsay men neither emigrated nor joined the merchant navy on the same scale as men of other districts, preserving their fishing industry through hard times; on this was based their prosperity in the late 1960s. The population continued to rise until 1911, since when the decline has not been very great and more recently the population has been increasing sharply. The population structure is good, recruitment to fishing is high, and Whalsay in 1969 was among the most vigorous and successful communities in the Highlands and Islands.

The less favoured parts of Mainland have been much less fortunate. The population figures for the parish of Aithsting and Sandsting are typical of the west and north Mainland, similar to the pattern for the whole of Shetland but with all the main features exaggerated.

TABLE 3
POPULATION: AITHSTING AND SANDSTING, 1733–1966

Total Population				Age	Sex Differences in 1792	
					Male	Female
in 1733	987	in 1871	2806	0– 10	175	144
1755	911	1881	2902	11– 20	131	103
1775	1223	1891	2562	21– 30	100	143
1792	1285	1901	2396	31– 40	64	76
1801	1493	1911	2100	41– 50	46	55
1811	1617	1921	1871	51– 60	46	55
1821	1884	1931	1552	61– 70	46	54
1831	2194	1941	–	71– 80	11	15
1841	2478	1951	1225	81– 90	1	7
1851	2603	1961	957	91–100	0	4
1861	2670	1966	888			

By 1969 only 32 per cent of the maximum population remained, and the decline has been rapid, with a seven per cent drop between 1961 and 1966. Declining population has brought about changes in the population structure. Aithsting and Sandsting is the only parish from which an analysis of population can be made from data in the *Statistical Account*, which shows large numbers of children and comparatively few elderly. But although the population is now less than it was in the 1790s, the number of elderly has increased. In the 1790s the sexes were evenly balanced, a fact which supports the conclusion that there had been little emigration by that date. It is more difficult to draw conclusions about the number who were serving in the royal or merchant navy. The parish minister's enumeration in the 1790s would very likely have included the temporarily absent. By 1871 the population structure was very different, as illustrated by the neighbouring parish of Walls and Sandness. The main feature here is the great disproportion between the sexes. Men were generally leaving in their late teens, either emigrating or more often serving in the merchant navy and thus excluded from the census totals. The contrast with the present structure for the parish in 1966 is striking. Apart from the expected shrinkage there has been in population structure, the 1966 pattern shows the typical wasted shape of areas of declining population—a large proportion of elderly, very small numbers in the reproductive age groups, but (with the family size in Shetland slightly above the national average) quite a large number of children in relation to potential parents. The consequences of such a structure is a low crude birth rate, a high death rate and a natural decrease of

TABLE 4
POPULATION STRUCTURE: WALLS AND SANDNESS, 1871 AND 1966

1871				1966			
Age range	Males	Females	Total	Age range	Males	Females	Total
0–5	149	115	264	0–4	15	22	37
6–10	153	156	309	5–9	15	18	33
11–15	158	157	315	10–14	22	13	35
16–20	112	153	265	15–19	8	8	16
21–25	39	111	150	20–24	17	7	24
26–30	47	117	164	25–29	5	14	19
31–35	43	93	136	30–34	9	13	22
36–40	43	105	148	35–39	10	11	21
41–45	42	105	147	40–44	12	18	30
46–50	39	83	122	45–49	10	20	30
51–55	47	87	134	50–54	19	19	38
56–60	36	58	94	55–59	16	32	48
61–65	37	54	91	60–64	31	22	53
66–70	27	33	60	65–69	28	31	59
71–75	39	44	83	70–74	15	29	44
76–80	24	29	53	75+	20	42	62
81–85	16	19	35				
86+	9	7	16				
	1060	1526	2586		252	319	571

POPULATION AND DEPOPULATION

population. The declining population resulted in a reduction in services; for example, the secondary school is to be closed in 1970 and that has altered the entire character of the community. In 1871 the most numerous age group was from 10 to 15; in 1966 it was the over-75s, a fact bound to affect community attitudes.

For the whole of Shetland this general structure is to be found, but much less severely. There was a small natural decrease in most of the 50 years since 1921, but this was not very significant and was to be changed by quite small alterations in the volume of emigration. As emigration is the cause of this population decline, and was the cause of the unsatisfactory structure, it is important, firstly, to identify the emigrants and, secondly, to explore the nature of their move. In the following table the numbers in each group in the 1961 census are compared with the numbers in the same cohort five years later.

SHETLAND: AGE STRUCTURE OF POPULATION

Age in 1961	1961	1966	Increase or Decrease
0– 4	1260	1217	−43
5– 9	1348	1275	−73
10–14	1406	1157	−249
15–19	1157	1010	−147
20–24	950	975	+25
25–29	973	916	−57
30–34	1003	948	−55
35–39	1117	1095	−22
40–44	1005	963	−42
45–49	1186	1121	−65
50–54	1275	1160	−115
55–59	1236	1132	−104
60–64	1079	959	−120
65–69	908	754	−154
Over 70	1909	1156	−753

Losses are from two causes, death and emigration. The table shows that emigrants are largely in the 15 to 25 age-group. It is no longer the case that emigration is an escape from poverty as it was in the past. Nor is unemployment basically the cause of losses in this group indeed in 1969 there was a shortage rather than surplus of labour, although it was certainly the case that many were rather unsatisfactorily employed in part-time occupations, and that the labour shortage is of recent origin. Nor have the attractions of the bright city lights proved particularly important for, although Shetland may seem rather restricting to a certain group, the majority have a strong attachment to their islands. The cause of emigration in this age group was largely due to the educational pattern which caused young people to emigrate without making an explicit decision to do so. Young people leave for further education or training and it can be seen that there is a small gain on the completion of this training. But return is not always easy. They leave unqualified, single, property-less and mobile and may acquire qualifications, a wife, home and family which may bind them to remain away, even unwillingly. At a lower level of academic attainment the same kind of factors tend to draw country children to apprenticeships, shops and offices in Lerwick. The grass roots of emigration (and centralisation in Lerwick) can be seen from the following tables:

FOLLOW-UP OF 48 PUPILS ATTENDING AITH JUNIOR SECONDARY SCHOOL

Still in District		Other country areas		Lerwick		Outside Shetland	
Males							
Agricultural labourer	2	Fish workers	2	Garage	1	Services	1
Casual labour	2			Apprenticeships	4	At sea	6
Garage	1			Shop assistant	1	Apprentice	1
Fishing	2					Family left	1
Shop assistant	1						
	8		2		6		9
Females							
At home, knitting	1	Clerkess	1	Cook	2	Shop assistant	1
Married	1	Domestic service	1	Nurse	1	Nurse	1
Knitwear unit	4			Clerkess	4		
Domestic service	1			Waitress	1		
Canteen cook	1			Institutional management	1		
				Shop assistant	1		
				Receptionist	1		
	8		2		11		2

A small island community can never cater for the complete range of careers and ambitions; but, rather than an overall lack of employment, it is for the upper end of academic attainment that employment is lacking and this proved in the later 1960s, to be the main cause of emigration. Not many years ago many able people, for financial and other reasons, received minimal formal education, but in the future few are likely to escape the net. Thus, in the later 1960s Shetland was being drawn into a national pattern with greater mobility of population—but for Shetland that mobility was mostly in one direction. In the past education has been seen as an escape from poverty to security and attitudes have changed slowly, although a successful Whalsay skipper probably handles more valuable equipment and earns more money than many university graduates.

In conclusion, it may be helpful to compare the Shetland pattern with the pattern of population in other island groups in the period before 1969. The most obvious comparison is with Orkney which has a population of approximately the same size following very similar

FOLLOW-UP OF A CLASS OF 71 PUPILS ATTENDING
THE ANDERSON HIGH SCHOOL, LERWICK (SENIOR SECONDARY)

Males

Outside Shetland		In Shetland	
Secondary teaching	3	Secondary teaching	3
Law	2	Butcher	1
Doctor	1	Crofter	1
Veterinary surgeon	1	Garage work	1
Pharmacist	2		
Welfare work	1		
Armed forces	1		
Radio operator	1		
Car salesman	1		
Merchant navy	2		
University student	1		
Research students	2		
Unknown	6		
Family left during schooling	1		
	25		6

Females

Housewives	2	Housewives	11
Nursing	4	Nursing	1
Primary teaching	2	Primary teaching	4
Secondary teaching	2	Post Office	1
Librarians	2	Catering	1
Research student	1	Unknown	3
Family left during schooling	3		
Ship's stewardess	1		
Unknown	2		
	19		21

trends since the beginning of the nineteenth century. In 1969 the Orkney population was slightly the greater, but on three occasions the position had been reversed, in 1841, 1871 and from 1900 to 1925. It seemed at the close of the 1960s likely that Orkney, so much more dependent on agriculture, would suffer the more severe depopulation in the immediate future, and that Shetland would again have the greater population. The other inevitable comparison is with Faroe. From a population of 5265 in 1801 it rose, incredibly, to over 35,000 in 1969 and rapid growth still continued. In many respects the Faroese situation was quite different, especially with regard to emigration, and there were dangers there in a rapidly increasing population in islands which were so completely dependent on fishing. But from Faroe Shetland may at least take comfort that decline has not been an inevitable fate for island communities in the twentieth century.

NOTES

1 Many of these necessary adjustments to census material are made in R. S. Barclay, 'Population changes in Shetland during the past two centuries', a series of five articles in the *Shetland News*, 30 March to 4 May 1954.
2 A. W. Brøgger, *Ancient Emigrants* (Oxford, 1929), 6–7.
3 G. Donaldson, *Shetland Life under Earl Patrick* (Edinburgh, 1958), App. C.
4 J. Adamsone and others, 'Zetland, Parish of Nesting', in *Reports on the State of Certain Parishes in Scotland made to H.M. Commissioners for the Plantation of Kirks* (Edinburgh, 1627).
5 MSS Letter Book of Sumburgh Estate quoted by A. C. O'Dell, *The Historical Geography of the Shetland Islands* (Lerwick, 1939), 192.
6 John Campbell, *Political Survey of Great Britain* (London, 1774).
7 Webster's census is most readily available in J. G. Kyd, *Scottish Population Statistics* (Scot. Hist. Soc., 1952).
8 A. Edmondston, *A View of the Zetland Islands* (Edinburgh, 1809), ii, 135.
9 *OSA*, Unst, 43. All references to Shetland parishes in the *Statistical Account* are from E. S. Reid Tait, ed., *The Statistical Account of Shetland, 1791–1799* (Lerwick, 1925).
10 G. Low, *A Tour through the Islands of Orkney and Schetland in 1774* which includes the *Substance of a Paper by Andrew Bruce of Urie anent Fetlar* (Kirkwall, 1879), 174–5.
11 A letter from Rev. James Buchan of Northmavine read and minuted at the General Meeting of the S.S.P.C.K., 22 Mar. 1722 (in Scottish Record Office, Edinburgh).
12 For example in the parish of Tingwall–

	Total Merks	Merks Ley	Per cent Ley
Udal	648	50 (?)	8
Propertie	140	39½	28
Feu	79½	7 (?)	9 (?)
	867½	96½	11

13 T. Gifford, *Historical Description of the Zetland Islands in the Year 1733* (London, 1879, 56.
14 J. Brand, *A Brief Description of Orkney, Zetland, Pightland Firth and Caithness* (Edinburgh, 1701), 92–3.

15 G. W. Spence, 'The history of smallpox in Shetland', in the *Shetland Advertiser*, 19 Jan., 1863.
16 Edmondston, *View of Zetland*, ii, 87.
17 *OSA*, Mid and South Yell, 18–21.
18 *OSA*, Aithsting and Sandsting, 61.
19 T. McKeown and R. Record, 'The reason for the decline in mortality in England and Wales during the nineteenth century', *Population Studies*, xvi (1962), 94–122.
20 T. Ferguson, 'Mortality in Shetland a hundred years ago', *Scottish Medical Journal* (1960).
21 Brand, *Brief Description*, 92–3.
22 Edmondston, *View of Zetland*, ii, 138.
23 Low, *Tour*, 174–5.
24 Spence, 'History of Smallpox'.
25 A paper relating to ley lands in Unst by Andrew Ross, factor to the Dundas Estate, in Gardie Estate Papers.
26 P. E. Razzel, 'Population change in eighteenth-century England: a re-appraisal, *Economic History Review* (1965).
27 *OSA*, United parishes of Cross, Burness, etc., in J. Storer Clouston, *The Orkney Parishes* (Kirkwall, 1927), 286.
28 A. Peterkin, *Notes on Orkney and Zetland* (Edinburgh, 1822).
29 *OSA*, Birsay and Harray, 153–4, in Clouston, *Orkney Parishes*.
30 *OSA*, Northmavine, 82.
31 *OSA*, Unst, 42.
32 Information about weather and harvests in the years 1782–86 is taken mainly from J. Mill, *Diary of the Reverend John Mill 1740–1803* (Scot. Hist. Soc., 1889).
33 *OSA*, Northmavine, 78.
34 Edmondston, *View of Zetland*, i, 183–4.
35 Report on the Shetland Islands Petition.
36 A. Clark, *Miscellaneous Correspondence*.
37 *Shetland Journal*, 3 Jan. and 1 Feb. 1836.
38 Based on *OSA*, Walls, 110.
39 Mill, *Diary*.
40 J. Fea, *The State of Orkney and Shetland* (Edinburgh, 1884), 133–4.
41 *OSA*, Aithsting and Sandsting, 59.
42 *OSA*, Delting, 7.
43 *OSA*, Mid and South Yell, 22.
44 Based on *OSA*, Delting, 8.
45 E. M. Riley, *The Journal of John Harrower*.
46 R. Sibbald, *Description of the Islands of Orkney and Shetland, 1633 to 1845* (ed. R. Monteith: Edinburgh, 1845), 17.
47 *OSA*, St Andrews and Deerness, 13, in Clouston, *Orkney Parishes*.
48 'Zetlandicus' in *Edinburgh Weekly Magazine*, 1 June 1775.
49 O'Dell, *Historical Geography*, 194.
50 *OSA*, Delting, 7.
51 *OSA*, Delting, 8.
52 Edmondston, *View of Zetland*, ii, 67–8.
53 Clark, *Miscellaneous Correspondence*.
54 *New Statistical Account of Scotland* (Edinburgh, 1845), xv (Shetland), 155–6.
55 O'Dell, *Historical Geography*, 206.
56 R. S. Barclay, 'Population changes'.
57 *Report of H.M. Commissioners of Inquiry into the Conditions of Crofters and Cottars in the Highlands and Islands of Scotland*, [Napier Commission], (Edinburgh, 1882).
58 *Ibid*.
59 Donaldson, *Shetland Life*.

60 J. Shirreff, *A General View of the Agriculture of the Shetland Islands* (Edinburgh, 1814).
61 The reconstruction of the stages by which the Veensgarth farm came into existence is mainly based on population lists for 1802 and 1804, the censuses and valuation rolls after 1856. See also: G. Bruce, 'On the Improvement of Natural Pasture without Tillage', *Transactions of the Highland and Agricultural Society of Scotland*, 4th ser., iii (1870–1); H. Evershed, 'On the Agriculture of the Islands of Shetland', *ibid.*, 4th ser., v (1874) and R. S. Skirving's article, with the same title, in the 1874 volume.
62 J. Tudor, *The Orkneys and Shetland* (London, 1883), 469.
63 S. Hibbert, *A Description of the Shetland Islands, 1822* (Edinburgh, 1931), 137.

CHAPTER XII

Shetland and Norway in the Second World War

MAGNE SKODVIN

IN DEALING with my topic, I can make no attempt to tell the countless sagas of the women and men deeply involved in the emerging relationship of Shetland and Norway during the Second World War, what they did, how they did it; yet no discussion of that topic would be complete without glimpses at least of the human element. Human drama unfolds itself in brief episodes against a more general background. History is shaped, among other things, by geography; and Shetland and Norway are linked in history through their geographical proximity.

At the end of July 1940 the small Norwegian fishing boat *Traust* crossed the North Sea carrying two passengers who, with the Norwegian campaign over, wanted to join the Norwegian forces in the United Kingdom. The *Traust* was quite new, a good boat, but it had never been equipped for ocean sailing. The skipper decided that he needed at least a compass, and had bought one in Bergen before leaving. While it had worked all right on his way back to the boat, as soon as they got outside the skerries it started jumping around and was of no use whatsoever. Skipper Langöy went on anyway. When, according to his estimate, he had covered the best part of the distance

Editor's note On the evening on which, in the secondary school hall in Scalloway, Professor Skodvin rose to speak to a very representative audience of that district of Shetland, including many who had been prominent in the events which he was to discuss, he stated that he found the paper he had prepared both dull and—for the occasion—unsatisfactory. Dr Skodvin, therefore, decided to depart considerably from his written text: and the essay presented here is a reproduction, insofar as he has been able to reconstruct it, of his improvised lecture.

to his desired destination, he saw a British aeroplane on coastal patrol. Crew and passengers together took a sail, stretched it out on deck and painted on it in huge, crude letters: SHETLAND? The aeroplane immediately straightened out and indicated the course to follow. After a while they saw land ahead and that same evening they landed in Lerwick.

This story demonstrates the basic fact of geography which has for centuries determined the relationship between Shetland and Norway: if one goes due west from western Norway, one's nearest landing point is likely to be in the Shetland Islands. For this reason Shetland played a very prominent rôle in Norwegian history during the Second World War.

To most people on both sides of the North Sea, Shetland in the Second World War is best known as a base of operations in the north, as the theatre of war where forces of the United Kingdom achieved perhaps their most intimate and efficient cooperation with free Norwegian forces in a total joint effort within a well-defined area. People came to Shetland to escape from occupation; from Shetland people went back to occupied Norway on missions, some of them very special indeed. But before turning to these topics, it may be worth while to examine briefly the considerations of grand strategy that linked Shetland with Norway even before the German invasion of the Norwegian mainland.

The relatively short distance between Shetland and Bergen played a fundamental rôle in strategic thinking on both sides in 1939 and 1940. In the early months of the Second World War it dominated the problem of how Great Britain could deny the German navy access to the North Atlantic; and, seen from the other side, it was a decisive factor in German attempts to break the blockade. In terms of modern naval warfare, the 220 miles which separated Shetland from Bergen was a fairly narrow passage. German planning of the landing in Norway may to a considerable extent have been influenced by its narrowness.

The lessons of the First World War had not been forgotten in Germany. Before the outbreak of the war in 1914 German naval planners expected a very close blockade, with British warships patrolling close to the short strip of German seafront between the borders of Denmark and the Netherlands. As things turned out, this tight blockade did not materialize. Nevertheless, the grand blockade of the First World War proved that it was possible to keep the North Sea closed, and to do so with a high degree of efficiency. The southern exits could be almost sealed in the Channel, and the famous Northern Barrage extended across the North Sea at its narrowest, all the way to where Norwegian territorial waters began.

When he returned to the Admiralty after an interval of 24 years, in September 1939, Winston Churchill made it his policy to establish the same kind of Northern Barrage. But, eventually, the pattern of the First World War was to be repeated, in that the blockade line was moved farther away from the Continent. An Iceland-Faeroes barrier was instituted in July 1940 and was built up considerably during 1941. But the Iceland-Faeroes barrier was not established until after the German invasion of Norway. During the planning period for the invasion, the German admiralty had anticipated the same kind of Northern Barrage as it had experienced in 1917–1918, reaching Norwegian territory somewhere in the neighbourhood of Bergen—an assumption which was to have great importance.

On 9 October 1939, six months before the invasion of Norway, Admiral Dönitz—who was in charge of German submarine warfare—wrote a note on possible German bases in Norway. He suggested to the commander-in-chief of the German Navy, Grossadmiral Raeder, that two points on the Norwegian coast seemed especially valuable as German bases. These two points were Narvik and Trondheim. He gave a number of reasons for his choice, one of them being that both ports were situated north of the narrow passage between Bergen and Shetland: once German naval units were based there, they would be outside the barrage that Dönitz confidently expected the British to build up across the North Sea. This would assure the German navy much freer access to the North Atlantic, and to the seven seas, than they had ever had in the First World War. Dönitz wrote his note in response to questions which had been put to him by Raeder: and the German navy's strong interest in an invasion of Norway stems from such considerations of naval strategy.

The German decision to strike at Norwegian ports which lay even north of the Shetland-Bergen gap influenced the whole planning of the German invasion. The operation, under the code-name of 'Weserübung', i.e. Weser exercise, was planned and carried out as a strategic assault, possible only if executed as a surprise. German naval operations on the Norwegian coast north of the Stavanger region had never been anticipated. In Hitler's strategic thinking, this provided an additional and decisive chance of success since nobody was prepared for it. In other words, both the German need for bases in Norway and the way they were acquired were conditioned to a very considerable extent by the fact that Shetland is where it is.

Thus the stage was set. With the German invasion of Norway and the Norwegian campaign from 9 April to 7 June 1940, the action began and began immediately. Instead of a barrage and boundary, the waters between Shetland and western Norway became a main line of communication through a naval non-man's-land. The traffic ran both ways and was, in some of its aspects, unique even in a European context.

The passage from east to west served primarily as an escape route, but its multiple purposes and varying conditions will be obvious even from such a short survey as this. Eastward went a succession of expeditions for activities as different as minelaying, attacks on shipping, the landing of agents and ammunition, general intelligence purposes, and so forth. The 'Shetland-gang', operating with fishing boats mainly, was active from the very first summer: later, Norwegian MTBs were stationed in Lerwick. Many Shetlanders had immediate personal contact with these activities.

A considerable amount of information about escapes to Shetland has so far been available only in Norwegian. The main source of this are the two volumes of Ragnar Ulstein[1] to whom every future research worker in this field will have to pay tribute. The author himself came to Shetland across the North Sea in June 1941, and later returned as a parachutist to serve in occupied Norway. Thanks to Ulstein it is possible to be fairly accurate about the number of ships and sailings and passengers transported, about escape techniques, losses and successes, about the composition of crews and other related topics.

During the five years of German occupation, more than 5,000 civilians were taken across from Norway to the United Kingdom. Some of them joined in British-Norwegian large-scale raids and were brought back by the raiders. This was the case in all three of the major raids, the two to Lofoten and the one directed against Målöy. Others should be classified as special: for example, the evacuation from Söröya in the extreme north of civilians who managed to stay behind when the Germans carried out a very efficient scorched earth policy during the retreat from north-eastern Norway in 1944. The Norwegian population in Svalbard was brought to the United Kingdom by naval units in similar circumstances. But when such groups have been excluded, we are still left with over 3,600 evacuees who, astonishingly, crossed the sea in small vessels. Some ten per cent of these were picked up in Norway by fishing boats and by smaller naval units, both operating mainly out of Scalloway. The remaining ninety per cent came from Norway in such boats as they were able to procure themselves; and, as we shall see, there was a great variety of these.

According to Ulstein's statistics, they numbered 3,629 altogether: even with a certain margin of error, this estimate is as close as we can get. Remember that these were the ones who were successful: we shall have to deal with losses a little later. True, the 3,629 persons who are known to us did not all end up in Shetland—quite a few landed in the Faroes, and others reached Orkney. But Shetland received the overwhelming majority of them. The Norwegian consulate in Lerwick has been able to provide reliable statistics for each month of 1941, and from these we know that a total of 1,881 Norwegian escapees passed through Lerwick in that year—with the flow reaching 518, its highest point, in September. Since Ulstein published his study, more complete statistics have been made available, but these are not expected to change the general picture he drew in one respect at least: most escape-sailings were bound for Shetland.

The statistics reveal clearly that more than half of the escapees crossed in the course of 1941. Most arrived in September, with October in second highest place and August in third. If we count boats and not persons, we arrive at a total of 109 over the same three months, in other words an average of thirty-six a month. This corresponds closely to the number of thirty-four boats which had arrived in May 1940, most of them landing at some point on the east coast of Shetland—at Baltasound, Haraldswick, Bressey and elsewhere. The others went to mainland Scotland, to Orkney, to the Faroes or to Iceland. How, then, do we explain these clusters of arrivals, in May 1940 and in the autumn months of 1941? And how do we explain that escape-sailings from Norway, across the North Sea, mostly occurred in the first two years of the war?

As far as May 1940 is concerned, the answer is easy. The exodus had started immediately after the end of fighting in southern Norway. Some wanted to join the anti-German forces, and expected the crossing to Shetland to be easier than a long northern trek (under the eyes of the Luftwaffe) to territory that was still in Norwegian and Allied hands. Others simply wanted to escape from German rule. Three examples will show how they came. The *Disko* carried five families, twenty-six persons in all, half of them were children: this boat, incidentally, landed in Torshavn. The *Glimt*, a vessel of 29 feet, sailed with fifteen persons on board: they ran into bad weather and had to spend four very uncomfortable days and nights afloat until they reached Sumburgh Head and then went on to Lerwick. The fifteen were all men, mostly students of various kinds between 17 and 23 years, including one army sergeant. General Otto Ruge, the Norwegian commander-in-chief, had already ordered Air Froce captain Bjarne Öen to take his staff to the United Kingdom and start building a Norwegian Air Force unit there. The boat they sailed in was badly damaged by machine gun-fire from German planes, but they found a new one called *Sjögutten* (*Sailor*) and were able to carry out their mission. Many of these men were later killed in action, and two became generals.

The sudden rise in departures from Norway in the period August–October 1941 has no such obvious explanation. Meterological conditions do not account for it, since the wave of departures from Norway actually continued well into November when storms have to be expected. In fact the weather was unusually rough and stormy in November 1941 and caused the heaviest loss of all, the shipwreck of the *Blia*. It was her second crossing, for she had brought twenty young men to Lerwick in March and was used for naval purposes thereafter from a Scalloway base. On the November mission she was to pick up a Norwegian agent who operated in occupied Norway, and he offered to bring refugees back with him. The *Blia* never reached Shetland again, and forty-two persons were lost. The crew of six men all belonged to the group that came to be known in Norwegian history as the 'Shetland gang' (Shetlandsgjengen).

If November was a bad month for weather, it might be conjectured that August—the month of most crossings—would be fine: but we have to take into consideration that August is still a month of long days and good visibility, so that a small boat would be rather helplessly exposed if spotted by German planes. In short, all months of the year had advantages and disadvantages: people left from occupied Norway when they felt that they had to or wanted to. And the high number of departures beginning in August 1941 can probably be best explained by the increasing severity of the enemy occupation. The German invasion of Soviet Russian inaugurated a period of heavy reprisals even outside the combat area, and these were specifically directed against resistance movements throughout occupied Europe. According to directives that came from Hitler himself, those active in resistance groups were to be dealt with in such a way as to discourage any further opposition from within. Hitler had great faith in reprisals, and there is little doubt that frequently the policy was an effective one: for acts of sabotage had to be carefully weighed up—would they be worth the price? On the other hand, under certain circumstances, such a policy of terror might have the opposite effect, engendering resistance instead of preventing it. In the case of Norway, after the beginning of the Russian campaign, the increased threat and fact of reprisals were reflected in the statistics of escape.

In the second half of the war, however, escapes took a different direction. It was not that Shetland and the United Kingdom appeared less attractive but that easier (and, under the circumstances, safer) channels were opened up. As the German commitments on eastern and southern fronts became heavier, Germany lost much of her ability to exert pressure on Sweden. Correspondingly, Swedish restrictions on Norwegian activities in that country were relaxed and, from the end of 1943, Norwegian training camps were opened in Sweden itself. In spite of the most energetic supervision, the Germans found it impossible to establish complete control of the Norwegian–Swedish boundary, with its enormous distances of forest and mountain; not even the death penalty for attempts to leave the country could stop the crossings. By the end of the war, indeed, more than 40,000 Norwegian citizens had reported to the Norwegian refugee administration in Stockholm. Yet, even in this period, Norwegian boats travelled westwards and most of them, somehow, found their way through Lerwick.

Crossing to Shetland, throughout the entire war, was not an easy undertaking. German military personnel, police and secret police kept a constant watch and led a constant offensive against the 'Englandsfahrt'. Suitable boats were hard to get and were strictly guarded. In order to protect the owners, boats had to be 'stolen'. Boat-owners were instructed by the Germans to take vital parts out of their engines whenever they left their boats: and thus spare parts had to be found somehow. Also, passengers had to be hidden away and fed during what might be long periods of waiting. Assembling before departure was, in fact, a critical operation: in a sparsely populated country, and in such remote places as seemed most suitable as departure points, groups of strangers equipped for travelling could hardly escape notice and attention. Moreover, the permanent danger of infiltration of the escape organization by informers created an atmosphere of permanent strain and suspicion, with elaborate secrecy-measures making the simplest communication both difficult and time-consuming. Heavy losses frequently occurred before departure. But even if the party successfully managed to sail, there was still danger ahead. German planes patrolled the coast and did not hesitate to use their machine guns once suspicion was aroused. And, more than that, many refugees were entirely unfamiliar with the sea and with sailing.

To those who think of Norway as primarily a seafaring nation, it seems logical that so many should escape by boat. And many escapees, in fact, were experienced seamen—naval officers and professional sailors. But others knew next to nothing about motors or about navigation. They had engine trouble, went adrift and returned to occupied Norway to have emergency repairs made under the eyes of the enemy occupiers; or they continued under sail, sometimes using old blankets. One 'skipper', who had never been outside territorial waters, was instructed by a more experienced navigator before leaving to keep taking soundings: if, after some 24 hours, he found depths of 200 fathoms or more instead of the usual 60, he was to turn back immediately on the assumption that he had 'missed' Shetland.

The 5,000 Norwegian civilians who came to the United Kingdom across the North Sea during the war were a representative cross-section of the Norwegian population as a whole, a mixture of seamen and landlubbers. Their boats also varied, in size as well as in quality. Two young men are known to have set out in canoes—and one of the canoes was brought back by the current, empty. Two boys went off in a rowing-boat: when they realized that they were fighting a losing battle, one of them wrote a note to his mother and put it in a bottle—the Gulf Stream carried the bottle to northern Norway, where it was found a long time after, and the note eventually forwarded to the mother. Two other young men managed a successful escape in a rowing-boat, after rowing for five days and nights: but they ran out of water on the second day. These two were picked up by a British ship, given tea and put to bed: 'but', said one of them, 'it took a few hours before I could manage to straighten out my knees'. The smallest vessel that is known to have made the attempt also arrived safely, also carrying two men. But the first ship of all to arrive at Lerwick after the invasion was a steamer, the *Bomma*, on 10 April 1940, while Norwegian agents later captured a coastal steamer, the *Galtesund*, and took it across in March 1942. Four naval officers in a pleasure boat were picked up by a British submarine and witnessed a torpedoing before being set ashore on British territory. But, for all the use made of such different craft, most of the escape sailings were made in fairly small fishing boats of a type well known to everybody in Shetland. Until Ulstein published his books, the extent and importance of the westbound crossings were little known, perhaps even in Shetland. If we turn our attention to the eastbound sailings, those to Norway, then we arrive at a point where many Norwegians are less well informed than people in Scalloway.

Throughout the war, Shetland was the main base for a number of very important activities directed against occupied Norway. For obvious reasons, Shetland was used by all the armed services. Flights of the Norwegian air squadrons were occasionally stationed at Sullom Voe. Parachutists and special agents passed through Shetland on their way to Norway or on their way back. But it was naval operations which predominated, for even more obvious reasons: and these are usually associated with the 'Shetland gang', the 'Shetland Bus' and MTBs.

The first Norwegian warship to arrive in Shetland was the destroyer *Draug* which came to Sullom Voe on 10 April, the day after the German invasion, carrying sixty-seven German prisoners of war from the German transport ship *Main* which the *Draug* had sunk. The crew immediately transferred to British ships serving in the North Sea while the *Draug* was being repaired. Another destroyer, the *Sleipner*, followed at the end of April when the fighting ended in southern Norway. In June, at the close of the campaign in northern Norway, such Norwegian planes as could reach Shetland were instructed to go there. But, with all its close connections with the regular forces, Shetland was to have a predominant place in more special operations across the North Sea.

Some sailings on these special missions belong to the period before the organization of the 'Shetland gang'. In the first days of June 1940 a veteran in the business, Mons Storemark, took back to Norway a group of saboteurs who carried out a mission that has been frequently described as the first SOE-operation. They were brought back to Shetland later in the month by another skipper who was, even at that early time, making his second trip. After the 'Shetland gang' started operating, special trips were still made from Peterhead in Aberdeenshire, usually carrying intelligence personnel from the Norwegian High Command: and some of these trips took their passengers as far as Finnmark. But the overwhelming majority of the sorties have to be credited to the 'gang'. Frithjof Sælen, in his *Sjetlands-Larsen*, lists almost exactly 200 trips between Christmas 1940 and the end of the war. This gives an average of one sortie per week. If, towards the end of the war, the MTBs were used occasionally, until the beginning of 1943 it was fishing boats that were used, with—later—the submarine chasers taking over and operating out of Scalloway.

The 'Shetland gang' is a nickname for what was officially the Norwegian Naval Special Unit. Its base in Scalloway was under the authority of the British Admiralty and the admiral commanding Orkney and Shetland, and it took its orders from British Intelligence Headquarters in London. The highest positions in command, both in London and Shetland, were held by Britons: but operations were carried out in the closest cooperation with the Norwegian High Command and other Norwegian authorities. The British chief in Scalloway, Captain Sclater of the Royal Marines, was most widely known as Captain Rogers; there are persistent rumours in Norway that, even in Shetland, very few knew him by his real name. One reason for his adopting a *nom de guerre* was the fact that he had numerous relatives in Norway. His second-in-command, David Howarth, is best known as the author of *The Shetland Bus*.

The special unit landed arms, intelligence personnel and various equipment; and also Norwegian special agents, mostly from the Norwegian independent company, called Kompani Linge after its first commander who was killed in action during a raid against Måløy in December 1941. The numerous adventures of this unit were among the most thrilling to be recorded in the Second World War: but to repeat the highlights of their epic actions before a Scalloway audience would be carrying coals to Newcastle indeed. Even the briefest sketch of this period, however, would be strangely incomplete without mentioning at least the name of Leif Larsen ('Shetlands-Larsen'), who ended the war with fifty-two expeditions to his credit and is frequently mentioned as the most decorated naval officer of the Second World War. If an example has to be selected from his many exploits, perhaps the attempt to sink the *Tirpitz* with midget submarines, the so-called 'chariots', should be the one. This trip started as usual in Scalloway—this was after the base had been moved there from Lunna Voe—and took him past the German coast guards into the Trondheimsfjord. But, so close to the target as they had got, the mission ended in failure: for the 'chariots' which had been suspended under Larsen's boat, sank. Larsen himself proceeded on foot to Sweden and was soon back in Britain again. Another, even more dramatic example from his adventures, can be seen in his escape after the sinking of the *Bergholm* on her way back to Shetland in March 1943 from delivering supplies to a resistance group on northern Norway. On this occasion Larsen first tried to reach Shetland but then turned back towards Norway, found shelter and assistance there and was later picked up by an MTB stationed at Lerwick.

In 1943 the submarine chasers took over and altogether made 110 trips. The Shetland base continued to exist officially until 1 August 1945, but for all practical purposes it had its final moment of triumph when the three chasers *Hitra*, *Hessa* and *Vigra* were able to enter the ports of Bergen and Ålesund in May 1945, flying the Norwegian flag in a free country.

During its period of operation the 'Shetland Bus' took more than 400 tons of arms and military equipment from Shetland to secret bases in Norway. These materials were partly used for acts of sabotage against the German occupation army, partly for the training and equipment of a secret military force (the Milorg) that was to join the Allied forces in the final fight for the liberation of Norway. The 'Bus' also brought a considerable number of men from the Kompani Linge, who acted as instructors and advisers for the home forces in Norway: radio transmitters and then operators were also brought in, in sufficient number to keep the Allied High Command informed of enemy movements and undertakings in Norway. (At the end of the war, more than sixty radio stations were in operation.) On their way back, the men of the Shetland bus took with them some 340 persons, most of whom were wanted by the Gestapo. Of the great value of these activities, the official history of Norwegian naval operations in the Second World War says: 'A small unit of about 100 men in Scalloway on Shetland was able to maintain contact between the out-front in Great Britain and the home-front in Norway in spite of all German efforts to stop communications. In Norway most people—not to say everybody—knew that the Shetland Bus kept the line open between Norway and Shetland at all times and this helped more than a little to keep faith and hope alive both in the home forces and in the great majority of the Norwegian population . . .'.

A number of smaller Norwegian vessels were stationed in Lerwick from August 1943, patrolling around the islands and also providing an escort service between Lerwick and mainland Scotland. These small units—originally whalers—were also used for a different purpose, towing MTBs toward the Norwegian coast. The MTBs with their strong engines and high speed used an enormous lot of fuel, and had to be towed in this way so that they had full tanks when they entered Norwegian territorial waters. The MTBs also carried a little extra fuel in small containers as a safety-first measure.

Norwegian MTBs first of all joined a British flotilla in the Channel in the beginning of July 1940 and they served in this area through the Blitz. It was in September 1941 that a Norwegian officer suggested that they should rather be used close to the Norwegian coast; and the first operation they carried out there was successful in sinking a tanker with fuel intended for the German Luftwaffe. From November 1942 a Norwegian MTB flotilla was stationed in Lerwick and operated against German shipping in the Norwegian waters. Its official name was 'Shetlandsavdelingen', which indicated its land base; and, operationally, it was under the admiral commanding Orkney and Shetland, attacking German shipping and coastal fortifications and laying mines. But in addition to its offensive operations, this flotilla carried out activities of the same kind as the special naval unit in Scalloway: escape service, the landing of agents and of military equipment in Norway.

The story of the communications between Shetland and Norway is here told from a Norwegian angle. British sources would doubtless provide interesting further information on a number of points: among others, about how German intelligence tried to infiltrate and make use of the route to Shetland. British intelligence scrutinised arrivals here very closely, sometimes to the point where newcomers from Norway felt offended. Considerable worry, for example, was caused by fishball crates, where every tin might contain a secret transmitter smuggled into Britain. Norwegian sources show that there was some reason for suspicion.[2] On the whole, though, it seems that German intelligence and counter-intelligence was not at its best in this area. It is generally assumed that they were not adequately prepared since they expected the war to be won by assault on England. When this did not seem to materialize in the summer of 1940, they decided to send as many potential agents as possible, hoping that their numbers would compensate for lack of skill and training. Thus, while there was a considerable amount of infiltration, it was usually on an amateurish level.

There is a general conclusion to be drawn. No other German-occupied territory in Western Europe had such possibilities of direct communication with the free world outside as did occupied Norway.

Its main lines of communication led to Great Britain, directly or via Sweden, in both cases permitted by the factor of geography. Even Denmark was in a quite different position. Where the coast of western Norway offers shelter and hiding places everywhere, opens up the possibilities of sudden action and then sudden retreat, of secret meetings, of boardings and unloadings, Jutland has only its open and unsheltered beaches and the sandbanks that have been deathtraps to European sailors throughout the ages. Immediate contact with free Danes abroad had to be by air: and it is a way that leads in more than it brings out. Only personnel with special and important tasks could be sent in by air, and it took top-level decisions to send them. The only other route was to Sweden, and even this included a short and dangerous crossing by sea.

The Netherlands, Belgium and northern France are situated on England's doorstep. During the Napoleonic wars, we know that a continental blockade could not stop trade across the Channel. But in the last war, with the German breakthrough on the Western front, the British Channel became a no-man's land, more of a barrier than an ocean would have been because the distance was short and easy to patrol. Not until 1942 were the Dutch able to organize reliable contacts between the occupied territory and the government in London, and this was by way of Stockholm, with Dutch sailors acting as intermediaries. Another escape route led towards Switzerland, or sometimes Portugal, and even through Franco's Spain.

In 1940 two young Dutchmen in London, planning to land an agent, decided to try the short route. Difficulties kept piling up. While they needed high speed for the main Channel crossing, they wanted a battery-operated boat to run noiselessly on the last stretch. Even when they solved these problems there remained the choice of a landing point. They finally selected the parkland of a large hotel, in fact one where German units were stationed. At fairly regular intervals it was known that the German held parties there, attended also by certain Dutch civilians. So they worked out a plan to put a man ashore in evening dress who, relying on luck and strong nerves, was to make his way through the hotel grounds to the hotel and then into the town. Several attempts were made before they were successful. As no taxis were available at the time, the agent found he had to take an early morning streetcar, and that he attracted attention by paying for his ticket with silver coins: his briefing in London had not made it clear that taxis were extremely scarce nor that silver coins were then being hoarded.

This shows how difficult it was to get ashore in the Netherlands and, for tht matter, how difficult it was to follow daily events and developments closely in occupied Dutch territory. Even wireless contact was difficult to maintain with safety. France may not have been so easily isolated, particularly its south-western area. But the difficulties there were also considerable, as much of a political as of a geographical nature. Thus, in spite of great and seemingly unavoidable losses, in spite of the high price that had to be paid, the way to Britain nevertheless came more naturally to the Norwegians than to anybody else.

How important were the Norwegian losses? So far as is known, 166 persons disappeared while making crossing, most of them in total shipwrecks. Seven boats with a total of 77 passengers were captured by the Germans in attempted crossings. Of those arrested for attempting to escape or for assisting in planning executions, 67 were sentenced to death and executed. Another 91 died in prison or concentration camp or in the course of arrest. The total loss amounted to 321 dead, or roughly one in ten of escapees. But it must be observed that many of these evacuees were saved from the heavy sentences they would likely have experienced if they had been taken in Norway.

Was it worth it? With all due respect one might ask: how much did it all count in the contest? A few hundred men were able to join the services including the merchant marine, a few hundreds were saved from prisons or concentration camps, the free Norwegians abroad were joined by a steady trickle of newcomers. It was all immensely important for these individuals, but these were paltry numbers when compared with the totals engaged in the Second World War. Nonetheless, the escapes of these few had effects far beyond the mere counting of heads.

In the first place, they represented a victory in themselves—an act of resistance which could not be stopped, a series of German defeats at a time when the Germans were not used to being defeated. Every boat that escaped safely had won its own small battle. Those who were left behind heard about each escape and it gave them much-needed courage. The Germans were never able to break the contacts with the free world, and they were perfectly aware of this. On 24 September 1941 the Abwehrstelle Norwegen agency (the German counter-intelligence) wrote to Armee Oberkommando Norwegen and to the German admiral for occupied Norwegian territory that it seemed impossible to stop the 'England trade' from the Norwegian west coast. Could the situation somehow be used for German purposes? The Abwehr office in Trondheim was instructed to plant false rumours in the coastal areas in the hope of leading the enemy astray. They had no doubt that the rumours would reach Britain.

The relatively easy escape-route to Britain itself helped to create an important working condition of the Norwegian resistance. Most resistance movements in Europe in the Second World War were under permanent strain from the need to look after those in hiding from the Gestapo. Active resistance fighters frequently had short 'working hours' and had to be hidden away. If those in such safe-keeping had to be kept hidden *inside* the occupied territory, then a great deal of effort was tied up in this; and it, in turn, for ever created new dangers of discovery. Hardly less important was the mental strain on everybody involved, including those forced into inaction, because they had earlier distinguished themselves by characteristic acts of initiative and daring. Resistance groups in Norway never gave that priority to 'permanent unrest' which others had to do. They had available escape routes as a safety valve to keep down these pressures.

After some very adverse publicity in 1940, the Norwegians gradually acquired an equally exaggerated fame as a nation of resisters. The truth, of course, lay somewhere between these extremes. There is little doubt that the resistance in Norway—as everywhere else—derived its strength from an active minority, but it was a minority strong enough to exert more pressure than could the occupiers and the collaborationists—no little achievement in itself. To say this is, of course, to raise the question of how we can possibly measure the strength of resistance. It seems to me that one central factor is what we may call 'solidarity'. In Norway we can find a quite extraordinary cooperation existing between very secret and highly specialized groups and whole communities. Hundreds of persons might be in on the secret when a ship was preparing to escape, or at least they could not avoid observing the signs and drawing their own conclusions from them. Men like Leif Larsen might spend long periods waiting under the noses of the Germans in a place like Ålesund. Meanwhile his compatriots were organizing transport and other assistance for him and his men. In small communities like Vigra (which gave its name to Larsens MTB), young men of military age were almost without exception to be found in Britain at the end of the war. Another small community farther south, on the island of

Bömlo, was a centre for escapes throughout a long and critical period. Such happenings were not possible unless almost everybody in the community took his share in the common effort.

The outstanding importance of organized leadership and of cadres in resistance movements is obvious to any serious student. But there is reason to warn against the idea of the Norwegian resistance as a smooth-running, easily-operated and anonymously-efficient organization. Those in the resistance were nothing more than groups of very ordinary people who joined together to do their best under the most trying and adverse circumstances without special training or preparation. They spent an enormous amount of time on it because even the simplest thing had become incredibly difficult: not least in a country where towards the end of the war one person in ten was a German and where more than one adult male in five was a German soldier. The point is that this vital group of dedicated persons could feel surrounded by loyalty and sympathy. It is true that we find informers more frequently than we would like to. But one informer may be watched by thousands silent in their support. The 'England trade' goes far towards showing us how deep-rooted were the Norwegian loyalties and also the community solidarity which was so readily mobilized.

But it is time to return to Shetland. No study of our topic could now be made without frequent references to Ragnar Ulstein's outstanding researches. The author appears himself in his study, rather modestly, as a passenger on a boat whose name he shared, which came to Shetland on 24 June 1941. They had had a long journey: the engine had failed but they had managed to turn back to Norway at a most difficult point of the coast in heavy weather; they had had their engine mended and had set out again. They had spent seven nights and days at sea, almost half of them without food. A picture of the group was taken shortly after landing. Ulstein used it as an illustration in the first volume of his work and he gave it the following caption: 'Well arrived and received in friendship by coastguards and civilians. The Norwegians were among their own when they came to Shetland'. I can think of no better conclusion than this.

NOTES

1 Ragnar Ulstein, *Englandsfarten*, 2 vols (Oslo, 1965–67).
2 One tale goes that a German intelligence man, who had been very active as a smuggler during the period of prohibition in Norway, was able to enlist a few Norwegians with

whom he had dealings then, and send them on an expedition to Shetland or to mainland Scotland: their story was to be that they wanted to get hold of some whisky and possibly tobacco, and take it back. They were given tin cans filled with explosives, to be used against possible targets they might run across. As things turned out, they never left Norway but decided to hide away for a couple of weeks and then come back and pick up the money which they had been promised. They are said to have explained how they had landed in Baltasound—a name they had picked at random from a small-scale map of Shetland. But the German infiltration was more serious than that.

CHAPTER XIII

Economic Changes since 1946

STUART B. DONALD

THE CHIEF problem in deciding how to approach this very large topic has been in assessing what might be omitted rather than in raking about for what might be included. It is in our dealings as a living community with the outside world that the success or failure of our society must be judged. That the events of today are history in the making is the oldest cliché in the world, but this has never been brought home to me more forcibly than in my researches into the pattern of events in Shetland's economic development in the forties and fifties. So many of the pronouncements, the prejudices, the misconceptions and dearly-held theories which marked the embryo stage of serious thought and action about the economic problems of the islands at that time seemed as remote from 1969 as if they had been voiced a hundred years ago. The Shetland Islands still have a long way to go in building, conserving and preserving their economy: but Shetland has come a long way since 1946.

This paper falls into two major sections: a discussion of what, for want of a better word, I might call the philosophy of development in the years since the war, and its relation to Shetland's metamorphosis in economic development from the chrysalis of 1946 to the emergent adult of 1969; and a more detailed analysis of the individual components of the economy, and their aggregate effect.

DEVELOPMENT THINKING

First phase

The agony of the war years affected Shetland in ways other than the obvious human and material depredation. Despite a brief period of national, and indeed international, notice during the First World War, Shetland had by 1939 become a quiet and virtually forgotten backwater in the United Kingdom. The islands relied too heavily on the herring fishing as the keystone of their economy, a herring fishing which had become but a pale shadow of its golden days. The tottering social structure reflected the slender economy. For every fine house in Lerwick there were a dozen or more archaic crofts in rural Shetland, on all too many of which families lived at or near subsistence level—happily enough no doubt, but with a standard of living which was a humbling and shaming reflection on mid-twentieth century Britain. Too few homes and too few townships enjoyed those individual or communal amenities—amenities such as water, electricity or good roads—which were taken for granted almost everywhere else in the United Kingdom.

London rediscovered Shetland when war was declared and the strategic importance of the islands was again recognised. In six years the islands were thrust into the twentieth century with a vengeance, in a compacted parody of a physical and psychological evolvement which should normally have taken decades to mature. Suddenly the government was spending money in the infrastructure of the islands with a prodigality born of a very specific wartime need. Suddenly there was employment, full-time and well-paid employment, for all those who had been left at home. Shetland's standard of living rose dramatically during the war years. Troops outnumbered civilians: and it was like some monstrous tourist bonanza, a captive market of thousands which, despite shortages and austerity, needed services and supplies and was prepared to pay for them.

Then, as suddenly as it had developed, that boom was over and the bubble was pricked. Shetland, abandoned and derelict, became in the eyes of the South a temporarily valuable base which had outlived its usefulness and could now be consigned to limbo, and forgotten. While the islands were left with huge numbers of unemployed, the only assets in the economy were the knitwear and tweed industries which were riding still on the crest of an artificial wartime demand: even that was a demand which the industry was structured neither to bolster nor to replace. The islands were left with an ageing fishing fleet, still largely geared to a seasonal herring industry, which could not hope to satisfy the employment needs of the community; left with an outmoded, undeveloped, unmechanised, fragmented and necessarily neglected agricultural system, offering at best a subsistence level living to which Shetlanders returning from money-earning wartime jobs were understandably reluctant to resign themselves.

The problem of adjusting from an expedient wartime economy to a balanced peacetime economy was of course not unique to the islands. What made the Shetland case unique was that there no longer existed an acceptable, balanced economy to which the islanders could return. Even worse, there seems to have been an unnerving number of pessimists to the fore—pessimists whose view of Shetland's future was, to say the least, jaundiced by their own despair. Lemming-like they abjured self-preservation and sought self-destruction. Tom Johnston's encouragement and offers of aid to a regeneration programme were scarcely heeded in the manner which he had intended.

To absorb the huge numbers of unemployed male labour, a series of costly public works schemes was mounted. The purpose of such schemes, of course, was to buy time—they were to contribute usefully towards building the social infrastructure of the community while waiting for the country and the world to recover sufficiently from the economic devastation of the war to permit the reintroduction, or the new development, of normal commercial and economic activity. With one or two notable exceptions, neither the purpose of this breathing space nor the opportunities which it offered were grasped in the islands. As a result, too great a reliance was placed on the public works schemes so that by 1949, as money available for the schemes began to be reduced, unemployment rose alarmingly. Ninety Shetland men had been unemployed in September 1948: 480 were out of work in September 1949, and by January 1950 the figure had risen to 1000.

Part of the responsibility at least for this tragic situation rested with the central authorities. A leader in the *Shetland Times* put the point succinctly:

> Shetland has been coming to this end for a long, long time. When the war ended, many men were glad to turn their backs upon the sea and seek a livelihood within their native isles, but few were absorbed into new industries. With the exception of a few who went into tweed weaving, most simply meant another mouth to feed from some small croft and another job to be found on some scheme of public works. Schemes of public works should be in relation to the productive potential of the areas they serve. There should have been evidence of a Government desire to create anew, rather than patch up the old system by piecemeal improvements.

It was in fact a prime example of an over-rigid and unimaginative application by the government of the finances at its disposal. Whereas in the Highlands and northern Islands, exchequer funds tended to be used in building good roads leading nowhere, in Scandinavia they were used to finance a fish-factory at the end of a dirt track.

Yet there was a degree of local responsibility as well. It is both surprising and sobering to find the opinion that industry was 'unnecessary and irrelevant' in the Shetland context: yet this was said in a local authority debate on the economic problem in the first half of 1950. It is incredible to find the belief that work on more roads and water schemes was all that was required to cure Shetland's ills. Fortunately this remarkable assessment was a relatively isolated appreciation of the situation in the early phases of the local authorities' acceptance and understanding of their economic responsibilities. Otherwise one imagines that Shetland by now would just be one huge mass of concrete, interspersed with water holes, stretching from Sumburgh Head to the Muckle Flugga.

While government activity in Shetland was indeed inadequate to cope with the peculiar problems posed by a remote island community, the remote island community itself failed to recognise that the public works schemes had given it an artificial breathing space which should have been used to initiate self-help, but which was in broad terms wholly neglected.

There were of course exceptions to this general rule. The government in 1946, at the pressing instigation of Lerwick Town Council, financed the construction in Lerwick of an experimental factory for the Herring Industry Board. Even the usefulness of this, however, was diminished by the Board's refusal to contemplate the canning of Shetland herring on the grounds that they were 'too big'. Nor was the Board prepared to consider the processing of white fish—perhaps not surprisingly—and so the contribution which this huge factory was making to Shetland was but a fraction of what it might have been. Even the creation of the White Fish Authority did not help. It proposed that the processing and marketing of white fish, utilising the Herring Industry Board's plant, should be undertaken by a mutual trading organisation operating under the umbrella of the Shetland Fishermen's Association. But both capital and expertise were lacking locally and there was still an almost ostrich-like reluctance in certain sectors of the community to accept the value, even the necessity, of factory development. The correspondence columns of the Shetland papers bear mute witness to the quite astonishing pessimism which existed in certain quarters. One letter in 1953 proclaimed: 'It does not require a lowly intellect like mine to point out that Shetland is too far from the mainland for the erection of factories here ever to be a paying concern'.

Yet some national bodies such as the Scottish Agricultural Organisation Society, more clairvoyant than most, could anticipate the much later creation of the Highlands and Islands Development Board, stating in their 1947 annual report that 'the magnitude of the Highlands and Islands problem requires attention by the Government on a basis never before contemplated'. In Shetland itself, however, a request to the Secretary of State to designate the islands a development area was followed the next month by a debate which deplored the seasonality of existing employment but still shied away from the tricky paths of industrial development in favour of the smooth, known road of public works as the panacea for all ills. This first phase of development in post-war Shetland ended, in 1950, with chronic unemployment and widespread gloomy forebodings.

Second phase

The seven years from 1951 to 1958 consitute a second phase. In one sense these were depressing years for development prospects. Although the correspondence columns of the local papers show, by the pages of letters on development week after week, that people were beginning to be more generally aware of the problems which faced the community, few solutions were mooted; with no direction to all the talk and thinking and with little realism in the proposals, there was a great deal of pessimism. But a series of editorials, highly critical of the general apathy, began to appear in the local press. One typical and timely example claimed that

> there are many who feel that more emphasis should be placed on the Shetlanders' responsibility towards a solution of the problems. It must not be thought that there is no progess in Shetland, or that Shetlanders regard Government aid as a pre-requisite of all development.

These were certainly seven lean years for the community as a whole. Unemployment stayed at a high rate and emigration rocketed. More people left Shetland in the ten years between 1951 and 1961 than in the preceding twenty years. There was considerable soul-searching about the future of the hosiery industry. The herring fishing collapsed and from a value of more than £400,000 in 1948 slumped to a tenth of that figure in 1953. Despair abounded, and envious contrasts were made by the pessimists with the prosperity of Orkney. One letter in the *Shetland Times* in 1953 sums up the sorry state of morale in the islands. 'It is hard', stated the correspondent, 'to foresee a stable economy whereby prosperity of any high degree would be enjoyed by the majority of the Shetland people'. In 1955, indeed, the Althing debated and then carried the self-destructive motion that 'Remote areas are a liability to the nation'. What would be the voting if a similar motion were debated today? The Chamber of Commerce was in such retreat that in 1957, significantly, it was only after several unsuccessful attempts that it succeeded in raising a quorum for its annual general meeting.

Third phase

What may be perceived as a third phase then followed. In 1958, undramatically and without any hint of the minor industrial revolution that was to come, things started to change for the better. The catalyst was the formation of the Shetland Development Council. At first this was a huge body on which sat nominees from every conceivable corner of Shetland life, from the Yachting Association to the Tennis Club. For the first time, many new minds were committed to the serious consideration of Shetland's problems. For the first time there existed a body specifically charged with the responsibility for analysing Shetland's position—assessing its potential, pressing for action within the framework of what was practical and possible. Development in the future was to be positively encouraged; a definite lead was to be given to the community; self-confidence had to be restored and initiative encouraged. The then County Convener, later a full-time member of the Highlands and Islands Development Board, summed the whole situation up in a few words at the inaugural meeting of the Development Council. 'Development today', said Prophet Smith, 'does not come by accident: we can no longer sit back and wait for something to turn up. Unless we are prepared to plan, we cannot hope to progress'.

The new Development Council appointed five sub-committees: in addition to the predictable executive, general purposes and finance groups, a sub-committee was given responsibility for tourism and publicity and another for economic and indudstrial matters. There were no funds, of course, but the stated aim of the Council was to try to raise sufficient money to allow the appointment of a full-time secretary and the establishment of an office which could function also as a tourist information centre. They started in the traditional way, with a sale of work; and the first £110 went into the bank account.

The watershed came in 1959. The burden of planning for and supporting a tourist centre was removed when the generosity of local firm provided both office accommodation and voluntary staff. And in the same year the Council transmuted itself into the Shetland Council of Social Service. In this new guise it received a substantial grant from the Development Commissioners and was therefore able to appoint, jointly with Shetland County Council, a secretary who combined his work for the Council of Social Service with that as County Development Officer.

Two years later the functions were split, a full-time appointment being made to each post. Another year passed and the Development Office added an assistant to its staff. With three men working full-time on development matters, Shetland then became—and has remained—more fully staffed than any other Highland county in this sphere of activity. While development is still relatively new on the local government scene, it can surely be said to have a vital rôle to play in it.

By the time that Mr R. J. Storey, Shetland's first Development Officer, left the islands in 1963 he had promoted in the County Council much basic thought and action on development problems. Such enterprises as the Yell conference of 1962 brought that aggressive, realistic and effective attitude to development matters which has typified the elected representatives of Shetland ever since. It is difficult for an official to speak well of his councillors without appearing to flatter them for reasons of self-preservation. But I can pay honest tribute to the willingness and the speed of action demonstrated by the Council in voting to use their statutory and financial powers to the limit in assisting new factory projects: this played a crucial rôle in the regeneration of the sixties. I doubt if, in proportion to its size, any other Council had done more.

The creation of the Development Council thus provided a focal point for the initial dialogue on development problems and prospects. In the 1940s and 1950s the problems of some particular sectors of the community had been considered to some extent, even if not always in a particularly constructive light, by those engaged in those particular spheres of activity. The local authority in the early years debated economic problems only rarely and superficially. Its pronouncements tended to be limited to a pious hope that some form of remedial action would be taken by the government: there was some talk of self-help, but there were few ideas as to how this could be achieved. In retrospect this was not so surprising. Shetland, even in 1969, because of the relatively small scale of industrial operations, lacked a powerful voice in its economic affairs such as that provided by the trade unions or business federations which have always played a vital rôle in pressing for development in the urban south. The

County Council remained the principal voice for Shetland in most aspects of community life, including economic affairs. In the 1940s and 1950s this voice was not being properly heard; and therefore no corporate voice was being heard.

This situation altered completely in a third definable phase, between 1958 and 1965. In the Shetland Development Council, in the Shetland Council of Social Service, and in the Development Committee of the County Council were debated and dissected all the preconceptions, the prejudices, the possibilities and, above all, the embryo practical schemes for future development. This brought a dual benefit—long, serious and involved examination of the problems, and then the experience in practical involvement. Shetland, from having been a community where development was lacking, prepared to show the way. The islands rejected both wild optimism and blind pessimism, and adhered strongly to a new pragmatic realism.

Fourth phase

The fourth phase of post-war development in the islands was the most significant of all. In 1965 the Highlands and Islands Development Board was created and the four years after its inception brought dramatic changes in the Shetland economy. Shetland was ready for the Board, ready to take advantage of the financial assistance it could give to those with ideas and initiative. More will be said about the Board later: it is enough here to see that the creation of that body was, in Shetland, like finding the missing piece of the jigsaw. The lethargy of the forties, the apathy and pessimism of the fifties, the soul-searching of the early sixties, seem—in retrospect—an almost inevitable progression towards the pragmatic confidence, the initiative, the preparedness which the Shetlanders came to show in the years 1965–69. Shetland lacked only the financial assistance and the encouragement which could make it all happen. The Board saw that it did happen. But how was the community at large moulded and influenced by the events of the years since the end of the war? How did particular industries fare during this time?

DEVELOPMENT SINCE 1946

Textiles

In 1946 the Shetland knitwear industry was enjoying an unprecedented boom. Demand was high, and so were prices. The industry was based almost entirely on fully handknit garments, and had consequently a very definite limit on what could be produced. Because of this method of production, prices were high and yet represented but a poor return for the many hours spent in knitting a single garment. The tweed industry was also growing; weaving sheds were going up in several areas, and demand for tweed was also brisk. Much more than in 1969, these were cottage-based industries. There were only eight knitwear units—four in Lerwick, one in Scalloway, one in Hillswick, one in Voe and one in Sandwick—at which tweed was usually also produced. Of the knitwear production 90 per cent was being sold in the United Kingdom, a contrast with 1969 when more than three-quarters of total output was for export.

The few years after the war were traumatic years in which a succession of troubles beset the industry. Some of them were to reappear spasmodically, others had an effect reaching down to the late 1960s.

Most apparent immediately after the war was the violent antagonism by the 'old hands' against the introduction of hand-flat knitting machines. The passions raised by this issue were fierce indeed, and argument raged widely. It was suggested that under the 'corrupting influence' of the new machines, the Shetland hosiery industry would collapse. 'Knitting machines', said another opponent, 'will be the downfall of the Shetland industry'. And in 1948 there was indeed a serious slump in the demand. But it was a slump only in the demand for the pure handknit. It was machine-knit which the great mass of the market demanded, and it was the introduction of the machine that was to transform the Shetland knitwear industry into a powerful and priceless cornerstone of the economy.

The trouble with the handknit was basically one of price. It had sold very well during and immediately after the war when, with little available as alternative, customers had been happy to pay the necessary high price for the sake of obtaining knitwear at all. With the easing of rationing restriction, the mass-market manufacturers in the south stocked and sold garments at a fraction of the price of Shetland handknit and the demand for it collapsed. But the name 'Shetland' was then, as it is today, a symbol of quality, a desirable product. There was therefore good demand for the new, cheaper, hand-flat garments, machine-made in the islands. The other snag about the handknit was the lack of professionalism which attended much, though by no means all, of its marketing process. A lot of handknit was going out of Shetland in small quantities, unbranded and unpromoted, extremely vulnerable to market change. A leader in the *Shetland Times* in 1948, as the slump in the demand for handknit began to bite deep, claimed that 'This stiffening market serves to warn knitters of the need for a real co-operative marketing system and trade mark'.

The successful knitwear operations in the post-war years were those based on factories and on marketing units where foresighted men invested in buildings and equipment, in presentation and promotion, and competed for sales with a realistically priced product backed by a professional management organisation. But this concept was new to the islands. It was going to take years for the world market-places to come to know, respect and demand 'Shetland'. Only then did the real explosion take place. That still lay in the future. As late as 1951 one merchant was stating that 'the industry is unlikely ever to reach the peak dimensions in demand and money value experienced and enjoyed for some ten years during and after the war'. As if these production and marketing problems were not enough, the industry also had troubles on the raw material side at the same time. Suspicion of the United Kingdom Wool Marketing Board which had been set up after the war prompted Shetland wool producers to seek to form their own body, and efforts were made to gain government approval for a Shetland Wool Marketing Scheme. By 1950 when this proposal was finally rejected by the government, the U.K. Board was already in existence, and Shetland was not part of it. Even in 1969 Shetland wool producers had no guaranteed outlet for their clip, no guaranteed minimum price and no subsidy payment.

There were innumerable attempts to establish a locally-based yarn-spinning mill which could handle the entire island clip and then supply the local manufacturers with their yarn requirements. There were private negotiations with individual firms in the south, government reports and investigations, even the brave attempt in the late forties to start a mill in Baltasound. But the islands were still in 1969 waiting for their spinning mill—though it is probably true that at no time before were the portents so favourable, or the likelihood so strong, that after years of struggle Shetland would then ultimately get its mill.

With exploration of new markets in the mid-1950s resulting in the opening up of America, with about half the entire output going to the U.S.A. in the later fifties, more knitwear units were operating in the islands. In 1957 the Shetland Woollen Industries Association—a body drawing its membership from wool growers, manufacturers and home knitters alike—succeeded in obtaining from the Board of Trade new galley marks to cover not only handknit Shetland garments but also hand-flat machine garments and the products of a booming tweed industry. By 1959 there were four additional knitwear units, based at Northmavine, Mossbank and two in Lerwick, and demand for hosiery was brisk. But large areas of the county still had no knitwear units and, while home knitting was widespread, there was still a very considerable scope for further growth.

This growth came in the sixties. The twelve knitwear units of 1959 ten years later became twenty-seven, and their annual production of Shetland knitwwear was then valued at almost £1,500,000. Knitwear units then existed in every part and corner of the county. Long an exclusively female prerogative, the industry had come to employ a large number of men in factories and, at home, in knitting the plain part of the garment on hand-flat machines. Yell provided a particularly good example of the benefits which were brought. In 1962, the year of the Yell conference, the island was in desperate straits. In 1969, besides developments in other fields, there was employment for men in three knitwear units. In the Shetland Knitters Association's factory at Mid Yell, work was then on a shift system—6 a.m. till 2 p.m., 2 p.m. till 10 p.m.—so that a man with a croft or a lobster boat had daylight hours, no matter which shift he worked in the factory, for his other activities. The largest of the knitwear units employed about fifty people on the premises, plus, of course, hundreds of outworkers doing the linking and knitting of the yokes. It is well to remember, however, that even the smallest of the units had considerable significance in the economy of the township in which it was located. Production throughout Shetland by 1969 was at saturation point: it was doubtful if one additional jumper could be produced in the islands, and yet international demand for Shetland knitwear was far from being satisfied.

Fishing

The fishing industry at the end of the war faced problems probably greater even than those of the knitwear industry. The great strength of the Shetland fisheries was traditionally in the herring fishery. Although it had dwindled throughout the twentieth century from an incredible peak in 1905, when no fewer than 650,000 crans were landed in the islands (to be compared with 46,000 crans in 1968), herring fishing had still been at the outbreak of the Second World War of very great significance to the economy. Of the thirty or so herring curing stations in Lerwick and elsewhere in the islands, most closed down during the war years and mostly closed for good. If the herring fishing had been one of the strengths of the Shetland economy, it also had been one of its weaknesses because it was highly seasonal. On its own it could not provide a year-round prospect of full employment in the fisheries, and the Shetland fleet in 1946 consisted largely of elderly, unadaptable drifters.

What Shetland lacked in the post-war years was cohesive planning and direction for the fishing industry as a whole. Thus the modern, versatile fleet which fished out of Shetland harbours in 1969 and the diversified shore-processing facilities providing hundreds of permanent jobs were a long time a-growing. And it was growth attended by more than its share of growing pains. A first attempt to end the seasonality of the fishing came from Howarth's Scalloway yard which, immediately after the war, started to build dual-purpose boats for the Shetland fleet. But progress was slow and not helped by lack of shore-processing. Marketing weaknesses contributed to the general decline but, worst of all, was the collapse of the herring fishing after the post-war peak, in 1948, valued at £420,000. Landings declined through the 1950s. But there was to be a welcome resurgence—the figures for 1969 were well ahead of those for 1968, with more than £300,000 having been earned by the herring fleet in the first seven months. During the 1950s landings of white fish improved but could not compensate for the decline in herring values. Once again, dramatic growth came only in the later 1960s, despite a decline in 1967 and in 1968 because of poor spawning coupled with two bad winters. White fish were back in 1969 in such quantities that the boats were on a quota system, and brought again that pattern of alternatively good and relatively disappointing catches which seems inevitable.

In 1953 the value of local landings—throughout this section I have ignored figures of direct tripping to Aberdeen—had fallen to only £195,000, a great contrast with a valuation of £535,000 just five years previously. Local processing facilities would have helped to slow the decline, yet in that disastrous year of 1953 the White Fish Authority rejected a plea from Lerwick Town Council for the setting-up of a local processing market for white fish, on the grounds that additional freezing facilities in the islands were not needed. The situation was so bad that several skippers left Shetland for good, taking their boats with them. This was no time to replace older boats with expensive modern vessels and the number of boats of 40-feet and over in the Shetland fleet fell from 85 in 1955 to 47 in 1963. Thereafter, however, there was a steady increase and in 1969 there were almost seventy boats in an impressively modernized fleet. Burra Isle took delivery of the first steel purse-net boat in Shetland; another was nearing completion for a Whalsay skipper. The total value of fish landings in 1968 was almost £600,000 and that figure, because there had been a bad winter and a bad white fish season, was 25 per cent below the comparable figure for 1966.

As well as better fishings and better boats, the new success of the islands' fisheries depended on the build-up of shore-processing, providing a steady market for the catches of the smaller vessels which did not trip to Aberdeen and also bringing very substantial employment opportunities ashore. In 1959 there were two processing factories in Shetland—an old-established family firm in Scalloway, and the Fromac organisation in the Highlands and Islands Development Board plant in Lerwick: two years later Fromac pulled out but, fortunately, the build-up of new factories was under way by then. There were in 1969 no fewer than ten factories either in operation or under construction. Iceatlantic Frozen Seafoods opened up in Scalloway in 1960; Claben, subsidiary of an Aberdeen company, in 1964; and in 1966 Shetland Seafoods, then part of the Ross Group and later an Imperial Tobacco Company subsidiary, moved from small premises in which they had been mainly crab-processors to the empty H.I.D.B. factory in Lerwick and proceeded to mechanise and modernise it into the largest and most diversified of the Shetland processors. In 1966, too, the Scalloway firm of T.T.F. Ltd. which had opened on Blacksness Pier the previous year made substantial growth. The Sullom Voe Shellfish Company decided to set up in 1968 a new lobster, crab and scallop factory on the Out Skerries; and a branch of Shetland Seafoods was opened at Mid Yell, an 11,000 square-foot cannery for the Shetland Norse Preserving Company. There were two particularly exciting things about this last project: firstly, it was a Norwegian venture launched by two long-established and successful Norwegian firms in partnership; secondly, it was the first Shetland cannery and added a new dimension to the shore-processing picture.

Expansion of the fishing fleet was absolutely essential to all these new ventures. Whereas in 1959 the fleet was very much concentrated in Whalsay and Burra, by 1969—though the Burra and Whalsay fleets were as important as ever—there was, with the introduction of boats to the North Isles, an extension of the traditional fishing communities: in addition six modern, transom-stern, multi-purpose 34-foot boats were under construction, due to be delivered in 1970, to help supply the new factories in the north. Meanwhile the shellfish industry soared in importance from the first beginnings in 1947 when lobster worth £2,500 was landed. In 1968 this branch of the Shetland fisheries earned over £100,000, a figure which was soon to climb much higher with the new developments taking place in the north isles.

In 1969 Shetland had a diversified fishing industry, with a modern fleet and with shore facilities for processing of every type of fish landed in the islands. Every week several planeloads of crab left the Shetland Seafoods factory at Lerwick for Scandinavia, while from T.T.F.'s plant in Scalloway frozen fillet was shipped direct to the U.S.A. in an Icelandic refrigerated ship. The markets were universal, there was a great variety in the produce and the catching fleet was constantly growing. Despite problems, for no industry and least of all the fishing industry is every totally free from problems—the main one being that shifting imbalance where catching power outstrips processing capacity which then expands to overtake catching power and so *ad infinitum*—fishing became ever more important to the Shetland economy; and in 1969 there was much confidence in the future of this vital industry.

Agriculture

Agricultural production in the islands was valued in 1969 at about £1 million. Although there were some large farms in the more fertile parts of the county, these agricultural returns were earned from crofting. Whereas in 1946 there was scarcely so much as a tractor in the islands, by 1969 the industry had modernised itself. And Shetland agriculturalists have a superb record in reseeding and reclamation, having led the 'league table' in this for many years in the returns of the Crofters' Commission. At the end of the 1939–45 war, Shetland was importing milk from Orkney because of inadequate local production: but dairy farms were established throughout the county and excellent herds of beef cattle raised in a general period of more intensive and more productive land use. The disastrous effects of high shipping costs for feeding-stuffs, meanwhile, extinguished the pig and poultry industry which existed for a short time in the 1950s. While the nature of the land inevitably dictates that farming will never be to Shetland what it has always been to Orkney, there was still tremendous scope for improvement; the later 1960s gave every indication that it would be sought by young go-ahead men pioneering modern methods. Sheep and ponies are still the two products most readily associated with the islands and they are still very important in the agricultural economy. The sheep population in 1969 approached a quarter of a million, and the excellent work of the Shetland Flock Book Society had helped to preserve large numbers of pedigree, pure Shetland sheep. The pony industry too, thanks to the activities of the Stud Book Society, maintained a fine breed which commanded higher and higher prices: there was great acclaim in 1957 when a pony was sold for 116 guineas at the autumn sales, but this figure was far outpaced in October 1968 when an animal in Unst was bought for 570 guineas.

Tourism

Tourism was relatively stagnant between 1946 and 1956 but there has since been a growth of about 70 per cent in the number of holiday-makers coming to the islands. Although the season is still a short one, in the late 1960s the only limitation on tourist growth in the season was the amount of accommodation available in the islands: efforts were being made by bodies such as the Shetland Sea Angling Association to provide amenities and attractions which would extend the season both early and late. In 1959 there were fourteen hotels in the islands. Including the big new Lerwick Hotel, still under construction, the number had risen to eighteen. In the ten years since 1959, in fact, seven new hotels were established while, for various reasons, three others were closed. This was a very different story from the rather unhopeful attitude to tourism (as an aid to the economy, that is) which was prevalent at the time when the building that in 1969 had become Sumburgh Hotel was sold for demolition—fortunately, the contractor concerned had a change of heart at the last moment.

Other industries

Knitwear, fishing, agriculture and tourism are what might be called the traditional facets of the Shetland economy. In the 1960s there were other and newer elements, however—small as yet in comparison with these and other industries but full of promise. There are many individual craftsmen in Shetland who produce quality articles in basketwork, pottery, silver and gold, sheepskin and sealskin; and in the 1960s some extended their businesses by opening craft workshops and employing between two and ten people. One business of this kind was started in the 1950s, five began in the following decade: thus a stone-polishing factory was established in Whiteness, using the rich mineral resources of the islands. Also using the resources of Shetland—its climate and the plentiful supply of feeding obtained in fish offal from the processing factories—were the Wormdale mink farm, opened in 1964, and the rainbow trout farms at Strom and Olnafirth. One of the more esoteric indicators of the economy was the thriving business of publishing: the islands maintained in 1969 two presses which, since 1945, produced a remarkable number of good books on all aspects of Shetland life. Nor must we forget the growth in two decades since World War II in the service trades, the construction industry, and in transport and communications.

The future (as seen in 1969)

Where did this leave us in autumn 1969? What was the state of the community? What were the problems? What were the prospects?

Shetland in 1969 was a community imbued with that most vital of all emotions; confidence in its own future, instanced by the evident willingness to put faith *and money* into the future of the community. The help which Shetland received from the Highlands and Islands Development Board would never have been forthcoming if there had not been people of enterprise and initiative in the islands who were prepared to take advantage of it and, at the same time, to stake their own faith in the future by taking a calculated risk in their own projects. Shetland had then some 6 per cent of the population of the Highlands and Islands. In the first year of the Board's existence Shetland received help for 17 projects, bringing in sums equivalent to 10 per cent of all the funds which the Board disbursed; by 1967 that share had risen to 12 per cent for 27 projects; in 1968 Shetland claimed 17 per cent for 44 projects. The actual cash sums involved showed a remarkable growth over the three years, representing a total investment by the Board of about £650,000 in support of almost 90 different projects.

Many things happened in the late 1960s which twenty years before would probably have been deemed impossible. Individuals were prepared to back themselves: more importantly, the community at large was prepared to back individuals. There was, for example, substantial local shareholding in the new Lerwick Hotel and in factory developments elsewhere in the islands. Ordinary folk were ready to put their money into somebody else's project, buying their own stake in its and the community's future. A further indication of the changed regard for the future of these islands was the way in which it had become possible to attract investment from outside. Scandinavians, Scots and English invested their money, expertise and enterprise in Shetland. In the mail which arrived at the Development Office in one week in August 1969 there were, almost unbelievably, letters from three large firms in the south contemplating setting up in Shetland and from two individuals who had money they were prepared to invest in island projects. Large capital sums were required to develop on a large scale the existing industries, in terms of both technology and production—bigger and better fishing boats, power-looms in a new mass-market hosiery industry which would supplement but not supplant hand-frame production. Large-scale farming of trout and ultimately of white fish was also expected to make high demands.

There were problems as well as prospects. The press had lately announced that yet another 10 per cent increase in sea freight charges was to be inflicted on the islands. Freight rates were six times their pre-war level, and savage increases had become an annual event. Shetland was more than fortunate in having natural resources to exploit—this, indeed, was the sum and substance of the reason for recent growth—but there were fears for the viability of natural resources in the face of constant increases in freight charges which had already squeezed out certain activities and might well threaten others in the future. Agriculture, in particular, suffered dreadfully from penal freights; and the enthusiasm and ambition of the farming community was all the more to be praised in view of this fact. It seemed impossible to persuade the central authorities that a community as remote from London as Prague or Genoa had its own peculiar problems and prospects, but Shetland showed its determination to fight on against these impositions.

This raised the most crucial problem of all. How could London understand Shetland? I submit that London can understand Shetland no more than Shetland can understand London, but we in Shetland do not decide what is best for London. Yet in London were and are taken decisions which affect the basic fabric of social and economic life in these islands, taken it would seem, on all too many occasions, by persons with little or no knowledge or understanding of the Shetland situation. Who could imagine that a Transport Bill, specifically designed to encourage greater use of rail-freight facilities on the mainland, could have anything but a totally disastrous effect on rural haulage firms in the North Isles of Shetland? London could. London could in the 1960s also imagine that it made sense to amalgamate two water authorities—those of Shetland and Caithness—which were not linked by water resources or needs, but were actually *separated* by one hundred and twenty miles of it. The central authorities also cheerfully assured us that police amalgamation would bring economies, and in the first year of the amalgamated Northern Police Forces, Shetland's policing costs were levied from Caithness and rose by 66 per cent. These are but a few examples from the later 1960s. We have suffered episodes such as that which occurred when a civil servant who visited the islands believed that Faroe was part of the same county as Shetland. In view of all this, is it surprising that my greatest fear for the future in 1969 was that Shetland would be totally swallowed up, muffled and administered by people who just would not accept the simple, obvious fact that special circumstances demand special remedies, that the proof of the development pudding was there for all to see in Faroe and in Scandinavia, that the whole future of a community which in 1969 was alive, prosperous, dynamic, and an above-average contributor to the United Kingdom export drive was in jeopardy so long as its self-contained identity was threatened and its right questioned to take at the local level at least a smattering of the decisions which affected its life and livelihood?

CHAPTER XIV

Social Changes during the Quinquennium

JOHN J. GRAHAM

A LOCAL writer, commenting on the quincentenary celebrations, said: '... for centuries the common people of these islands have been going about their business, working hard and earning little, and nobody has paid much attention.... Their voice is heard occasionally, feeble, and far away. Nonetheless, they are the stuff of real history, the lives of those without whom the elect would not exist. One day their story, real history, will be told, and the cause for celebration become clear.'

Comparatively little has been written about the social history of Shetland; much remains to be done. What I hope to attempt is an exploratory review of territory which I trust will become the subject of more intensive research in the near future.

The lives of the common people cannot be regarded as something separate, something lived in isolation from other sections of the community. However much one may divide society into classes or castes, it is impossible to see historical change in terms of isolated groups within a particular community. Earl and bishop, merchant and minister, laird and crofter, each can be placed in his own particular sociological pigeon-hole, but each one's life and activities were affected in varying degrees by each of the others. The Shetland crofter himself must to a great extent be considered through the economic, institutional and cultural framework within which he had to live his daily life.

In attempting to make this vast subject rather more manageable within the limited space at my disposal, I have divided the period into five phases:

(1) 1469–1568—all but a century, during which the Scottish landed interest began progressively to acquire property in Shetland.

(2) 1568–1615—the short but violent period of the Stewart earls.

(3) 1615–1712—almost a century again when, with the overmighty earls out of the way, the lesser magnates got to work acquiring and consolidating their estates.

(4) 1712–1872—the long period of 160 years which bound the landlord and his tenants together within the system of fishing tenures.

(5) 1872–1969—almost a century again, marked by ever-increasing intervention from central government through commissions, legislation and financial support.

The acquisition of Shetland by the Scottish crown would have meant little change for Shetlanders during the succeeding century. They were a class of crofter-fishermen living off the produce of their land, disposing of their fish to Hanseatic merchants for cash or in exchange for fishing equipment, grain, ale, spirits, articles of clothing. Their native speech was Norse, their houses and steadings were built in the traditional Viking long-house pattern which determined the domestic architecture of Shetland folk for over a thousand years. Their laws, their customs and traditions, their entire fabric of living had evolved from their Scandinavian roots. They lived a reasonably secure and ordered existence, with great faith in the force of established custom as exercised by their lawmen at the representative meetings of the Lawthing. A measure of their autonomy can be gauged from the fact that they had even established commercial agreements with the German merchants, whereby the foud and 'certain honest, discreet men' negotiated annually the prices of fish sold and goods purchased.

During the first hundred years the Scottish infiltration proceeded steadily, affecting land, trade and religion. But with the arrival of Earl Robert Stewart and his half-brother, Lawrence Bruce of Cultmalindie, the pace of change increased dramatically. Stewart and Bruce were not mere land-hungry colonisers: they were real predators, out for the quick kill. Within a few years their oppressions, carried out with a blatant disregard of law or person, roused the whole islands into indignation. In 1577 some 760 udallers assembled at the Lawthing to give evidence of the tyranny of Bruce. This was a remarkable and historic gathering. About one-quarter of the adult male population of Shetland must have been present; their complaints were noted and Bruce dismissed as foud. But for the Shetland udaller it was the end of an auld sang. Not for another 300 years would Shetlanders be able to raise their united voices in protest. Until the Truck Commission of 1872 they were to endure exploitation, hunger, hardship, but in silence. And when at last their voice is heard again in 1872 the results of three centuries of silence and subjugation are only too obvious. Whereas the witnesses against Bruce spoke starkly and fearlessly, the evidence before the Truck Commission is all too often tentative and inhibited.

The period of Earl Patrick has been dealt with so thoroughly by Professor Donaldson that I propose to dwell only slightly on it. Between 1568 and 1615 the Stewart earls created a major convulsion in our local history. This period saw the end of Norse law in Shetland and the final assimilation of the isles into the structure of Scots government. It witnessed a trial of strength, not so much between the Stewarts and the lesser magnates, who felt the shadow of Scalloway Castle more ominous than did any udaller. It ushered in a period of lawlessness and anarchy at all levels of the community. When the chief administrator of the islands authorised his henchmen to rob, despoil, and evict, when ministers of the gospel were guilty of exploitation, common assault and intimidation, it is not to be wondered at that unruliness prevailed generally. The removal of Earl Patrick from the scene in 1611 did not improve matters. Then the coast was clear for the lesser predators and throughout the remainder of the seventeenth century the fight was on for the accumulation of bigger and bigger personal estates at the expense of the smaller landholder.

In 1620 the privy council sent a commission north to investigate 'multifarious oppressions and legal mal-practices in Shetland', while the case of Ninian Niven in the 1620s reveals evidence of considerable exploitation and tyrannising of small farmers. The reformed Church and its kirk sessions were actively in the field and in close alliance with the civil authorities. But the churchmen were encountering much opposition. In 1629 the privy council reported that it had received information 'of the great and high contempt of the ministerie and kirk discipline within the bounds of Zetland . . . by the presumption and boldness of lewde and dissolute persons.' These persons were accused of '. . . vile raylings and imprecatiouns spewed out aganis the ministrie in their faces, the upbraiding of thame in thair pulpits . . . the threatening of thame to break thair heads . . . the lying at await for the ministeris awin lyffes . . . coming to the kirks on the Sabbath day with unlawful weapouns to persew the ministeris of thair lyffes. . . .' Those responsible for such ongoings were no doubt followers of the Scottish landlords who were mainly episcopalian, but however much the ordinary folk might have been out of sympathy with their actions, such acts of violence must have created a climate in which law and order were held in some contempt. Indeed the Baillie Court Book for Dunrossness at the close of the seventeenth century suggests this prevailing mood of lawlessness: in 1694 there were 20 cases of assault in a community of 90 families.

And so we come to the end of the century and the third of the five periods I outlined earlier. How had the life of the individual Shetlander changed during these two hundred years or so? His house and its furnishings would have remained unchanged. His daily round of living would have altered little. He continued to look to the land and the sea for his livelihood. The land, in normal years, could be expected to keep him and his family for perhaps six months out of the twelve, and for the remainder of the year the fish he sold or bartered to the German merchants eked out his existence and paid his rent. The majority were now tenants of Scottish landowners. Fewer of them had land valued at more than 5–10 marks. The fairly prosperous middle class of farmers which Professor Donaldson saw as forming the core of Shetland society at the beginning of the seventeenth century had now shrunk considerably. Whereas Dr Donaldson mentions Whiteness and Weisdale as a district which seemed to have had a higher proportion than others of the relatively well-to-do, a century later this area had 120 holdings averaging 6 merks each. Of the 120, only 15 tenants had land of 10 merks or over, while 56 had land of under 5 merks.

But even the whittling down of the size of the holding would have made little appreciable difference to the tenant. The major change during these 200 years occurred in the social fabric affecting the individual's feeling of security, his place in the overall scheme of things. During these centuries the structure of Shetland society had undergone considerable dislocation. Any community is held together by institutions and customs. Institutions control social relationships at a formal and impersonal level, while customs operate on an informal, more personal basis. Prior to the seventeenth century, local institutions and customs had worked together as integral parts of local society. The old legal and administrative system had evolved from the same background as had the customs and traditions of the people; it was the explicit recognition of their desire for an ordered existence; it was administered by individuals identified closely with the local community, who used the common language of the community. The sixteenth and seventeenth centuries disturbed this equilibrium. Law and people, ruler and ruled were alienated—socially, linguistically, culturally, and economically.

It seems that most Shetlanders were bilingual at the beginning of the seventeenth century. By 1630, according to information supplied to Sibbald for his account of Scotland, the people of a northern parish in Shetland '. . . seldom speak other [than Norse] among themselves, yet all of them speak the Scots tongue more promptly and more properly than generally they do in Scotland'. This competence in the new tongue, at a time when there were apparently no schools in the area, is quite remarkable and reveals just how urgently the local people felt the need to come to terms with their new situation. But in making this accommodation their native speech suffered. If a language is to continue in its vital function of knitting together, expressing and explaining social relationships, it is essential that it should not lose any of its richness and flexibility; and, even more important, that it should be so capable of evolving as to describe changing situations, new experiences. To be able to do this it must have a recognised social status. And this is what Norn no longer had. When it ceased to be used as the recognised language of law and administration, this status declined, and its use was restricted to the Shetlanders' workaday world. In 1700 Brand reported that 'many of the people speak Norse . . . especially in the Northern Isles where in some places it is the first language of the children'. Norn, as a distinctive language, was in its death throes, confined only to remoter pockets of population. Soon it would cease to exist as such and become absorbed into the speech patterns of Lowland Scots. Its passing diminished the cultural identity of the Shetland people, and as the eighteenth century opens we find them exposed and vulnerable on every quarter.

The fourth period (from 1712 to 1872) is, in many ways, a major watershed in the history of the Shetland people. Three new factors began early to affect local society and were to exert enormous influence on Shetland life for well over a century. Firstly, the local landlords moved in to capitalise and operate the fishing after the decline of the German traders. Secondly, the presbyterian church, with its apparatus of kirk session and presbytery, began to operate really effectively. And, thirdly, there were the beginnings of formal education.

To mention the word 'laird' in Shetland is to move into waters muddied by bitter memories, distortion and prejudice. For generations one of our favourite blood sports has been 'hunting the laird'. The evil, grasping laird has become one of our figures of folklore, but like all legends this contains a dramatic truth, rather over-simplified.

With the decline of the German trade during the early years of the eighteenth century, Shetland found herself in an economic crisis. The merchants of the Hansa had for over two hundred years brought a measure of prosperity to Shetland. Fish, agricultural produce and hosiery were sold at agreed prices, while the local people were supplied with bread, linen, liquor and other requirements. The amount of German currency which remained in circulation for most of a century after the departure of the German merchants is some indication of the value of this trade, but there were others: for the landlords had benefited through the leasing of sites for the Hanseatic trading booths, while their tenants' rents were frequently paid to them in cash.

Both landlords and tenants found themselves victims of the collapse of the fish trade. The local economy was threatened and the only obvious hope of reviving it lay with the lairds, for they alone could contribute the necessary capital. But these lairds found the Continental markets extremely unpredictable. The letter books of Thomas Gifford, perhaps the most enterprising of all the early merchant-lairds, are full of grousings about the precarious nature of the trade in dried fish. He writes in 1718: 'I have the last year met with many disappointments in my small trade to Hamburgh, and unless something can be raised that way, the earle [of Morton] needs expect nothing from me, for I have been travelling through the greatest part of the country to gather the rents and not received above £40 sterling, and that all in German stoyvers and double stoyvers, a coin that passes no way in the world but in the country where it is made, and in this poor place where we are content to take anything. . . .' This wry observation captures vividly the economic situation at the time: both laird and tenant were caught in the grip of a depression.

It was the laird alone who had the freedom to manoeuvre. Committed to the rôle of capitalist he could not readily withdraw, and if the profits were precarious, they were at least there to be won, however marginal. The obvious answer lay in increasing the turnover of fish exported, and to do this he had to increase his labour force. And what more readily available source of man-power than his own tenantry? Thus began a situation which resulted in the fishing tenures, whereby occupancy of a croft involved a commitment to fish for the landlord who exercised the right of pre-emption in securing the total catch at a specified price which he himself would fix. In 1726 we find Thomas Gifford spelling out the obligations of tenants on his estate. It is interesting to note from the following agreement both the patriarchal tone which he assumes and also the implication that the policy he is laying down is for the common good: '. . . that the fishing Trade is the principal Means providence has ordained for the support of the paroch . . . without which ye could neither subsist your families nor pay the land rent and other publick burdens . . . But having the benefit and prosperity of the paroch of Northmaven more in view than any profit or advantage I possess by the trade, I am satisfied to goe into the following agreement. . . . And as I have a natural right and power to oblige my own tenants to accept thereof so I hope it will appear so faire and reasonable to all that no honest man in the paroch who other regairdeth his own Interest or the publick good will refuse the same'. The agreement which was signed by 103 Northmavine tenants stipulated that Thomas Gifford would undertake to furnish them with all the necessaries required for fishing and would buy their fish at the 'common price', if they guaranteed to sell to no one else. Failing this they were to be liable to a fine of £6 Scots for each parcel of fish sold to any other merchant. This was no merely private agreement negotiated between landlord and tenant, but was given legal status by being presented before a stewart court. Here was the complete, ironclad monopoly: invoked by law and secured by penal sanctions. But the most iniquitous aspect of it all was that Thomas Gifford was steward-depute for Shetland and as such the principal justice of the local courts. On this occasion, however, he had his local depute officiate. Perhaps he felt his presence as judge might be construed as legal intimidation. After all, the memory of Bruce of Cultmalindie, who exploited his position as foud for personal gain, was only five generations away. But the most likely explanation is that he would have seen nothing irregular in reinforcing a monopoly by legal sanctions. He regarded his paternalistic rôle as vital to the whole community. If he failed to prosper, his tenants would suffer accordingly and in their own interests would have to toe the line. This attitude continued throughout the eighteenth and nineteenth centuries, forgetful of the fact that the self-styled patriarchal eye had all too often been blind to the sufferings of the people. An official observer of the British Destitution Committee of 1847 commented of Shetland: 'I could find only a few cases where individual landowners had made any extra-ordinary effort to relieve the wants of their tenantry or had proposed to have done so had the external aid been withheld.' Not that they were without the means to have done so. The Gifford estate in the 1750s was worth at least £10,000 sterling, and in 1819 the Garth estate was valued at over £13,000.

But there is another side to the activities of the landlords. If we look further into the operations of Gifford of Busta we find neither philanthropist nor tyrant, but a man who often acted humanely and in the interest of his tenantry. He was the focal point of the whole community—touching, through a whole network of relationships, the lives of the local people on every quarter. By the 1740s he owned almost three-quarters of Delting and practically two-thirds of Northmavine. Apart from his basic rôle as land-master and merchant, we find him organising education for the area by admitting local children to schools run by private tutors employed for his own children, arranging apprenticeships for local boys, playing a dominant part in kirk sessions and presbyteries. When tenants fell into arrears he arranged with them to work off debts by building dykes, repairing houses, casting peats, foddering his animals, salvaging whales, selling produce. He was essentially a business man committed to a system, in itself pernicious, but one which he operated not without humanity. Two examples from his Day Book are fairly typical of the way in which the system worked:

'*Robert Sinclair in Burraness*: July 27th, 1715—Given him a Tack of my 3 mks. land in Burraness for 5 years the first being Crop 1716, the debt payment at Lambas that yr. and obliged to pay service and powltrie fowls. Conform to the Countrie practice given him ane order to gae to Unst and get timber to repair the houses.' Robert Sinclair proved unable to pay his rent and in 1721 the account is closed with Robert declared bankrupt and his debt standing at £17.11s Scots.

'In 1718—Set to Gilbert Manson the old roum besouth the Voe lying in the Scattald of Flett called Curkagarth—To be laboured by him for three years free of any duty and thereafter to pay for it according to the worth thereof, the first year being Crop 1718. Have also given him Timber for house.' Gilbert Manson managed to keep his head above water, balancing his account mainly by foddering Busta's animals.

The worst aspect of this system was that it made the tenants economic vassals, deprived of any independence or opportunity for initiative or means of registering complaints. The landlords' will became the tenants' law. It placed the tenants absolutely in the hands of the landmaster who could, by the whims of nature, vary from the bullying tyrant to the genial master. As time consolidated the system, it is not to be wondered that the crofter-fishermen became submissive, even servile, accepting their lot as something pre-ordained. And the presbyterian Church, with its authoritarian framework and Calvinist doctrine, confirmed them in the view that life was 'a vale of tears' and that only by humility and acceptance could spiritual rewards be attained.

The presbyterian Church did not operate really effectively in Shetland until after 1700. In that year the Rev. John Brand visited the isles as a member of a General Assembly commission. He found the body of the people to be very ignorant of God and religion. This assessment is amply confirmed by reports from a series of presbyterial visitations which Brand's visit set in motion. These reveal evidence of the material and spiritual poverty of the Church at this time—derelict buildings, lack of manses and glebes, infrequent celebration of the sacrament, people illiterate, immoral and lawless, with assault, drunkenness, witchcraft, slandering and petty theft rife throughout the country. When we contrast this situation with the reports of parish ministers and visitors from the south at the close of the century, we realise that the eighteenth century saw a considerable reformation of morals and manners among the Shetland people. Parish ministers in their contributions to the *Old Statistical Account* are unanimous in commending their parishioners as decent, respectable people. Indeed practically the only vices they single out for condemnation are excessive tea-drinking and an addiction to fine clothes. The district of Whiteness and Weisdale had 555 births registered between 1727 and 1761, with only 15 or 2.7 per cent recorded as illegitimate. In 1852 the officer in charge of building the 'meal roads' reported that he 'had never met with a more sober, docile, or tractable people, or any so susceptible of kindness shown to them. During the operations of over four years only £2 worth of tools went missing although at the end of the works many came forward eagerly to buy tools. There were only three or four complaints about drunkenness or improper conduct'. And we must recall that the people referred to were living at that time through a period of extreme poverty and destitution.

It would be an oversimplification to claim that this transformation from lawlessness to social order was solely the work of the Church. We must not forget that during this period there operated a series of Country Acts designed to maintain good neighbourhood and keep in check petty crime. Each district had its local bailiffs, or ranselmen as they were called, with authority to enter and search houses on suspicion of theft. At the same time there is no doubt that the kirk of the eighteenth century set a pattern of behaviour which had an enormous effect on the whole community.

The kirk session was one of the most powerful instruments of the presbyterian system. At its best it was the people's court, moral watchdog and welfare service: at its worst it was an agency for petty espionage, peddling in gossip and scandal. We tend to think of the old kirk sessions as chastisers of the immoral, and certainly many eighteenth-century session clerks inscribed in their records the charge of 'ante-nuptial fornication'. But their responsibilities were infinitely wider than that. They looked after church finance and fabric, they were community bankers offering loans to those in need, they administered poor relief, looked after lepers and other unfortunates, provided home helps for motherless children, fostered orphans, supervised local schools, ran small libraries, and were in general the only organised body operating within the parish.

Although the disciplinary powers vested in the kirk session gave Holy Willies too much scope for petty tyranny, exploitation of scandal-mongering, and sheer sadistic pursuit of the unfortunate, their very sternness and rigidity were perhaps what the situation at the time demanded. They were certainly uncompromising and no respector of person or rank. Lairds, doctors, ministers themselves, were all liable to the same moral law, and this impartiality must have impressed the people, as did the authority and rigour of the action taken by the session. For example, in 1760 at Sandness Andrew Twatt's son was charged with abusive language and imprecations against a neighbour, bidding the Devil break his neck. It was discovered by the session that Andrew Twatt had not chastised his son for the same, and he was not only rebuked for so wickedly disregarding his baptismal vows but ordered to bring his son before the session and chastise him in their presence. Which Andrew Twatt did.

The ministers themselves wielded enormous influence. In many instances they spent their entire working lives in the one parish. The Revs. Grierson and Mitchell spanned virtually the whole eighteenth century in Tingwall; John Mill was 62 years in Dunrossness, James Buchan 43 years in Walls, John Morison 36 years in Delting. These men knew their parishes and congregations intimately; and many of them in their contributions to the *Old Statistical Account* are eloquent in their condemnation of the system of fishing tenures operated by the lairds. But there is no evidence in kirk session or presbytery records that they took any practical steps towards alleviating the burdens of the tenantry. On the other hand, it cannot be said that minister and laird always presented a united establishment front at this time. Certainly there were marriage alliances between the manse and haa-house but frequently relationships were strained. The Revs. Mill and Morison engaged in lengthy disputes with their local heritors over manses, glebes and teinds, while Gordon of Fetlar complained bitterly to the presbytery in 1802 of the lack of interest by the landlords in the ruinous state of his church and the fact that he was living in a hovel of a manse where he had to set the kitchen fire in the middle of the floor lest it set fire to walls built partly out of turf. The major contribution towards stipends and upkeep of kirks and manses had to come from the landlords and it is not surprising that ministers were chary of antagonising their principal paymasters.

The Rev. John Mill has left in his diary the record of his long and rancorous incumbency of the parish of Dunrossness. He appears as a man of great personal integrity but the harshness of his spiritual outlook, in which he used disaster and destitution as signs of divine displeasure, makes one wonder if anything but fear kept his flock around him. During the famine of 1783 the sheriff sent circular letters to all local parish ministers requesting them to distribute the parish allocation of government charity meal. Mill replied that this was 'a trade I was never employed in and have no mind to undertake now. Merchandise is more becoming Persons of their [i.e. landlords'] character than ministers of the Gospel who have matters of greater moment to mind if faithful to their trust.' He added that, moreover, he was very busy catechising at the time. Five years later when the best harvest in seven years was being taken, he writes: 'People were publicly warned to beware of abusing it to God's dishonour, as in 1781, by fiddling, and ranting, and gluttony, drunkenness and all unclean abominations, and thereby provoke a just and holy God to send sore judgments on the land, by famine and a plague, to sweep such obstinate vermin off the earth into the pit of destruction.'

I am convinced that the presbyterian Church, however bleak and authoritarian, made a major contribution to the social stability of Shetland life. It can be argued that what was achieved was not so much a stable as an inert community, with independence and the creative instincts stifled. Certainly very little folk music or literature emerges from this period, but there is no direct evidence to suggest that the Kirk, apart from zealots such as Mill, campaigned against these activities. What it did do was to provide a unifying influence and a certain sense of spiritual community.

The third important factor influencing eighteenth-century life in Shetland was the beginnings of formal education. The seventeenth-century legislation for the establishment of parochial schools had been entirely ignored in Shetland. At the beginning of the eighteenth century the only education being carried on was by private tutors of lairds' and ministers' families, the occasional small church school conducted by a reader, and a few private adventure schools frequently run by women. Very few people could read and ministers reported that it was difficult to find sufficient literate elders to form kirk sessions.

In 1709 the Society in Scotland for the Propagation of Christian Knowledge was formed with the object of bringing 'piety and virtue' to the Highlands and Islands, designated as 'Popish and Infidel parts of the world'. In 1711 Zetland presbytery petitioned the Society for erection of schools in its area, and in 1713 the first was set up in Walls under a teacher from the Scottish Borders. Within a fortnight 40 pupils were enrolled and every indication was given that the community was eager for education. The Society's funds were limited and although pressed for more schools, only three had been established by 1740. Parishes were clamouring for education and to make the most of the Society's local allocation it was agreed in 1740 that the three schools be ambulatory: to remain within specified parishes for two years at a time then to move on to another three areas. At this time the landlords were under constant pressure from the presbytery to fulfil their legal obligations and establish parochial schools. This met with no initial success, not only because many lairds were unwilling to make their statutory contribution of one half the cost, but because the whole concept of the single parish school supported with a stipend of at least 100 merks was quite unsuitable for an area with such scattered pockets of population as Shetland. To expect the heritors and people of a parish such as Bressay, Burra and Quarff to contribute towards one school for the whole area was unrealistic, and in varying degrees most parishes were in similar straits. In fact, it was not until 1827 that the act of parliament of 1696 was formally implemented and Shetland had a legal school in each parish, and then only because the extension of SSPCK and Church schools into the remoter areas made the establishment of a central parochial school a feasible proposition in the eyes of the parishioners.

During the eighteenth century a very limited number of children attended school but there was general diffusion of learning throughout the islands, parents often engaging women to teach reading to their children in exchange for bed and board. In the early 1820s investigations suggested that while the Hebrides and other western parts of Inverness-shire and Ross-shire—all predominantly Gaelic speaking areas, it should be noted—had 70 per cent of their populations over the age of eight who could not read, Shetland had only 9 per cent of that age group who were illiterate. The degree of literacy was, however, extremely low and consisted mainly of an ability to struggle through the Scriptures. Indeed, one of the SSPCK rules stipulated that arithmetic was not to be commenced until the pupil had read through the Bible at least once. Inability to read the Scriptures came to be considered a social and spiritual disgrace. On 8 November 1823, the parochial schoolmaster pinned the following notice to the Mid Yell kirk door: 'I am very sorry to say that some families are without the word of God altogether. . . . Their names have already been taken up and may be made public in the Parish to their own disgrace if they continue much longer insensible to their eternal welfre'.

There was a real hunger for education. The erection of schools aroused great local enthusiasm. In 1768 the building of Happyhansel School at Walls involved the whole community—minister, landlord and tenants. Eleven young men offered to supply tobacco and 'strong waters' to the men engaged in the building and forty-two more were to be invited to make similar contributions. The East Yell parochial school was to open on 11 November 1822, but on the appointed day no furniture had arrived from Lerwick. The teacher records that people were so anxious for the school to commence that they offered to send planks to be placed on stones as forms. In the circumscribed world of the Shetland crofter of these days education offered a glimpse of wider and better things.

Between 1755 and 1851 the population more than doubled. Although this meant more and more sub-division of townships to accommodate the additional families and less and less homegrown food to maintain these families, the lairds saw nothing in this but the hand of progress. For them an expanding tenantry meant in practice more fishermen and, in terms of prevailing economic theory, greater progress. But for the great mass of crofter-fishermen this was a period of marginal existence which a bad harvest or poor fishing season could precipitate into famine conditions. From 1780 to 1850 there was on the average one famine year in every four. The destitution during many of these years was appalling, although never on the disastrous scale experienced in Ireland or the Western Isles in the 1840s. Fish, particularly the piltock, was the salvation of many a Shetland family during the bad years. In September 1804 a visitor to Shetland encountered several families who had not tasted oatmeal or bread for five months and were living almost entirely on piltocks. In some districts oxen and young cattle were bled, and the blood mixed with meal for added sustenance.

During these hard years, however, there began the gradual breaking down of the close links which had bound tenant to landlord for so long. The French Wars of the late eighteenth century drew thousands of Shetland men—many of them press-ganged—into the Royal Navy. Those fortunate enough to return brought with them an aura of adventure and the lure of new horizons which the young were eager to explore. The whaling ships of Hull, Dundee and Peterhead were now calling regularly at Lerwick where hundreds of local men joined them for the spring and summer expeditions to Greenland and the Davis Straits. Lairds attempted to combat this intrusion into their monopoly by imposing fines on all who joined these ships, but this had little effect. In fact, by the end of the eighteenth century the landmasters were finding it increasingly difficult to maintain their stranglehold on the crofters. The growth of Lerwick had seen the rise of independent merchants who had made money in trade with Dutch fishermen, naval vessels, whaling ships, not to mention profits from that 'invisible import'—smuggled liquor. The great social gulf which had existed for over 200 years between the small upper class of landlords and the great mass of the people, was now being filled by these landless merchants. The ambitious man with a small nest-egg of naval prize-money or Greenland savings could escape the treadmill of crofting and fishing by setting up a small shop. By the 1850s and 1860s there were over 200 retail establishments in Shetland. Unst alone had over forty. But many of these small shops had inadequate capital to survive in a system where long credit had become a trading convention. They operated the usual barter system, trucking in knitwear, eggs, and sometimes fish, but bad debts accumulated and bankrupted many of these small businesses.

Meanwhile the great bulk of the population spent their lives in a daily round which had changed but little over centuries. In 1801 an average of over six people lived in each house, which in the majority of cases consisted of one or two rooms with no windows. In 1861, 1016 or 16 per cent of houses had no windows, the only means of light being supplied from an opening in the thatched roof which also served as an exit for smoke from the fire in the middle of the floor; 33 per cent of the houses had one window and 43 per cent two windows, while a mere 8 per cent had more than two windows. Dr Arthur Mitchell, a Poor Law commissioner, contrasted the Shetland house of this period with the traditional Western Isles house. 'There is', he wrote, 'a barrenness and desolation about the misery of a Harris house that is tenfold more depressing. It is a poor house and an empty one—a decaying, mouldy shell, without pretence of a kernel. Whereas in Shetland there is usually a certain fulness. There are bulky sea-chests, with smaller ones on top of them; chairs, with generally an effort at an easy one; a wooden bench, a table, beds, spades, fishing-rods, baskets and a score of other little things, which help . . . to make it a domus. The very teapot, in Zetland always to be found at the fireside, speaks of home and woman, and reminds one of the sobriety of the people. . . .'

Here is the core of the old Shetland—poverty but warmth of communion, of family togetherness, their links with the sea providing an added dimension to their cramped lives. Facts and statistics tell us little of the texture of daily life at any period of time. We know there was poverty and misery and it would be wrong to sentimentalise a way of life which contained these. But we must recognise the virtues which grew from adversity: the strong sense of kinship and community which took naturally under its wing the weak and the old, the orphan and the pauper; the feeling of continuity produced by folk memory, reinforced by the fact that often three generations lived together under one roof: the awareness of the world of love and legend which invested the daily round with significance. These qualities sustained and integrated life in these days and lay at the heart of the community. Time does not permit a closer look at the traditions and customs of this period, but I should, in passing, like to stress their importance in the lives of the people.

The pace of change had already begun to quicken by the middle of the century. In 1852 the completion of the so-called 'meal roads' gave Shetland 176½ miles of road compared with the previous five or so. The penny post of 1840 was welcomed enthusiastically: in 1856–57 no fewer than 134,000 letters and newspapers were delivered in Shetland. In 1862 came the first locally edited newspaper and the first secondary school. The *Shetland Advertiser* had a brief but tempestuous career of one year, but its forthright criticisms of the local establishment made a considerable impact. Those in authority had been immune from public criticism for so long that they exploded with remarks such as: 'We seem now to be under a new power; we have got the printing press amongst us'. The Anderson Educational Institute, established to provide education for the poorer children, was also viewed with suspicion by the privileged few, but it prospered and has in many ways been the greatest single influence on the social structure of Shetland. The first regular all-the-year-round steamer service commenced in 1858, and by 1862 more cattle and ponies were being shipped south in a week than in a year forty years previously. Change was in the air, but it was not until 1872 that the whole economic structure came under objective and critical scrutiny. The Truck Commission's extensive investigations throughout the islands revealed that the roots of the iniquitous barter system which affected every crofting family lay in the old relationship between laird and tenant based on the fishing tenures. As the commissioners put it: '. . . it has been so much the habit of the Shetlander's life to fish for his landlord that he is only now discovering that there is anything strange or anomalous in it. . . . It is evident that men brought up in such habits and with the tradition among them of a still more subservient time in the past, are prepared not only to submit to extreme oppression on the part of their proprietors, but also to become easily subjected to the influence of merchants who possess no avowed control over them.' To the fisherman, the forces which governed his daily life were natural and immutable. He accepted them and asked no questions. He was seldom aware of the price of the goods acquired from the shop in exchange for his fish, he rarely bothered to check his pass-book in the shop at settling-up time, and he never knew the value of the fish he was selling until four to five months after the season closed. When asked to give evidence about these aspects of the system he was frequently evasive and loth to criticise. But excerpts from the Report were published in *The Shetland Times*, which was launched in 1872. These would inevitably have sparked off discussion, involving a closer look at the local situation. For the first time the community became really aware of the crippling system in which they were enmeshed. They now realised that the authority which determined their lives was vulnerable to criticism and itself subject to a higher authority. And twelve years later, when they came to give evidence before the Napier Commission, they were no longer evasive and discreet. In 1884 they openly criticised the crofting system, its short leases, insecurity of tenure, inadequate housing, excessive rents. And with the passing of the Crofters' Act of 1886, which gave them security of tenure, compensation, and promises of re-assessment of rents, a new wave of confidence swept through the islands. The herring boom was under way and money circulated more freely than ever before. The new confidence is reflected in the spate of improvements carried out on houses in the 1880s and 1890s. In 1881 there were 695 houses with between 3 and 5 rooms: in 1901 there were 1,517.

It is one of the ironies of history that enlightened legislation, designed to ensure a brighter future, can also highlight a darker past. Many Shetlanders responded to the new freedom and opportunities of the 1872 Education Act, the 1886 Crofters' Act and improved communications by deciding to emigrate. And many of those who remained began to associate the old, traditional way of life with all that was crude, outdated and non-progressive. In 1892 Laurence Williamson, a scholarly Yell crofter, wrote: 'This is a transition time such as never was before. The old Northern civilisation is now in full strife with the new and Southern one, and traditions, customs, which have come down from hoary antiquity, are now dying for ever. The young don't care for their fathers' ways. I mean what was estimable in them. The folklore and family traditions and picturesque stories yield fast to the "People's Journal", "Glasgow Mail", "Ally Sloper's Half Holiday" and such like'. This perceptive man saw with remarkable insight the beginning of the end of the indigenous native culture. He mourned its passing but he accepted the challenge of the new society being ushered in.

The fifty years since Laurence Williamson died have seen more sweeping changes than the previous five hundred: changes in the physical and cultural environment leading to greater personal opportunities, diversity of employment, enhanced prosperity and comfort. These are the subject of a study in themselves and I would merely add in conclusion that although they have inevitably brought with them a disruption of the old closely-integrated society, they have to some extent been absorbed, and there still remains at the heart of our island life a sense of community and local identity to help carry us more confidently into the years ahead.

SOURCES CONSULTED

Books

D. Balfour, *Oppressions of the Sixteenth Century on the Islands of Orkney and Zetland* (Edinburgh 1859).

Rev. John Brand, *A Brief Description of Orkney and Zetland, etc.* (Edinburgh 1883).
Gordon Donaldson, *Life in Shetland Under Earl Patrick* (Edinburgh 1958).
Gilbert Goudie, ed., *The Diary of the Rev. John Mill* (Scot. Hist. Soc., 1889).
Patrick Neill, *A Tour through some of the Islands of Orkney and Shetland* (Edinburgh 1806).
Sir Robert Sibbald, ed., *Description of the Islands of Orkney and Zetland*, 1845.
E. S. Reid Tait, ed., *The Hjaltland Miscellany*, vols, 3 and 4, (Lerwick 1939, 1947).
E. S. Reid Tait, ed., *Old Statistical Account for Shetland* (Lerwick, 1925).
New Statistical Account for Shetland (Edinburgh, 1841).

Government Commissions, Official Reports, etc.

Register of the Privy Council.
Second Report of the Commissioners appointed to enquire into the Truck System (Shetland), vol. i (1872).
Commission to Enquire into the Conditions of the Crofters and Cottars of the Highlands and Islands of Scotland, vol. ii (1884).
Moral Statistics of the Highland and Inlands of Scotland (Inverness, 1826)
Report of the British Destitution Committee, 1847.
Registrar-General's Census Reports, 1861–1901.

Manuscripts

Baillie Court Book of Dunrossness, 1694.
Skatt Rental for Zetland, 1716 (in Scottish Record Office).
Parish Registers of Whiteness and Weisdale, 1727–61 (in Scottish Record Office).
SSPCK Committee Minutes (in Scottish Record Office).
Kirk Session Minutes of Dunrossness, Tingwall, Walls.
Presbytery Minutes of Zetland.
Letter-Books of Thomas Gifford.
Day-Books of Thomas Gifford.
Papers relating to Distribution of Charity Meal, 1783.
Andrew D. Mathewson Papers.
Laurence Williamson Papers.

Newspapers

The Shetland Advertiser, 1862–63.
The Shetland Times, 1872–73.

Index

Aberdeen, 64, 116–17, 145, 158, 164, 169, 209–10
Aberdeenshire, 16–17, 77–8, 189
Africa, 169
agriculture, 23, 26, 28, 107, 111, 153, 159–60, 165–7, 172, 211–12
Aith, 53
Ålesund, 191, 195
America, 11, 132, 162, 164, 169, 207, 211
Amsterdam, 89, 95, 100, 129–30
Angus, 77–8, 122, 137
Angus, earls of, 28
archaeology, 22, 25–8, 108
Ard, Alexander of, 28, 44
Australia, 164, 169

Baltasound, 17, 91–2, 103, 115, 125, 136, 185, 197n, 207
Banffshire, 21, 77, 122
Bergen, 3, 23, 34, 39, 42, 52–4, 56, 58, 61, 83, 87–91, 94–5, 108–9, 120, 181–3, 191
bilingualism, 71, 73, 75, 220–1
birth-rates, 159–61
Black Death, 36
Boddam, 21
Breckin, Sands of, 23
Breiwick, 69
Bremen, 90–3, 95, 109
Bressay, 11, 27, 53, 76, 92, 102–3, 141, 170–1, 185, 227
Bruce of Cultmalindie, 11–12, 14, 128, 217, 222
Bruce of Muness, 125
Bruce of Sumburgh, 123, 128
Bruce of Symbister, 12, 125, 129, 134
Bruce of Urie, 151, 155–6
Buckie, 117
Burgundy, Charles the Bold of, 97–8
Burra, 76, 116, 126, 170–2, 210

Caithness, 12, 21, 28, 33–4, 36, 162, 215

Caithness, earls of, 33–4, 36, 38
Canada, 111, 162, 164, 168
Clapham, Alexander of, 40–1, 45
clearances, 165–8
Clickimin, 26
climate, 22–5, 107, 156–9
Copenhagen, 42, 44, 125, 143
Crofters Act, 130, 164, 166, 168, 231–2
Crofters Commission, 211
Crofting, 131–2, 134, 159–62, 164–6, 219, 225, 231
Crofting Commission (Napier inquiry), 165, 168, 231
Cunningsburgh, 22, 27, 125

Dale, 69
Danish East India Company, 130
Danish influence in Shetland, 41, 47, 53, 57–8, 86, 88–9, 99, 114, 116, 120–1, 124, 182, 193
Danzig, 88, 90–1
death rates, 154–9
Delting, 80–1, 126, 134, 162, 170–1, 223, 225
Denmark, king of, 88
Denmark, Sweden and Norway, kings of, 1, 4, 29, 41–5, 53–9, 61, 64–5, 67n, 83, 88–9
destitution, famine, 127, 133, 152, 154, 156–9, 162, 228–9, 230
Douglas of Spynie, 153
Dundee, 12, 16, 230
Dunrossness, 11–14, 21, 75, 80–2, 126, 134–5, 143, 159, 170–2, 219, 225–6
Dutch influence in Shetland, 3–4, 17, 90–1, 94–5, 96–105, 108–9, 110, 120, 125, 162–3, 193–4, 229

economy since 1946, 198–215
Edinburgh, 129, 132, 140, 157, 169
Edmonston of Buness, 128

emigration, 5–6, 22, 116, 131, 158, 162–78, 202, 232
employment, 175–8, 199, 202
England, King Cnut of, 63
English influence in Shetland, 17, 72, 108–10, 157
exports, 109, 221

Fair Isle, 20–1, 103, 126, 137, 143, 154, 168, 170–1
Faroe Islands, 20, 35, 51–3, 55–6, 58, 86–90, 112, 143–4, 157, 163, 178, 183, 185–6, 215
ferries, 116, 145–7, 163
Fethaland, 112, 134
Fetlar, 13, 75, 80, 126–7, 135, 152–6, 170–1, 226
Fife, 12, 40, 46, 110, 141
Finland, 23, 62, 206
fish-curing, processing, 16–17, 115–16, 172, 200–2, 209–11
fishing, fishing tenures, 1–3, 5–6, 16–18, 26, 92–5, 96–105, 107–18, 131, 163, 169, 172, 199, 201–2, 208–11, 217, 221–3, 225
fishing boats, 98–110, 112–17, 131, 191, 209–11
Fladdabister, 158
Flemish influence in Shetland, 88, 97–8, 100, 193
Floorevag, battle of, 35, 52
Fort Charlotte, 16, 81–2, 121, 130, 136
foud, foudrie, 11, 43–7, 58, 92, 94, 123, 207
Foula, 112, 143–4, 146, 154, 165, 170–1
France, kings of, 41, 97–8, 101
French influence in Shetland, 87, 92, 97, 102, 163, 193–4
French wars, impact of, 102, 113, 130, 150, 157, 193, 229
Fraserburgh, 117
Fugla Ness, 21, 75

Gaelic language, 3, 18, 70, 77–9, 84, 228
Garth, estate of, 168, 223
geography, influence of, 20–9
geology, 20–2, 25–6
German influence in Shetland, 53, 111, 181–97, 220 (see also Hansa)
Gifford of Busta, 111, 133, 221–3
Glasgow, 117
Gloup, 112
Greenland, 33, 101, 113, 163, 229
Greenock, 168

Grierson of Quendale, 134
Gruting, Ness of, 24
Gulberwick, 82

Hamburg, 86, 88, 90–2, 94–5, 100, 130, 221
Hansa, Hanseatic League, 3–4, 36, 83, 86–95, 97, 109–11, 113, 217, 221
Haroldswick, 185
Harrower, John, 162
Hay of Laxfirth, 128
Herring Industry Board, 201
Highlands, 78, 165, 228, 230
Highlands and Islands Development Board, 1, 118, 146, 202–3, 210, 213
Hillswick, 155, 206
Houlland, 69, 72, 79
housing in Shetland, 26, 199, 121, 217, 229–30
Hudson Bay Company, 162
Hull, 157, 230

Iceland, 33–5, 51, 54–7, 62–3, 67n, 86–9, 110, 113–14, 183, 185
immigration, 6–7, 9–14, 26–7, 116, 169, 199
imports, 92, 94, 109, 124–5, 221
Ireland, 11, 17

Jarlshof, 26, 28, 108

Kincardine, 77–8
King's Lynn, 100
Kirkcaldy, 12
Kirkwall, 11, 40, 46, 53, 55, 65, 126
knitting, knitwear manufacture, 2, 172, 202, 205–8, 214

law, feudal, 3–4, 36, 43, 45, 123–5, 224–5
  Frostathing, 49, 63
  Gulathing, 49–51, 53–4, 56, 63
  udal, 3–4, 35, 41, 49–66, 123, 133–4, 217–18
Leith, 120–1, 125, 140
Lerwick, 17, 22–3, 25, 27, 69, 72, 76, 79, 81, 101, 103–5, 113, 115–17, 121, 124, 127–9, 132, 135–6, 143, 145–6, 151, 154–5, 169–72, 175–8, 182, 184–8, 191–2, 206, 208–9, 210–12, 228, 230
Linga, 69, 72, 79, 83
London, 111, 190, 193, 199, 214–15
Lübeck, 88, 90–1, 125

INDEX

Lunnasting, 27
Lunna Voe, 190

Mauritius, 101
Mediterranean, 111
Melby, estate of, 56, 69, 76, 165
military service, 199
mink farming, 213
Moray, 77–8
Morton, earls of, 129–30, 221
Murray of Tullibardine, 122

naval service, 128, 162–4, 173, 229
Nesting, 14, 74, 130, 135, 158, 170–1
Neven of Windhouse, 128
Newcastle, 125, 157
New Zealand, 164–5, 168–9
Norse language, Norn, 8–9, 19, 19n, 49, 58, 95, 120, 144, 217, 220
North Roe, 21, 27, 76
Northmavine, 10, 40, 45, 126, 134–5, 152, 157, 170–1, 208, 222–3
Norway, kings of, 28, 33, 34–6, 49–50, 52, 54–5, 63, 100
Norwegian influence in Shetland, 6, 8–9, 20–1, 28–9, 33–47, 49–57, 62, 66, 69–76, 78–80, 83–4, 87, 89, 97, 101, 108, 113, 117–18, 120, 132, 146, 169, 181–97

Olnafirth, 126, 213
Orkney, 8–12, 14, 20–1, 26–9, 32–47, 51–6, 59, 61, 64–6, 74, 77–8, 83, 86–90, 101, 120–3, 130, 132, 137, 143, 157, 168–9, 177, 185, 190, 192, 202, 211–12
Orkney, earls of, 8–10, 29, 32–6, 38–41, 44–7, 66
Out Skerries, 129, 143, 146–7, 170–2, 210

Papa Stour, 75, 170–1
Papil, 27, 75
parliament, 119–20
Perth, treaty of, 34
Perthshire, 12
Peterhead, 117, 189, 230
Pictish influences, 26–8
place-names, 3, 69–84, 143–4
pledging of the islands in 1469, 3–4, 10, 29, 32–47, 83, 120
pony-breeding, 2, 212
population, 12–13, 16–18, 28–9, 131, 150–78, 228
Portugal, 193

potatoes, 156–8
press gangs, 162–3, 229
privy council, 58–9, 119–20, 123, 218
public works, 200–1

Quendale, 23, 134

Raefirth, 53
religious denomination:
    Church of Scotland, 9–11, 16, 18n, 20, 27, 33, 125–7, 131, 137, 143, 166, 218–20, 223–8
    Free Church of Scotland, 126
    Methodists, 126, 143, 163
    Quakers, 158
    United Presbyterians, 126
roads, bridges, 130, 199, 201, 230
Russia, 23, 186–7

St. Ninian's Isle, 4, 22, 27, 62–4
Samphrey, 56
Sandness, 27, 56, 75, 158, 163, 170–1, 174–5, 225, 227–8
Sandsair, 131
Sandsting and Aithsting, 75, 81, 126, 130, 135, 146, 152, 156, 159, 170–1, 173–4
Sandvoe, 134
Sandwick, 23, 75, 125–6, 206
Scalloway, 12, 16, 26, 39, 81, 92, 113, 116–17, 145, 172, 181n, 186, 190, 206, 209–11, 218
Scandinavia, 1, 3, 8–9, 20, 36, 125, 211, 214
schools, schooling, 127–31, 151, 175–7, 225, 227–8, 231–2
Scotland, kings of, 34, 36, 41, 42, 99, 100, 120
Scottish influence in Shetland, 2–4, 8–18, 20, 27–9, 33–6, 72, 74–5, 80–1, 216–17
Scottish Record Office, 7, 119–35
sheep, wool, 165, 167, 207
Shetland, Stewart earls in, 11, 15, 54, 57, 59, 125, 169, 217–18
'Shetland Bus', 190–1n
Shetland Council of Social Service, 203–5
Shetland County Council, 203–5, 214
'Shetland Gang', 184, 186–9, 190
silver craft, 2, 213
skatt, skattlands, 4, 35, 45–7, 57–9, 61, 133–5, 152–3, 166, 223
Skeld, 113
smallpox, inoculation, 152, 154–9, 161
smuggling, 113, 130

social developments in Shetland, 216–32
Spain, 111, 120, 124–5, 193
Sperra, Malise, 36–40, 46
Statistical Account, 152, 160, 173, 224–5
Staxigoe, 124
Stenness, 91, 112
stone-polishing, 2, 213
Strathearn, earls of, 28, 36–8, 40
Stromness, 137
Sullum Voe, 2, 189
Sumburgh, 41, 82, 140, 186, 201
surnames, family names, in Shetland
  Anderson, 14
  Balfour, 132
  Bruce, 11–14, 167
  Bult, 83
  Cant, 10, 65
  Chalmer, 10
  Cheyne, 11
  Christie, 14
  Clephane, 40
  Coghill, 83
  Davidson, 14
  Doull, 16
  Dundas, 129, 141, 157
  Edmonston, 11, 48n
  Fallowsdale, 11
  Foster, 83
  Fraser (Frissel), 10
  Gifford, 11, 111, 133, 221–3
  Gray, 12, 14
  Greig, 16
  Grierson, 16, 134, 225
  Hafthorsen, 39
  Halcrow, 167
  Hay, 11, 167
  Henderson, 14
  Henry, 16
  Hill, 11
  Hognason, 132
  Hughson, 14
  Hutchison, 14
  Inglis, 12
  Kennedy, 12, 14
  Lauder, 11
  Magnusson, 10, 65, 83
  Malcolmson, 11
  Manson, 223
  Mitchell, 12, 16, 225
  Murray, 11–12
  Mowat, 83
  Nicolson, 16, 83
  Nisbet, 10, 13–14
  Niven, 128, 218
  Noble, 14
  Norsk, 11
  Ollason, 83, 133
  Reid, 53
  Ross, 12, 16
  Schlaitter, 83
  Short, 12
  Shuardson, 15
  Sigurdson, 15
  Sinclair (St. Clair), 10–11, 13–14, 37–41, 133, 223
  Smith, 83
  Spence, 13–14
  Stewart, 11–12, 14–15
  Stewartson, 15
  Strang, 13
  Thomasdochter, 14
  Thorvaldsdatter, 39, 48n, 55
  Tomasson, 53
  Torrie, 16
  Tulloch, 9–10, 13
  Turheimsdochter, 133
  Twatt, 225
  Wishart, 11, 83
Sweden, 23, 42, 53, 59–60, 62, 120, 187, 193
Switzerland, 193

Tingwall, 14, 21, 39, 52, 69, 75–6, 79, 82, 127, 135, 143, 166–8, 170–2, 225
tourism, 2, 6, 18, 136–47, 212, 214
traders to Shetland, 12, 86–95, 217, 220
Trondheim, 100, 183, 195
Trondra, 26, 171
trout-farming, 213
'truck' system, 111–12, 217–18, 229–31
treasure trove, 27, 62–6
Twatt, 69

Underhoull, 28, 108
Unst, 10–11, 14, 20–3, 25, 74, 76, 80–1, 126–8, 131–3, 135, 141, 152–4, 156, 163, 165, 170–1, 212, 219
Uyea, 27, 134

Veensgarth estate, 166–8
Vlaardingen, 96, 98, 100–3, 105
Voe, 69, 113, 206, 223

Walls, 11, 16, 56, 75, 82, 126, 135, 158, 163, 170–1, 174–5, 225, 227–8
Weisdale, 20, 113, 153, 159, 163, 219, 224
Western Isles, 12, 17–18, 28, 35, 41, 140

INDEX

whaling, 113, 123, 129, 157, 163, 229
Whalsay, 22, 83, 92, 109, 116–17, 126, 147, 170–3
White Fish Authority, 201, 209
Whiteness, 113, 153, 159, 213, 219, 224
Williamson, John (Johnny Notions), 155
Williamson, Laurence, 128, 232
World War I, 103–4, 115–16, 145, 182–3, 199

World War II, 1, 104, 115–16, 136, 181–97, 198–9, 209, 211, 213
Wormdale, 213

Yell, 10, 13–14, 20, 23, 52–3, 74–6, 80–1, 83, 92, 109, 117, 127, 130, 135, 155, 160, 170–1, 204, 208, 228, 232

Zeno, Nicolo & Antonio, 39